CHANGING

the *Odds*

for

CHILDREN

AT RISK

Seven Essential Principles of Educational
Programs That Break the Cycle of Poverty

SUSAN B. NEUMAN

 Teachers College
Columbia University
New York and London

Published by Teachers College Press, 1234 Amsterdam Avenue, New York, NY 10027

First published in hardcover in 2009 by Praeger Publishers, an imprint of Greenwood
Publishing Group, Inc.

Library of Congress Cataloging-in-Publication Data
Neuman, Susan B.
    Changing the odds for children at risk : seven essential priciples of educational
programs that break the cycle of poverty / Susan B. Neuman.
      p. cm.
    Includes bibliographical references and index.
    ISBN 978-0-8077-5048-3 (pbk. : alk. paper)   1. Poor children—Education—
United States.   2. Educational equalization—United States.   3. School improvement
programs—United States.   I. Title.
    LC4091.N44 2009b
    371.826'9420973—dc22

                        2009033468

ISBN: 978–0–8077-5048-3

Printed on acid-free paper

Manufactured in the United States of America

16 15 14 13 12 11 10 09   1 2 3 4 5 6 7 8

CONTENTS

ACKNOWLEDGMENTS

A book of this scope owes very much to very many. Throughout the three years of research on this book, I have visited over 100 early intervention settings and have benefited tremendously from the wisdom of colleagues who are working daily to change the odds for children at risk.

I owe a special debt of gratitude to my colleague of many years Donna Celano, professor at LaSalle University in Philadelphia. Despite the distance that separates our institutional residences, we remain close colleagues, committed to examining how community-based initiatives can improve the lives of city children and to writing about it in a way that makes this information accessible to people outside our fields of education and communication. Donna has been my eyes and ears on many occasions, and I thank her for her many thoughtful and inspirational insights.

I am particularly thankful for the opportunities to learn from program leaders in the fields of family support and health—areas that have traditionally been outside the boundaries of education. Colleagues who read and thoughtfully commented on the parts of the manuscript concerned with these areas include Kellie Teter, Robin Tutt, Eveline Hunt, Pam Davis, Gloria Rodriquez, Mercedes Perez de Colon, Carolyn Rutledge, Mary Cunningham DeLuca, and Nancy Willyard. They have helped in many ways, connecting me with committed professionals in the field, including Beth McClure, Mary Stout, Marva Williams, Krysti Myatt, and Heather Callister, who are working daily to improve the odds for children and their families. Many of these individuals have kindly read parts of the manuscript and fact-checked along the way; I am responsible for any errors that remain.

I have been blessed with wonderful colleagues in my professional and personal associations. Barb Pellin, Eric Smith, Ellen Frede, Libby Doggett, and Cathy Grace have all been jacks-of-all-trades in early childhood education, working doggedly at various administrative levels to improve services to the children who need them most. These people have often been fearless in their efforts to shake the system into new ways of thinking, all with one goal in mind—bettering the lives of young children.

I am indebted to colleagues Hedra Packman, a children's librarian in Philadelphia, and Theresa Ramos, as well as project officers at the William Penn Foundation, who helped me understand the power of community-based initiatives, especially libraries. These individuals have shown what can happen when creative leadership and out-of-the-box thinking come together to reach out to a broad constituency, especially disadvantaged children.

I also want to thank Shannon Christian and Bob Stonehill, wonderful colleagues in Health and Human Services and the Department of Education, whose extensive understanding of community programs helped to connect me with such fine colleagues as Stefan Zucker, Lucy Friedman, and others working in the field of after-school education, including Kim Baranowski and Kelley Harmer. Bob Slavin, Bette Chambers, and Nancy Madden have also been helpful, calling people on a moment's notice to allow me to visit and interview their programs.

There are also hidden stars, people working "in the trenches" who deserve special notice. Because of the sensitivity of their roles, in some cases I have given them pseudonyms, but I wish to acknowledge and thank Nancy, Leanora, Bill, Darlene, Val, Missy, Irene, Sylvia, Fanny, Maria, Hilda, Laurena, Mateo, Lincoln, Shana, Kelly, Carol, Susan, Debbie, Melissa, and so many more who have entered the pages of this manuscript. All of these individuals have given life to the definition and spirit of what it means to be a highly qualified teacher. Our whole society benefits from such talented and ethical professionals.

Deepest thanks are owed to people who are turning around the misperception that television is always the 'bad guy' in education. Judy Stoia and Beth Kirsch, along with their creative team of Chris Cerf and Norm Stiles, repeatedly demonstrate what television can do to improve children's access to learning. I am also grateful to Linda Rath and Mary Haggerty for their insightful comments and their understanding of the history of innovative television projects to reach people "where they are."

I am thankful to Dimitriy Masterov, Nathan Sterken, and Serene Koh, my cheeky and delightful students at the University of Michigan, for providing their wonderful research assistance. Their competence and creativity in helping me gather and display information was always accompanied by flexibility, kindness, and understanding.

I wish to thank my wonderful agent, Sharlene Martin, as well as the Spencer Foundation, for sponsoring this project. It would have been impossible to have visited, reported, or observed the many programs throughout the country that are changing the odds for children at risk without their generous support. And finally, to my best friend and husband for the last 40 or so years, Russell, who continues to support, listen, and inspire all those around him: thank you.

INTRODUCTION

America's poor children do not fare well in our society. The odds are if a child is born poor, he's likely to stay poor. He'll probably live in an unsafe neighborhood, landscaped with little hope, more neighborhood bars by corners than quality day care or after school programs. As he makes his way up through the local school system, he'll likely find his schools dilapidated, playgrounds distant memories where equipment once laid, teachers, though earnest, ready to throw in the towel. Being the have-not among the haves, he'll find that his skills are hopelessly behind his peers, only to drop further as academic demands get higher, his options increasingly narrowed to either staying behind, giving up, or dropping out. And perhaps, the most tragic element of it all is that this cycle of disadvantage is likely to repeat itself over and over again, until we are determined to do something about it.

Of course, it's not as though we haven't tried. Schools today are in the midst of the biggest educational reform movement in their history, grappling with federal mandates to leave no child behind. Redefining the federal government's role in education, the No Child Left Behind Act of 2001 consumes over 400 billion dollars of federal and state monies yearly. But although some efforts for investing resources will be substantially more productive than others, there is little evidence that any of these efforts will close more than a fraction of the differences in achievement for poor minority children in comparison to the achievement of their middle-class peers. Despite the many heroic attempts to beat the odds, these school reforms, like so many other reforms before them, will fail to close the achievement gap.

Schools will not fail for lack of resources, good teachers, high expectations, or rigorous standards. In general, America's schools spend more per student and have higher-quality teachers and standards than do virtually any of the countries that routinely trounce us in international comparisons. Rather, schools will fail to significantly close the gap because so many children come from highly vulnerable and dysfunctional environments before they ever reach the schoolhouse doors. Despite America's vast wealth, nearly one out of every five American children lives in poverty—one of the highest poverty rates in the developed world. The painful fact is that, despite the billions of dollars poured into schools and the vast array of reforms implemented, whatever influence a school has on its students' lives is trumped by this reality. Today, despite the past 40 years of reform, we have done almost nothing to raise or change the trajectory of our poor and disadvantaged children.

This deeply unsettling fact was brought home to me one day when my staff made a mistake in my schedule and sent me back to a school I had visited two years earlier; instead of a school I had not yet seen. In my capacity as Assistant Secretary of Elementary and Secondary Education under President George W. Bush from 2002 to 2004, I had already visited a highly effective reading program for troubled readers at this particular school. At that time, the school was truly an example of beating all the odds stacked against it, and it had even attracted the attention of the First Lady and other dignitaries and prominent scholars. The media gathered the heartwarming individual stories that made up the school's overall success rate. It was a testament to what is possible for all schools.

Yet now, two years later, my staff inadvertently sent me back to this same school and what I saw there was a shell of what it had been. Academic leaders were in short supply, because professional development had lapsed after district mismanagement of funds. A highly successful curriculum program had been inexplicably dropped in favor of one that had gone untested. Frustrated teachers began to leave in droves after losing hope of changing the trajectory of failure. They were replaced with permanent substitutes or novices straight out of college. After the original media attention had turned to other matters and the specialists and scholars had moved on to other projects, the school once again slid back into the murk of poverty's inertia.

The idea that no school can cure educational inequity is hardly astonishing, but it's remarkable how much of our political discourse is predicated on the notion that it can. Failing to recognize the gravity of the problem, government has offered more platitudes than solutions, arguing that there are "no excuses for low achievement." And yet the fact that seems to have been lost in the ongoing debate that 6.7% of our country's population lives in the very poorest and most vulnerable census tracts, where there are also higher proportions of very young children, higher rates of single parenting, and fewer educated adults. Naturally, these census tracts are among those failing to close the achievement gap.

Good schools can go a long way toward helping poor children achieve better, but the fact remains that educational inequity is rooted in economic problems and social pathologies too deep to be overcome by school alone. And given this reality, there is every reason to stop thinking about placing all of our faith in school reform as if some magical thing were about to happen and every reason to thousands of children during their middle childhood years. These programs are confronting the conventional wisdom that says that poor children are unmotivated, beyond redemption, and unable to learn. Along with the magic formula of an adult authority figure, these programs engage students in learning and simultaneously begin to reverse the stranglehold of a starkly disadvantaged environment.

What these and other programs are demonstrating is that poor children have all the greater need of learning environments that are safe, secure, and nourishing, because their homes and their neighborhoods are so often not. And yet schools never have really had such all-embracing power to heal. Our best hope is to break the cycle of disadvantage that lies outside the influence of the school day.

The good news is that we now have a sound evidentiary base in the sciences to reduce these tremendous disparities in children's achievement and life changes. We also know *how* to do it. By capitalizing on the knowledge gained over the last 25 years, we can sharply raise the odds of success in life for children living in vulnerable circumstances.

How We Can Change the Odds: The Seven Essential Principles

We need to recast our priorities, to fund programs that have solid evidence of results—programs that stake their reputation on their abilities to exponentially improve the performance of at-risk children. This book demonstrates how the role of education can be reinvented to effectively change the odds for this army of otherwise lost children—and to do so over the long term.

The prescription begins with seven essential principles. Programs that work must

1. Actively target the neediest children.
2. Begin early in children's lives.
3. Emphasize coordinated services, particularly for children whose families present multiple risks.
4. Focus on boosting academic achievement through compensatory high-quality instruction.
5. Deliver instruction by trained professionals, not by aides or volunteers.
6. Acknowledge that intensity matters, defending against any dilution of program quality as a waste of public resources.
7. Always hold themselves accountable for results and for children's achievement.

When we fund programs on the basis of outcomes, or what works, we put in place a set of interventions that have been shown through accumulated trials to benefit families and to give back solid returns over time. Throughout this book, I will report evidence from cost–benefit analyses when available, along with economic forecasts that stand up to the highest level of critical scrutiny. Far from isolated assessments of program effectiveness, these programs have lived up to the replication challenge, changing the outcomes collectively for millions of chilto start thinking about other institutions that we might have to mobilize to solve the problem.

Learning in Communities

A good place to start is with some educational reforms that are actually working in communities all across the country. There's no shortage of exciting developments. You only have to visit New Song, a community-based early intervention program in a ravaged neighborhood in Baltimore, to begin to figure out that high-quality child care can drastically improve the educational readiness of inner-city children. Here, using a model founded by E. D. Hirsch and now in place in more than 400 centers throughout the country,[1] this philosophy is tied to helping children overcome their early knowledge deficits, recognizing that it is not the ability to learn that these children lack, but the knowledge, experiences, language, and opportunities for learning. Researcher Fred Smith tracked the effects of this intensive knowledge-centered program on student achievement and found that the achievement gap narrowed significantly for one cohort and was entirely eliminated for the other. This program confirms previous anecdotal evidence that high-quality child care with knowledgeable teachers trained to focus on prevention can go a long way toward changing the odds for poor children.

Or take the evidence on the costs and benefits of family intervention programs that have shown real returns on investments, adding more than five dollars for every dollar invested. Recognizing that many of the most pervasive and intractable problems faced by young children and their parents can be traced to maternal health–related behaviors during and immediately after pregnancy, David Olds created a program that sent registered nurses to make home visits both before and after pregnancy,[2] helping young mothers prepare and care for their infants' nutritional, health, and social needs. These mothers are no longer casualties of a failed system; a voluminous literature of over 100 articles in peer-review journals attests that when growth-fostering interventions are put in place, families can rebound and lead highly productive lives.

Community-based programs in libraries and health clinics are now demonstrating our abilities to go beyond isolated models to replicable, scalable, and affordable interventions that not only reduce health disparities but also increase children's positive outcomes in a myriad of ways. Programs such as Reach Out and Read, now located in over 2,000 hospitals and health centers in all 50 states,[3] where it shows low-income parents and children the techniques and pleasures of looking at books together, are demonstrating that literacy-promoting interventions by pediatricians can improve the language scores of young children dramatically. Studies from 19 clinical sites in 10 states report a tenfold increase in parents' reading aloud, as well as large, statistically significant increases in references to reading as one of the three most favorite things to do with children.

After-school programs that use an altogether distinctively different form of learning[4]—engaging students in communities of practice—serve as "places of hope" dren at greatest risk. What sets them apart from all other programs are the immediate and long-term benefits that accrue to us all from preventing problems from spiraling upward. The linchpin holding them together is accountability.

Smarter Government on Six Fronts

Once these priorities are set, we need to move from principles to action. Preempting more years of tired thinking and incremental tinkering with programs that have long failed our children, the following solutions will make it possible to produce results for an American public increasingly impatient with the status quo.

1. Mobilize other institutions. Placing all of the burdens of poverty upon the school system as if it can cure all but the common cold only derails its central mission of high-quality education. Rather, we need to mobilize other institutions that are integrally tied with family and community supports, early childhood, and after-school programs as part of the critical equation for changing the odds.

2. Eliminate unnecessary programs. Federal formulas for reaching high-poverty children are fundamentally flawed and are likely to increase rather than decrease the achievement gap. Strategic reviews and the elimination of programs that are not central to our core priorities are necessary to adequately focus and direct high-quality services to children who most need them.

3. Pursue outcomes. Education is about rewarding performance, not good intentions. The only way the public will know whether it is getting what it paid for is by monitoring programs continuously. The solution is to set performance targets, measure performance against them, and reward results. Compliance-driven monitoring in the past snarled too many programs in needless red tape. Today's monitoring must be about one thing, and one thing only: outcomes.

4. Consolidate. Consolidate and streamline policies and programs aimed at improving early care and education programs. Consolidate funding streams and give broad waiver authority for funds to be used in ways that demonstrate the greatest impact.

5. Put the public in charge. Put the public in the driver's seat by making government programs and policies more transparent. State-of-the-art assessments that provide continuous reviews will help to inform the public and to build the public trust, as well as holding everybody involved accountable for children's successful entry into schools. The assessments also present an ongoing picture of what these children need in order for their development to be ensured.

6. Evaluate programs empirically. Revolutionize methods for evaluating programs; soft process measures and anecdotal reports will no longer do. All programs must be subject to empirical, rigorous research specially designed for multifaceted intervention needs.

This book explores these key principles and concludes by discussing the kinds of actions necessary to implement them. It takes an in-depth look at programs that are efficiently and effectively changing the odds for children for the long term. Together, it tells a story of priorities and choices. We can choose to ignore these risks and the harm done to children who grow up in a world without books or stimulating activities, whose natural curiosity is crushed early on, who are isolated from the world of learning beyond their individual neighborhoods. Or we can choose to use our knowledge to fund programs that fundamentally change their odds, breaking the bleak cycle of poverty and disadvantage. We cannot afford to continue the status quo.

My belief is that, as a pragmatic nation, we will choose the latter course—that we will realize it is in our collective interests to have more children socially, physically, and mentally healthy—children who then go on to become adults able to produce, year in and year out, exciting new innovations that improve the lives of us all: a citizenry committed to create a more civil society, where all people take responsibility for themselves and their communities. And, guided by a course of action to change the odds, we will not only enhance our productivity as a nation, but we will prove once and for all that we are a just and a great society.

CHAPTER 1

THE CRITICAL EARLY YEARS FOR CHANGING THE ODDS

A snapshot of two graduating high school classes, one from a middle-class community and the other from below the poverty line, could capture it all. By every measure, they couldn't look more different. Middle-income students would be more crowded in the picture than that of the low-income group, a reflection of the absolute numbers of students who graduate high school. The disproportionately small numbers of poor students seen in the picture are likely to represent the 50% or less of those originally entering the upper grades who have stayed in high school even as their peers have dropped out. Living in single-parent families, large families, with parents who are also high school dropouts, it's only their fortitude and sheer resilience that finds them gathered here. As a group, their fortunes have worsened over the past two decades, with graduation rates plunging to a new low of 17% in some urban communities.

Even more striking in our metaphorical snapshot will be the differences in their composition. The graduates from the middle-class community are largely white, with few minorities represented, but there is nothing but minority in the other group, a result of the growing resegregation in our schools. Poor students today are increasingly likely to attend predominantly minority schools—an increase of 13.9% since 1969—reports Gary Orfield of Harvard University; more than a third attend schools with a minority enrollment of 90–100%.[1]

Looking more closely at their faces, the sharp rise in the economic divide throughout the past two-and-a-half decades is even more evident. Graduates from the middle-income community smile confidently and widely, thanks to the local orthodontist, and many are wearing glasses, a sure sign of continuing health care and their families' regular incomes. In the other picture, the students look somewhat older, bruised, and sickly, probably reflecting the daily toll of living on the edge. Being raised in poverty, they have had less of everything—whether material resources (food, shelter, health care) or community resources (good recreational programs, safe neighborhoods, adequate governmental services)—than the others. Nine million of these students will have no health coverage at all—nearly 12% of our entire student population.

America might be a land of plenty, but this snapshot reveals that it is also a land of inequality. Differences between rich and poor children in the last two decades have more than doubled, causing the greatest economic disparity since 1979. Most recent statistics, according to Nobel Prize–winning economist James Heckman,[2] indicate that the top 20% of families have amassed 62% of total income growth, with more than half of that growth going to the very top 5%. Only 2% of total income growth comes from the bottom 20%. These statistics paint a picture of a polarized and static society; as Heckman has suggested, "Never has the accident of birth mattered more" in the United States.

The actual rate of child poverty in this country is astonishingly high, compared to the rates of other rich industrial countries. Average estimates place about 20.8% of all American children in poverty, and 42% of minority children. These rates are even higher for the youngest of our children—at least two to three times higher than most other major Western industrialized nations. Poor children in this country are suffering, and sadly, our nation is diminished by the wasted opportunity and productivity of such untapped potential.

Why do the students in our snapshot differ so dramatically? Certainly genetic endowment is sometimes part of the answer—being healthy, smart, good looking in this country gives you a leg up. But the reason that certain children end up on certain rungs of the ladder is more a factor of their social environment than their genetic composition. As prominent social scientist Christopher Jencks pointed out more than twenty years ago,[3] the biggest determinant of prosperity in the United States may simply be the good fortune born of such conditions, unforeseen opportunities, or other unfathomable set of circumstances as happen to place a child in a certain ZIP code. The advantages and disadvantages that children will inherit from the neighborhood they live in, their parents and the resources they provide, and the quantity and quality of their child care and early schooling will either support or seriously diminish their means for attaining marketable skills and school success.

Our portrait captures only a moment in time, but it reveals the history of our students, their earliest years, and how this period has often painful and lasting consequences. It shows how growing up poor can handicap children. While living in ravaged communities offering little work and less hope, families and children develop coping strategies that may be contrary to a culture of achievement, further reifying their underclass status.

When it comes to solutions for altering this ecology, the battle between the partisans of nature versus those of nurture has been particularly fierce and unrelenting. A century's worth of genetic studies, starting with those of Lewis Terman,[4] the titular father of intelligence testing, has concluded that all these circumstances basically come down to genes and heredity. Being that intelligence is "fixed" at birth, their argument goes, there is little to gain by intervention. This argument has been used as a rationale by conservatives for doing nothing about the seemingly intractable achievement gap and the widening income disparity. Nurturists, on the hand, are likely to argue that intelligence is not one skill but actually a bundle of crucial—and separate—mental abilities, all highly alterable. Predisposed to the hype of "Baby Einstein," liberals often seek to revive any and all outdated War on Poverty programs, embracing the all-too-predictable "we need more funding" refrain.

Though tantalizing to those who might seek neat, linear explanations of human behavior, neither explanation is correct. Genes and environment don't occupy separate spheres. They interact. It is not nature versus nurture; it is nature through nurture. The two must be considered in tandem. Psychologists such as Sir Michael Rutter of the University of London[5] argue for reciprocal causation—environmental factors have strong effects on intelligence, even if genetic heritability can range from 40% up to 80%. If heredity defines the limits of intelligence, his research shows, experience largely determines whether those limits will be reached. Given that experience is highly alterable, the prospects for improving the odds for children at risk and remedying social inequalities are far greater than we may have ever dreamed of before.

Starting Out

It starts with the child's developing brain. Americans have always cherished babies. But it wasn't until we began to hear about the rat-a-tat-tat of the brain of a human embryo about 12 weeks after conception and its physical transformations to the billions of neurons in a full-term baby that the public became totally enraptured with early development. Brilliantly described in the popular press, who would have thought that stories about neurons—those long, wiry cells carrying electrical messages through the nervous system, carving mental circuits into patterns over time—could be so fascinating? Developmental psychologists, after all, had studied children's development for years, observing and testing their behaviors and abilities at different ages. Now, for the first time, we had concrete evidence of the brain's activities shown in vividly displayed pictures, thanks to neuroscientists such as Kenneth Pugh and his many colleagues at Haskins Laboratories.[6]

What these pictures showed is that a tremendous amount of brain development occurs between conception and age one. Those rhythmic rat-a-tat-tats are actually the electricity of brain cells cobbling together and shaping the brain into patterns that over time will enable the newborn to respond to a mother's voice and perceive a father's touch. Most of a human's lifetime supply of brain cells, according to Dr. Bernard Shaywitz and his colleagues,[7] is actually produced between the fourth and seventh months of gestation. Once formed, the cells will later migrate to locations required for language, vision, and connections between the two.

A full-term baby comes into the world with billions of neurons, only to form quadrillions of connections between them. In response to environmental stimuli received through the sense organs, each of the brain's billions of neurons will forge links to thousands of others, forming synapses, or connections with which the brain recognizes the signals of the neural pathways. In a display of biological exuberance, an intense spurt in production will occur over the next three years—more than the brain can possibly use. It's like creating cable connections in all sorts of directions, wiring for any possible contingency.

Then, as if in a Darwinian competition, the brain begins a draconian pruning away of neurons, synapses, and even entire neural pathways that are not being continually stimulated. Although scientists don't fully understand how this all occurs, according to Rima Shore in her report on Rethinking the Brain,[8] it appears that stimulation actually creates chemical changes that stabilize various synapses. Those that are only seldom or never used get eliminated, literally sculpting masses of cells into patterns of emotion and thought that are, for better or worse, unique.

Deprived of environmental stimuli, the child's brain suffers. For example, researchers have found that children who don't play much or are rarely touched have smaller brains—as much as 20–30% smaller—than normal for their age. Animal studies provide another provocative parallel. Substantial evidence shows that neglect (including lack of touch) in the very early stages of life has long-term effects on coping, making it difficult for animals to respond to stressful events. In one study, rats that were rarely touched and handled as newborns were less able to regulate their responses to stressful events than those who had been gently touched as newborns.

It is clear from everything we've learned about how the brain works that stress can seriously inhibit the ability to learn. Young children who are physically abused early in life appear to develop brains that are exquisitely tuned to danger. At the slightest provocation, they are likely become aroused and stay aroused, retaining high levels of stress hormones long after the arousing situation has gone. It is as if the fear circuits go on and can't shut off.

Table 1.1.   Key Facts of Brain Development

- Brain development takes place before one year of age and is much more rapid and extensive than previously realized.
- Brain development is much more vulnerable to environmental influence than previously suspected.
- Early environmental stimulation has a long-term influence on brain development.
- Environment affects not only the number of brain cells and connections between them, but also brain-cell "wiring."
- New scientific evidence attributes negative impact on brain function, in part, to early stress.
- Good nutrition and nurturance support optimal early brain development.

Source: M. McCain and J. Mustard, "Early Years Study Final Report" (Toronto, Canada, 1999).

When overwhelming threats to physical or psychological well-being appear, changes are set in motion in the body and the brain, causing a literal cascade of neurochemical changes. As pediatrician and researcher Jack Shonkoff describes it,[9] the brain shifts the body's priorities, producing adrenaline and cortisol in sympathetic nervous system activity that supports vigilance. Future-oriented activities such as fighting off colds and viruses or learning things that don't matter now but might later, suddenly fall off the radar in the fight for survival. Because the stress system functions in such ways as to put growth-oriented processes on hold, a life of frequent or prolonged periods of trauma, says Shonkoff, "compromises brain development."

One of the more dramatic examples of the impact of stress and its long-term consequences has been reported by Megan Gunnar,[10] a scientist interested in the HPA (hypothalamus–pituitary–adrenals) axis, or what is more commonly described as the fight-or-flight response in moments of stress or danger. Gunnar visited Romanian orphanages right after the fall of Communism, rooms that looked like concentration camps holding 1,000 or more children from ages 0 to 12 months, in which they had been deprived of regular food and water. The children's cortisol (stress levels) were unbelievably high, and their ability to respond to caregivers was heartbreakingly absent.

Following 150 of these severely traumatized babies as they were adopted by Canadian couples, she found in the study, now its 11th year, that she could put these children into one of two groups. In the first group, the children seemed to grow up happy, normal, consistently responsible, and socially competent. But the other group looked as if something had hit them. These children appeared damaged, exhibiting severe antisocial behavior and troubled relationships with others. What separated these two groups of children was the age of adoption: The first group was adopted early on, before four months, and the second group between eight and 12 months. Gunnar's thesis is that because of the extraordinarily powerful role that environment plays in shaping a brain's capability, even these few months made such a difference in the children's behavior that in the 10th year of life, they were still fighting the effects of stress.

Emotional deprivation early in life seems to have a similar effect. Infants of parents suffering from depression show reduced activity in areas of the brain that serve emotional activity. Drugs such as cocaine, alcohol, and tobacco, often used as self-induced medicating devices for depression and stress, have been shown by the laboratories of William Greenough of the University of Illinois[11] to interfere with the formation of synapses, negatively affecting children's attention, information processing, learning, and memory. If a sight, sound, or experience has proved painful before—a drunken dispute between parents, an accident of spilled milk followed by a beating—the child becomes attuned to critical signs, facial expressions, and angry noises warning of impending danger. In this state, says neuroscientist Bruce Perry,[12] the brain remains on high alert. This happens so early in life that the effects of nurture can be misperceived as innate nature.

All of this raises a troubling question. If the brain becomes seriously compromised early on—either through physical, emotional, or sensory deprivation—is all hope lost? Once this intricate tapestry of mind is woven, can the circuits be rewired? What is the potential malleability of intelligence and the power of an intervention to turn things around?

It hearkens back to why the question of nature or nurture won't go away. Some of the most provocative discoveries addressing this question have come from behavioral geneticists who rely on studies of twins and adoptees. Identical twins share genes, but fraternal twins are siblings born together—just half of their genes are identifiable, making them ideal subjects for examining the complex interplay between nature and nurture.

For decades, conventional wisdom had it that the effect of being raised in the same family (adoptees) was less than the effects of genes (twins). Then came geneticists like Eric Turkheimer and his colleagues,[13] who questioned whether these relationships held true for all families, or just those from the oft-measured population of middle-class twins. Together with several colleagues, he examined scores on the Wechsler Intelligence Scale of children of a sample of seven-year-old twins from more than 50,000 infants. In a widely cited article published in 2003, he found that virtually all the variation in IQ scores for twins from the middle class could be attributed to genes. But for impoverished families, the opposite was true: 60% of the variance in IQ was accounted for by the environment. The role of genes was close to zero. In essence, the impact of growing up in poverty trumped children's genetic capacities.

When children who have gone from rags to riches take part in selected adoptee studies, a similar pattern emerges. In a study of such adoptees, French researchers Chriane Capron and Michael Duyme at the University of Paris[14] examined both rich (physicians and executives) and poor (farm workers and unskilled laborers) birth parents and adoptive parents. They found clear-cut differences in the adopted children's scores. When both birthparents and adoptive parents were well off, the researchers found a mean IQ of nearly 120; when both were low, the mean IQ was 92. But regardless of whether the adopting families were well off or not, adopted children raised by well-to-do families scored nearly 16 points higher. This means the difference between getting a high school diploma or a college degree.

These studies confirm that it is no longer a question of whether the environment matters. It matters—greatly. Rather, the question is when and how it matters: and this sets off yet another controversy. Might there be critical times when such neurological rehab is especially prone to environmental stimuli? Seeing the policy potential, media types and celebrities such as Rob Reiner, hoping to promote early childhood education, proclaimed the brain to be "cooked" by age 10. A widely circulated article in *Newsweek* claimed that "[c]hildren whose neural circuits are not stimulated before kindergarten are never going to be what they could have been." Wild claims about the timing of intellectual development when a young child's brain could be "stoked" by intensive neurologically correct stimulation was promoted widely in the press, as well by toymakers and educational marketeers. Mozart CDs, thought to stimulate the brain's wiring processes, started flying off the shelves in the hands of parents hoping to raise smarter children.

Realizing that the hype was getting out of hand, John Bruer,[15] in his controversial but carefully documented book *The Myth of the First Three Years*, put the case in perspective. Much of this problem with all the exaggerated claims lay in the belief that the first three years represent a "critical period"—literally a window of opportunity for wiring the brain, learning a set of skills impossible to learn later. But as Bruer argues in his book, the "stimulate-the-brain-early rage" ignored the fact that synapses, after having grown, wither away despite anything parents and teachers do. In fact, this natural pruning process is helpful for intellectual development, leading Bruer to indicate that "less is more" when it comes to synapses.

It turns out that the "window of opportunity" in the human brain, with few exceptions, is open for far more than the first three years. Only a few very basic capacities, such as vision and—to a far lesser extent—learning a new language, are connected with sensitive periods, or windows when the brain demands certain types of input in order to create or stabilize certain long-lasting structures. Realizing the potential destructiveness of using science so selectively, 15 internationally recognized developmental psychologists, in what has come to be known as the "Santiago Declaration,"[16] urged caution when interpreting the implications of neuroscience for policy, practice, or parenting. It is never too late to learn.

But as Bruer and his colleagues would acknowledge as well, all this does tell us that there's not a moment to waste. Early experiences clearly do affect the development of the brain. In fact, one of the chief problems about the disproportionate attention to the period from birth to three years is that it begins too late and ends too early.

The brain can be extremely forgiving. In what is referred to as brain plasticity, changes can occur in the organization of the brain as a result of experience. A surprising consequence of brain plasticity is that the brain activity associated with a given function, such as the ability to hear individual sounds in words, can move to a different location through experience or "brain recovery." Scientists have found that the brain is so malleable that very young children who suffer the consequences of injuries or devastating environments can still mature into highly functional adults. Geraldine Dawson and her colleagues at the University of Washington,[17] for example, who have monitored brain-wave patterns of children born to mothers who were suffering from depression, found that if a mother is able to snap out of depression, the child's brain activity in the left frontal lobe quickly picks up. Similarly, Sally Grantham-McGregor and her colleagues, in a randomized controlled trial in Jamaica,[18] demonstrated the resilience of the brain in infants with stunted growth caused by poor nutrition and poverty. Providing children with a stimulation intervention involving weekly play sessions with mothers at home, in two years the damage to children's brain activity was repaired, enabling them to reach about the same stage of development as a control group of low-risk children.

The same holds true, too, for children who survived the Holocaust, children left so traumatized that it appeared they could never function normally. Believing the in malleability of intelligence, Reuven Feuerstein[19] developed the concept of mediated learning, teaching these young children once more how to think for themselves. Using basic geometric shapes (triangles and a rectangle) within a scattershot of dots, he helped the children internalize strategies for solving problems, giving them constant feedback to help them avoid haphazard guesswork. Working one-on-one two hours daily with children such as Jonathan, who suffered from a spectrum of learning difficulties, as well as atypical autism, recovery was slow but progressive. With extensive treatment, Jonathan learned to read and write not only in Hebrew, but in English as well.

It is clear that brain development is not just based on genes. Genes cannot cause behavior. Rather, behavior is the product of a seamless interaction between heredity and environment. The effects of heredity depend crucially on environment. These discoveries about the brain's function and malleability in healthful environments offer not only hope but compelling evidence that highly vulnerable children can overcome glaring deficits in their early years. Even certain inherited disorders such as dyslexia are highly treatable with appropriate intervention, as Dr. Sally Shaywitz and her colleagues at Yale University have found in their studies: "[W]e can never underestimate the environment's power to remodel the brain."[20]

The Child Enters a Social Environment

The brain's architecture, exquisitely attuned to environmental inputs, is shaped by a child's social world. Children's first caregivers have profound effects on virtually every facet of their early development, ranging from the health and the integrity of the baby at birth to the child's readiness for school.

At six weeks, newborns are already craving to learn. Their eyes, ears, and other sensory organs are acutely attuned to new and unfamiliar events. Their eyes are drawn to sharp contrasts and movement, such as a shiny mobile twirling overhead—all these experiences help them derive sophisticated inferences about objects, shapes, sizes, and colors. Soon, their nascent theories about the properties of objects will come together and provide the foundation for an astonishing growth in concepts (including causation), memory, and even problem-solving in some basic form. Each of these accomplishments will reveal just how active the young mind is, demonstrating its desire to learn and how it continuously revises and reinterprets information as it responds to new initiatives and observations about the environment.

But humans are social beings. All of this learning takes place in social surroundings. Studies show that more than any other sights and sounds, newborns prefer the appearance of human faces and the sounds of human voices. In a unique experiment, Patricia Kuhl,[21] professor at the University of Washington, attempted to expose American infants to the sounds of Chinese either through 12 play sessions with an adult or through an identical number of language sessions delivered by DVD either aurally or both aurally and visually. After the play sessions, the American children performed nearly as well as infants in Taiwan who had listened to Mandarin being spoken all their lives. But, equally astounding, infants exposed to the tapes and videos versions demonstrated no learning whatsoever. The message was clear: learning is enhanced in a social setting. The young brain is at work early in development analyzing language, but adults play a critical role in that learning.

Babies turn their heads when they detect the sound of their mother's voice, even perceiving slight variations in pronunciation as totally different sounds. They respond in special ways to social stimuli, orienting themselves toward the people who provide their care and toward those who offer the most interesting and stimulating learning experiences. "Parentese"—that unique sing-songy pitch, with exceptionally well-formed phonetic units—may sound silly to adults, but the child gravitates to it. Kuhl has shown that by the age of six months, a young child allowed to choose whether to listen to women speaking parentese versus the same women speaking to other adults will chose parentese every time. It's the signal an infant prefers. Moreover, Kuhl's research has found that a strong positive relationship exists between the degree to which mothers use this form of speech and their infants' performance on tests of perception.

Disrupted parenting or otherwise negative environmental circumstances of extreme poverty and neglect may expose children to circumstances that one might euphemistically call "canaries in the mineshaft"—early warnings of serious problems to come. While studying early privation in the most wretched of circumstances, as in the infamous case of the Romanian orphans under the misrule of Nicolae Ceausescu, Michael Rutter and his colleagues[22] often confronted children who had virtually no social or cognitive stimulation and few opportunities to establish a relationship with a consistent caregiver. Children failed to babble or coo, making little eye contact with adults. When tested later on, the deficit was found to have increased over time.

This is why family and immediate kin have such power in young children's development: because early experiences can enhance or diminish inborn potential, the environment of early experiences shapes the opportunities and risks those young children will encounter.

The environment has many layers, however, almost like a set of Russian dolls. Noted developmental psychologist Urie Bronfenbrenner[23] described these multiple ecological layers as systems, including the family, the community, and societal environments, each fueling and steering children's development. Just like an old-fashioned teeter-totter, environments push and pull behavior in a well-orchestrated dance of activity, changes or conflict in any one system influencing all the others. Take a classic example: A large corporation decides to shift operations from one plant to another located overseas, causing hundreds of families to lose their jobs and health insurance. Families who have relied for generations on "the company" for work are no longer secure, with few resources to turn to. Things get really tough—so tough that as creditors closely nibble at whatever savings are left, the family faces the real terror of not being able to make the next mortgage payment. Stressed, depressed, and with little energy in reserve, the parents shut down, and the delightful verbal chatter with their baby, known affectionately as "parentese," simply stops. The child, once animated, now feels insecure. The home environment can't buffer all the difficulties that may come from the outside world.

Some years ago, Roger Barker,[24] a trained biologist and an ecological psychologist by trade, made a simple but stunning insight. Likening environments to "activity cages" with his laboratory-conditioned eyes, he found that he could predict human behavior based on people's habitats, or immediate environments. Observing behaviors in different places, he established a set of principles that recognized that although people demonstrate different behaviors in different settings, they seem to demonstrate strikingly similar behaviors in similar settings. Furthermore, these behaviors tend to be consistent and stable within a setting. Whether pumping gas at the local station, going to the city council meetings, or hanging out at the local bar, he found that he could anticipate consistent patterns of behavior within settings. The people you might see engaging in loud, raucous behavior at the local bar on Friday night would be the same individuals sitting quietly and pensively reading scripture in pews on Sunday. Looking at these implicit, set rules of behavior, Barker argued that environments "coerce" behavior, drawing people into a set of intuitive expectations, interactions, and patterns.

Although the magnitude of the effects, according to Barker, might arguably smack of determinism, there's no question that in densely populated poverty areas the environment appears to provoke deeply disturbing patterns. Examining forces that shape inner city neighborhoods, Harvard sociologist William Julius Wilson[25] found in a ground-breaking analysis that after dramatic shifts in the economy and the loss of manufacturing jobs, today's inner cities are more urban, more spatially concentrated, and more clustered in zones of poverty. Left behind in the out-migrations of minorities who have successfully moved into the middle class, ghetto residents are increasingly cut off from job networks, individuals, and institutions that represent the mainstream. What develops in this environment is highly troubling—a set of ghetto-specific norms, behaviors that make steady work seem less likely and a set of habits, skills, and styles running counter to any hope for social mobility and achievement. "Work is not simply a way to make a living and support one's family," Wilson reports. "Work also constitutes a framework for daily behavior and patterns of interaction, because it imposes discipline and regularity. Children who grow up in jobless families and in jobless neighborhoods are negatively affected in many ways, from a lack of working role models to the absence of regularity and routine in their home lives."

Poverty, even if brief, can be harsh and limiting. Every family member is likely to feel its reverberations. But when occasional hard times turn into years upon years of joblessness, or entrenched poverty, the situation takes on a ferocity that imperils children's chances in life. Studies report that the more chronic and persistent an experience of poverty is, and the earlier in life it occurs, the more adverse are its effects on children's development. Based on the Infant Health and Development Program, a longitudinal database of 985 infants and their families, Greg Duncan and his colleagues[26] estimate that five-year-old children exposed to chronic poverty in infancy were likely to average nine IQ points lower than non-poor children. Ripping away a family's dignity, status, and emotional, physical, and intellectual resources, poverty often leaves resentment, futility, and—frankly—irresponsible parenting.

Poor children in America fare worse than more affluent children on almost every measure of well-being for data are collected. It starts with health problems. Children in poverty are likely to suffer from a wide array of chronic health problems, as well as mental retardation, poor hearing, heart problems, digestive disorders, allergies, tooth decay, and obesity. Furthermore, Wilson's documentation of increasingly concentrated poverty in urban areas shows how the effects of poverty move from the individual to the neighborhood. Many neighborhood areas, such as those in Detroit, have lead "hot spots" where lead runs in the community's soil—in the water children drink, the dust in their hair, and on their finger-tips—from peeling lead-based paint. One study[27] reported that as many as 68% of children attending a local pediatric clinic had unsafe levels of lead in their blood. Asthma, the leading cause of children's trips to the emergency room, is on the rise, partially because of the poor quality of housing conditions. It is scarcely surprising that poor children are likely to suffer almost 12 times the number of restricted activity days, school absences, and learning disabilities than their more well-to-do peers.

But it doesn't stop there. Much as in the old adage—"the rich get richer, but the poor get poorer,"—disadvantage accumulates. According to the most exhaustive and reliable source of data, the Early Childhood Longitudinal Study, poor children score about 60% lower in cognitive performance when they enter school,[28] something that remains true through high school. An enormous body of research also demonstrates that these childhood difficulties become associated with adjustment problems in adolescence and adulthood, including delinquency and dropping out of school—not to mention psychopathological problems.

These children's problems become our problems. The exodus of millions of students before 12th grade exacts a tremendous cost on our society through higher unemployment, increased crime, and billions of dollars in lost revenue. A recent study in California,[29] for example, found that just 57% of African American and 60% of Latinos graduated in 2002—66,657 dropouts would cost the state $14 billion in lost wages over the students' lifetimes. Workers having only a high school diploma or less will almost certainly face a difficult future and may be consigned to the "working poor," just above the poverty line. On average, the male high school dropout might have earned about $13.61 per hour in 1973, but now he earns less than $9 an hour. By contrast, workers with advanced degrees earn 20% more per hour than they did in 1973. Perhaps for the first time in its history, America now has a caste-like underclass of unskilled and illiterate persons with no counterpart in the Western world.

This is why the environment of a child matters: it influences every opportunity and risk that young children will encounter. And this is why interventions targeted solely at the family environment will never sufficiently address the needs of vulnerable children. We might even ask ourselves whether there isn't something disingenuous in our professed faith in the omnipotence of the family unit against the thralls of entrenched poverty. Rather, we need to rally every group and institution in the child's social environment to help families thrive and produce healthy children. Little Benjamin might be the apple of his parents' eyes, but if he is living in a home filled with toxins such as lead and mercury, he will be at significant risk for impaired brain growth if the situation endures uncorrected. Baby Rebekah, the jewel of the family, will be at risk living in a community where slum landlords trigger fires in hopes of bilking their insurance companies. Despite all efforts to create a haven for her, toddler Tanya will be at risk in a neighborhood that is too unsafe and too violent for her to play outside.

Healthy environments produce healthy children. Environments characterized by trauma, fear, violence, and uncertainty produce insecure and unhealthy children. This is precisely why we need to mobilize social service agencies, community-based organizations, child care, schools, and clinics to solve problems when these systems break down. When environmental systems begin to crash down upon each other, they take vulnerable children in their grasp and overwhelm them in the undertow.

Poverty's Wake

The question of exactly what to do about child poverty is painful and immensely contentious. Although no social scientist believes that income alone determines how children will turn out, most do believe that parental income has an important influence on children. And it does, but its influence is nowhere near so large as many political liberals imagine, nor nonexistent, as many political conservatives believe. Harvard economist Susan Mayer,[30] in her analyses of two longitudinal datasets, describes the relationship between parent income and child outcome as both complicated and nonlinear: some additional monies improve children's chances, but once basic material needs are met, extra dollars don't seem to relate directly to increased outcomes.

The actual ways in which poverty and low income affect young children's outcomes make it plain that the solution has less to do with doubling parental income or other cash assistance strategies and more to do with culture—conscious values as well as unconscious behaviors. In fact, sociologist George Farkas[31] suggests that culture, as expressed by skills, habits, and styles is the crucial link between family background and education, occupations, and long-term earning capacity. Differences in culture, he argues, are central to the stratification of outcomes and to understanding inequality in American society.

But, as we shall see, differences between the "culture of achievement" and the "culture of material hardship" are neither trivial nor to be underestimated. Instead, they represent a major chasm between middle- and lower-income children, reflecting differing resources and differing kinds and degrees of support for early learning.

The Culture of Achievement

Strolling through town, I see a mother and her toddler as they encounter a beautiful golden retriever. The child squeals with delight, saying "Da, da, da, da" to his mother. Smiling broadly back to him, she says, "Yes, Benjamin, you're right. It's a doggie—*doggie.*" This sort of simple, poignant modeling behavior conceals a complex process by which children discover that patterns of sound take on meaning, and that language represents objects and events.

Many of us delight in the cooing and babbling of a baby's first utterances, those sequences of sound that begin to form words: "baba" for bottle and "wawa" for water, attempts that will become increasingly shaped by interactions with familiar adults. Before long, we know, these charming approximations will become distinguishable words, leading first to telegraphic speech—"Mommy get me"—and then whole sentences. By about three-and-a-half years old, children's conversational skills will grow enormously through several units of exchanges as they extend their vocabulary and develop stories in concert with their friends, family, and caregivers. As speech becomes more elaborate, children's vocabularies grow exponentially. Recent estimates put the average first-grader's vocabulary at about 6,000 words, or about eight words acquired daily between the ages of 18 months and six years.

But language is not just talk. Rather, children use language (increasingly sophisticated words) to learn about the world around them. Despite some differences in theory, both Swiss psychologist Jean Piaget[32] and Russian psychologist Lev Vygotsky[33] recognized the importance of the intersection of language and cognitive development. Children use words to develop important conceptual understandings; language actually drives cognition, with words standing for increasingly sophisticated ideas. Children use the natural medium of language to do their thinking.

However, it's not only what parents say that matters—it's also what they do. Middle-class parents build routines in their children's worlds—grocery shopping, visiting the library, eating out at restaurants: highly familiar events that become internalized over time. Within each of these settings, a set of oral language scripts develops—predictable language sequences conditioning children to anticipate what comes next and to know how to act, becoming almost second nature to children. Just watch a child who visits the library every week. Young Hannah strides confidently to the preschool area, summons the librarian to help her find her favorite *Curious George* book, and runs to the check-out counter—"I wanna check it out!"—without hesitating for a minute, demonstrating a fluidity and automaticity attributable only to a highly familiar routine. Even at these very early ages, parents are exposing children through everyday routines to a repertoire of behaviors and accompanying social conventions associated with learning.

Among the most common routines connected to cognitive gains and vocabulary development are activities centered on book-reading. Evidence of the importance of reading aloud to children abounds in professional literature, but that is not the reason parents read to their children. They read because they find it enjoyable and believe that reading nourishes children's minds and imaginations, enriching their relationships. Parents, usually sensitive to what interests their children, what scares them, what delights them, and what excites their curiosity, use the characters of stories to explore their children's thoughts and feelings, as well as the relationship of events in stories to their own lives.

The sheer volume of research activity around storybook reading captures both the subtlety and the intentionality of child-rearing practices in mainstream families. According to sociologist Annette Lareau,[34] it is a logic of "concerted cultivation," deliberate and sustained efforts by parents to stimulate their children's development and to cultivate their cognitive and social skills. Watch a parent read to her baby, and you'll see a highly repetitive routine that demonstrates this logic. Mother will first evoke Jessica's attention by pointing to a picture and saying, "Look!" She will then ask, "What's that?" If Jessica hesitates even a moment, her mother will answer her own question—"It's a ball!"—supplying the label for the picture. When Jessica points or makes any vocal attempts, her mother adds a confirmation, "That's right, Jessica. They are playing with a ball!"—filling in the response. This pattern of dialogue is repeated page after page as Jessica's mother carries out many of the conversational moves as necessary; in fact, at first little Jessica may contribute nothing more than visual attention.

But the format changes over time. As soon as her mother recognizes a vocalization that even closely approximates the actual label for a picture, she'll change her response. In Jerome Bruner's phrase,[35] a parent will "up the ante," withholding the label and repeating the query until the child vocalizes. She'll say, "Yes, it's a cow" and then extend the word's meaning: "Cows give us milk." She'll encourage Jessica to perform at the highest levels of which she is capable, increasing the demand while at the same time making sure Jessica is engaged and successful in responding to her questions. Through these remarkably intuitive strategies, parents organize progressively more complex learning situations, deftly tuned to the child's needs and inherently intellectually salient and emotionally satisfying to young children. Viewing themselves as cultural transmitters, parents enroll their children in numerous age-specific routines and activities—camp, lessons, tournaments—all designed to develop their talents and interests.

Together, these routines and activities begin to build a set of mental models, or structures that children use to anticipate events, reason, and gain new information. They are akin to architects' models of buildings and molecular biologists' models of complex molecules: a picture theory of meaning used to reason and make inferences. Probably one of the more common examples is the mental model of a story that children who have been well read-to typically develop by the age of three or four. Over time, children internalize a sense of story—essentially a road map of what a story contains, including characters, events, problems, and resolutions. A well read-to four-year-old, such as Jessica, learns to expect that a storybook begins with a literary device such as "Once upon a time . . ." and ends with phrases such as ". . . and they lived happily every after." You'll find that she'll even correct her mother if certain aspects of a story are missing (or shortened for bedtime). This mental model helps children quickly grasp the meaning of other, more complicated stories, a tool that will serve them well as they enter formal schooling.

All the while, like directors of a major production, parents are leading from behind, carefully guiding their children's activities in a rational, issue-oriented manner. They'll encourage verbal give-and-take, sharing their reasoning behind decisions and soliciting their child's objections when he or she refuses to conform. While setting demanding standards of contact, they'll offer freedom with responsibility, always careful never to hem children in with too many restrictions.

Laden with all these tools—a rich and varied vocabulary, a set of discourse practices finely tuned to different environmental settings, books, numerous age-specific activities providing knowledge and experiences about many different things, and a parenting style placing a tremendous emphasis on reasoning and negotiation—the young middle-class child has developed a culture of achievement, armed with the skills, habits, and styles of thinking that will serve her well when entering school.

The Culture of Material Hardship

The contrast for the child living in poverty couldn't be more stark. Money buys material resources, lessons, summer camps, and stimulating learning materials. Without money, these resources are in short supply. In fact, even when families are able to save a few precious dollars to buy materials, these resources don't exist in neighborhoods of concentrated poverty. They are simply not available.

Try walking in a city such as Philadelphia, known not only for its gentrified neighborhoods but for its stark differences in income levels. In the city's Roxborough neighborhood, a city community with a suburban touch, stores carry children's books, street and business signs are plentiful and well-maintained, and even local diners are conducive to reading the newspaper. Then visit Kingsessing in southwest Philadelphia, a poor neighborhood. Here you'll find that coloring books are about the only children's books for sale, billboards and signs are often deteriorated, and the neighborhood pizza shop is not exactly a place where customers linger to read. Children growing up in Roxborough encounter a wide variety of reading materials as they go about their day. For Kingsessing's children, print hardly exists.

These differences are critical, because young children begin to develop a sense of letters and words long before they're formally taught to read. They'll see a stop sign, a bus stop, or a McDonald's logo, and the letters and shapes will begin to take on meaning. As they repeatedly leaf through books at home or at day care, they begin to understand that the pictures and words go together.

But if you walk through poor neighborhoods and ask yourself questions such as these: Are there readable, formative signs in the business district? Can parents in this neighborhood buy children's books at the local stores? What are the quality and quantity of books in child care centers, school libraries, and the public library? Can people be seen reading newspapers or books in laundromats, restaurants, and bus shelters? you'll find the answers highly disconcerting. Whereas children from middle-communities would likely be deluged with a wide variety of reading materials, children from poor neighborhoods have to aggressively and persistently seek them out.

Take just a couple of examples. Walking through these neighborhoods, we found about one book title for every 3 children in Roxborough but one book title for every 300 children in Kingsessing. In Roxborough, just 4% of the signs were in bad shape, compared to 74% in Kingsessing. These contrasts held true at every turn—day care centers, schools, even local libraries.

Or try hanging out at a local restaurant such as Taylor's, a popular breakfast and luncheon spot in middle income area. You'll find newspapers stacked at the end of the front counter, with just about everyone called "hon." Waitresses don't shoo customers away if they sit and read; in fact, they promote it with endless cups of coffee, drawing in regulars such as Michael, a furniture salesman from the suburbs. "I like the environment—I like to sit at the counter. I like to read the paper and chat with the girls," he says as he eats a plate of eggs and French fries while paging through the *Daily News*. But in low-income neighborhoods, public places aren't reader-friendly because of bad lighting, uncomfortable seating, and move-along attitudes.

Libraries are terribly important in poor communities, for they are the single source of literacy for many people. They, more than anything else, hold the potential to level the playing field. But even here, differences in the numbers of books vary strikingly, with about four books per child available in the middle-income neighborhoods, compared to two books per child for the poor. In dangerous neighborhoods, libraries don't even have evening or Saturday hours that make it possible for working parents to come in with their children.

When you are in an environment without books for sale, in which no libraries are open, no one is reading, and all the print signs are covered with graffiti, every aspect of the environment speaks to you and says, "Don't read."

Contemporary poverty discourse often portrays the poor as trapped in concentrated, poverty-stricken neighborhoods beset by a multitude of social pathologies, including high crime rates, poor schools, and lack of jobs. But they are also trapped in other ways as well, including limited access to routines, activities, and lessons—the building blocks of experiences for developing children's language and cognition. Try finding a summer camp in poor areas. While Todd's middle-class mother wrestles over whether to enroll him in Adventure Land, or Breezy Point, both camps set on beautiful acres with basketball, soccer, tennis courts, computer labs, nature studies, and musical and dramatic outlets, Tanya's mother faces a very different choice. Tanya will be waiting until September for the local Head Start program to open (she's on a waiting list), hoping in the meantime to take advantage of the couple of slots that have opened at the Salvation Army camp. With recent budget cuts, the camp's going through hard times. "We're trying to do our best, but it's difficult with the town pool closed for the last umpteenth years," relates Rita, the camp counselor. "Most likely, the children will spend their time at the local library branch, which thankfully got its air conditioning fixed."

Routines are not routine in poor neighborhoods. With limited access to stores, (most of the local ones have closed), grocery shopping can take about four hours, by the time you take public transportation to the nearest store (not the high priced bodega), shopping and then returning home. In a cash-only neighborhood, you might spend your entire day paying for the electrical bill, starting at dawn at the cash checking store and then waiting for your turn at the local gas company store. Because of the hours and hours of waiting, parents often leave their children with kin or friends, giving the children long stretches of leisure time but few organized activities. Attempting to establish some clear boundaries to protect them, parents end up restricting children's autonomy, often favoring strict obedience and punitive measures when trying to keep them from straying too far. The verbal give-and-take so common is middle-class homes is replaced by absolute authority. In this highly constrained environment, children and families are likely to create an even thicker divide between themselves and the outside world.

Children who endure persistent family economic hardship and chronic poverty are likely to have difficulties with peer relationships, including delinquency, school dropout, and psychopathology. Parents' reports, teacher's reports, and self-reports reveal that children lash out, fight, and can't control their emotions or get along with others, externalizing their anger rather than internalizing it in anxiety, sadness, depression, and dependency. Connections between these factors are even more pronounced for boys than girls.

Two Different Worlds

Given these vastly different scenarios, it should come as no surprise that inequality arises and persists in these social environments, translating into enormous differences in children's school readiness skills. According to the results of Betty Hart and Todd Risley's study of language interactions of 42 families,[36] the accumulated linguistic experience of middle-income children when they arrive in kindergarten will total about 45 million words heard or seen, compared to an average child from a welfare home, who will have heard or seen only 15 million words—a 30-million-word gap in exposure to the use of language. The gap in school readiness scores will represent at least a six-month difference between low- and middle-income children. According to the National Household Survey,[37] twice as many poor children will have short attention spans, three times as many will speak in a way that is not understandable to strangers—stuttering or stam-

Table 1.2. The Culture of Material Hardship
• Families reside in poor neighborhoods • Few material resources or stimulating activities for children • Limited access to high-quality child care • Poor schools where achievement is chronically low • Parents speak a dialect of English differing substantially from that used in schools • Extensive health problems • Limited social capital • Threats/violence

mering—and almost five times as many will be in poor health. Only a small fraction of poor preschoolers will display any signs of emerging literacy and the small motor skills necessary to begin writing.

Although not being able to hold a pencil may not be so crucial in this day and age, knowing some letters of the alphabet, beginning sounds, and how to write one's own name certainly is. To become skilled readers, children will need a rich linguistic and conceptual knowledge base, a broad and deep vocabulary, and the verbal reasoning abilities that allow them to understand messages conveyed through print. They'll also need code-related skills, the understanding that spoken words are composed of smaller elements of speech (phonological awareness), the idea that letters represent these sounds (the alphabetic principle), an understanding of the many systematic correspondences between sounds and spellings, and a repertoire of highly familiar words that can be easily and automatically recognized.[38] But a national longitudinal analysis known as Family and Child Experiences Survey, or FACES,[39] indicated that economically disadvantaged children may know perhaps only one or two letters of the alphabet upon entering kindergarten, even as middle-class know nearly all 26. In fact, poor children will lack so many of these skills that they become easy targets for retention in kindergarten after only a few weeks in school.

Starting behind, they'll stay behind. Describing the downward trajectory as the "Matthew Effect"—derived from the Biblical passage: "For unto every one that hath shall be given and he shall have abundance: but from him that hath not shall be taken away even that which he hath" (Matthew XXV:29)— Keith Stanovich[40] has described an all-too-predictable pattern. Children with limited exposure to print before coming to school fall behind in breaking the spelling-to-sound code (phonics) and end up exposed to much less text than their more skilled peers are. With less practice, they become excruciatingly slow, plodding readers. Slow-capacity-draining word recognition processes glue children to the print but not the meaning behind the message. Comprehension breaks down, leading to more unrewarding reading experiences. As these events multiply over time, children eventually give up. To put it more simply—and more poignantly, in the words of a tearful nine-year-old already falling frustratingly behind his peers in reading—"reading affects everything

Table 1.3. Beginning Kindergarten Students' School Readiness Skills by Socioeconomic Status (SES)

	Lowest SES	Highest SES
• Recognizes letters of the alphabet	39%	85%
• Identifies initial sounds of words	10%	51%
• Identifies primary colors	69%	90%
• Counts to 20	48%	68%
• Writes own name	54%	76%
• Hours read to before kindergarten	25	1,000
• Accumulated experience with words	13 million	45 million

Source: S. B. Neuman, "From rhetoric to reality: The case for high-quality compensatory prekindergarten programs," *Kappan* 85 (2003): 286–291.

you do." Without reading skills in school, children start down the slippery slope of nonachievement, tracked in to low-level courses, all too frequently dropping out of school altogether.

Rather than changing the trajectories of children who start out behind, schools too often merely reproduce social inequality. According to social reproduction theorist Pierre Bourdieu,[41] schools begin by sorting students into stratified classes giving them access to different levels of knowledge. They then channel them into jobs at different levels in the stratified occupational structure. As a result—more often than not—students from various social classes and ethnic groups end up in positions highly similar to the ones occupied by their parents.

When observing classrooms, however, you'll probably see a sorting process far less intentional—though no less damaging—than Bourdieu suggests. Placed in charge of relatively large classes (20 or more), most teachers must teach to the average—those children who arrive in kindergarten with a reasonably broad fund of knowledge. Trying to activate children's prior knowledge even in the earliest stages of schooling, teachers refer constantly to concepts that they assume children already know. They'll discuss nursery rhymes and fairy tales, for example, in order to connect new pieces of information with things already familiar to children. When these analogies fail to connect with some children's knowledge or understanding of words, classroom transactions will be ineffectual, and learning will be lost. Sometimes, teachers will be compelled to slow down, stop, and teach—or reteach—but doing so often comes at the expense of other young children who want to move ahead. Conscious of the need to manage an increasingly restless and impatient group, teachers move on.

Many teachers are forced to triage, teaching to the "bubble" kids—the children who already possess some background knowledge and are able to learn new things more readily than those who lack it. Paced to cover certain material by days, weeks, and months, even the best teachers will have to make compromises for the sake of the larger group. Although teachers diagnose, refer, recommend, and suggest additional supports for the students who are falling behind, remediation for most will be outside their reach as they quietly and futilely fall further and further behind. Even of those lucky enough to get remedial help, only about one out of every three are likely to benefit and attain some level of success.[42]

Why Are We Waiting for Children to Fail?

The saddest part of this scenario is that all these findings could have been predicted before children ever enter the schoolhouse door. Policy makers refer to the complex set of environmental conditions related to low achievement as "risk factors." Children who live below the poverty line, speak a language other than English, have a mother with less than a high school education, live in a family with only one parent present, or live in a single-parent family will likely be identified as "at risk," meaning they will have fewer accomplishments and more learning difficulties after they start school. In fact, policy makers have delineated 15 or more risk factors all related to poverty, regardless of race or ethnicity.

In estimating the sheer dimension of the problem, the nonpartisan Child Trends organization reports that of the approximately 3.9 million kindergartners entering school, 2.2 million will lag behind in at least one area, 610,000 will lag behind in at least two areas, and about 5%—or just under 200,000 children each year—will lag behind in three. These children will have less than a 50–50 chance of making it through school and staying off welfare.

Although creating a terminology for characterizing low achievement may reduce policymakers' uncertainty about why so many children are not successful, it certainly hasn't influenced policies for the better. In fact, it may make things worse by stereotyping children by their social status. Rather than focusing on identifying those who may fail, it makes far more sense to identify pathways for how we may help such students succeed in schooling. Based on what we know about the culture of achievement through an enormous body of evidence, we can explain the reasons why poverty takes such a terrible toll on children's development and learning capabilities.

Materials and resources. Poor families are resource-poor. They lack access to educational resources such as books, newspapers, and magazines that may help them extend their worlds and increase their children's verbal skills. They lack cognitively stimulating games, toys, and activities, such as blocks and puzzles, to support their children's independent explorations and help them develop reasoning and problem-solving skills. Studies show the scarcity of typical tools of literacy in many of these homes, including paper for children's drawing, large pencils, markers, crayons, magnetic letters, and stencils—among many other educational resources.

Children also lack organized activities, sports, and social and recreational programs. As Milbrey McLaughlin and her colleagues found in their studies of inner-city boys and girls clubs,[43] children develop talents through special relationships with other adults described as "old wizards"—people having specialized abilities and interests. These clubs not only promote children's physical and social–emotional well-being, but they also provide children with new ideas, interests, knowledge, and vocabulary, taking them away from the insularity of their immediate environments.

Because so many families are cloistered in unsafe neighborhoods, high-quality child care is another institutional resource that too often eludes poor families. Early childhood programs are critically important, for they can act as mediators of neighborhood effects on young children's outcomes. Children need programs full of cognitively stimulating activities involving language, reasoning, and socialization that recognize that learning is as essential for human growth and development as nurturance and safety are.

These materials and resources can't replicate the advantages that children from middle-class homes have, but they provide a foundation, an indispensable safety net, a world of stimulation that allows children's natural curiosity and interest in learning to thrive, not atrophy.

Language Supports. The ravages of poverty may be catastrophic for poor children's language and vocabulary development. A half-century's worth of literature on language[44] indicates that they will hear a smaller proportion of words—with

---

Table 1.4.   Risk Factors for Young Children

- Poverty
- Infant and child mortality
- Low birth weight
- Single parents
- Teen mothers
- Mothers who use alcohol, tobacco or drugs
- Transience
- Child abuse and neglect
- Lack of high-quality day care
- Low-wage jobs for parents
- Unemployed parents
- Lack of access to health and medical care
- Low parent education levels
- Poor nutrition
- Lack of contact with English as the primary language

Source: Hodgkinson, H. "Leaving too many children behind" (Washington, D.C.: Institute for Educational Leadership, 2003).

more limited syntactic complexity—and fewer conversation-eliciting questions, making it difficult for children to quickly acquire new words or discriminate among words. In our studies, for example,[45] we found that our four-year-olds had difficulty discriminating among common object labels, referring to a pad, stationary, a letter, and an envelope each as "mail."

As the noted sociolinguist William Labov noted,[46] poor children may be highly competent in narrative structure, syntactic sophistication, and inferencing skills in the complex world of the inner-city dialects heard throughout the country. Nevertheless, language is an instant signifier—of class, race, ethnicity, and of educational level. These children will be deprived of the background knowledge and conventions they will need in order to understand what is being said by teachers and books. They'll lack experience in the uses of language for abstraction. "What breaks my heart is their talk," says Joann McCall, a middle school teacher of 20 years. "They almost seem to grope for words, using phrases 'Like, like, you know'." In order to understand spoken or written speech, experts estimate that a person will need to know about 95% of the words; 5% can then be inferred from the context. If we assume that an average kindergartner knows 95% of the words in a teacher's remarks, the result is that the child is gaining not only new knowledge, but also the ability to infer the meaning of the other 5% of words as well.

Now, by way of contrast, take the less advantaged child, who will suffer a double loss. From the beginning, he'll find the conversation puzzling, because he doesn't know enough of the words to understand it. Not only will he fail to understand the basic message, he will also fail to learn new word meanings from the context of the conversation. Added to the double loss is a potential triple loss—of the interest, self-confidence, and motivation necessary for learning.

Children in poor communities are likely to hear many "nos" and "don'ts," prohibitions that serve to restrict rather than excite the habits of seeking, noticing, and incorporating new and increasingly complex experiences. Hart and Risley, in their study of language,[47] found that although the average child in the professional home accumulated 32 affirmatives and 5 prohibitions each hour, the average child in the welfare home accumulated 5 affirmatives and 11 prohibitions, which in one year works out to 26,000 encouragements and 57,000 discouragements. Poverty-stricken parents, feeling out of control themselves, may attempt to overly control their children's behavior (sometimes through harsh punishment), restricting and disapproving instead of redirecting or extending children's capacities for categorizing and thinking about new experiences. Multiply these daily experiences by the number of years that elapse before any formal schooling begins, and you can understand the need for intensive language supports.

Human and Social Capital. Raising children involves an enormous investment in community resources. Social scientists[48] use the expressions "human capital" and "social capital" to describe and quantify these effects. *Human capital* refers to the basket of skills, education, and qualifications that individuals bring to the marketplace—the capacities to deal with abstractions, recognize and adhere to rules, and use language to reason. *Social capital*, or the benefits of strong social bonds, was first described by sociologist James Coleman[49] as "the norms, the social networks, the relationships between adults and children that are of value for the children's growing up." It works somewhat the same. Just as any other forms of capital, human and social capital accumulate over generations, part of the culture of achievement that children successfully bring to and deploy in school.

But in poor communities in which institutions have disintegrated and mothers often keep children locked inside, fearing for their safety, human and social capital hardly exist. Possessed of limited education and skills, parents face tremendous obstacles in their attempts to acquire human capital, often experiencing life crises greater frequency and intensity than others do.

Lacking human and social capital often leads to a feeling of powerlessness, especially when attempting to deal with complex bureaucracies, whether of clinics, emergency rooms, or schools. As Annette Lareau describes,[50] middle-class parents' superior levels of education give them vocabularies that can help them deal with institutional settings. Trained in the "rules" of the game, they can take over, dominating interactions. Poor families and working class parents, on the other hand, may not be familiar with the key terms and phrases professionals use, such as "tetanus shot" or "stanines, percentages, and norms," and they generally don't want to ask. Evidencing a sense of constraint, they may just accept the actions of those who are in authority.

Yet what may be perceived as a lack of caring and involvement—particularly in relation to academic activities—may actually be a lack of confidence on their part. This is why parents need mechanisms such as parent education groups with which they may forge connective ties and develop shared assumptions, as well as mutual responsibility. The provision of a coffee room where parents can informally chat in small groups may be far more effective than the traditional one-shot parent education meeting in which an adult, acting in an authoritarian manner, uses jargon and off-putting language.

We can all take a lesson from many Head Start programs that have elevated the role of parent education and involvement, creating real leadership opportunities among parents—much to the benefit of their children's learning and development. If you ever visit a Head Start, you'll find a homey atmosphere in many of the parent rooms. You'll feel comfortable and welcomed. Sometimes parents will be working on crafts together, getting ready for a tag sale, or listening to a speaker from the local community. Although these programs don't reverse all the ill effects that come with a starkly disadvantaged status in society, they show that parents can collectively accumulate social capital, gaining a better sense of control over their lives and the lives of their children.

"Creating circles of human connectivity," as Robert Putnam beautifully describes[51] "a bonding of people," won't make the problems associated with economic disadvantage, depression, and hardship go away for these families, but it will help, and it will give tangible and intangible support systems that may allow parents, in turn, to give greater support, stimulation, and nurturance to their children.

You'll find in the chapters that follow that successful programs aimed at changing the odds for vulnerable young children come in many varieties, shapes, and sizes. Some are home-based; others are delivered in centers. Some are small-scale and others more comprehensive, meeting a broad array of objectives. Nevertheless, they all share a common set of features. Recognizing that children's early development is highly susceptible to environmental influence, they provide stimulating materials and resources to help offset the devastating paucity of programs in many neighborhoods. They combine child-focused educational activities with explicit attention to parent–child interaction patterns. They also help parents develop "self-righting" tendencies through educational, social, and networking strategies to become more responsive to their children, acting as better advocates for their needs. You'll see that the scientific evidence resoundingly supports this basic premise: when we change the environment, we change the opportunities available. When we change opportunity, we give people hope for a better future.

Starting Out Right

Like a bleeding wound, poverty weakens one's defenses. It lowers resistance: by the time children reach adolescence, many show the signs of poverty's debilitating effects. Although we must do everything in our power to help youngsters at any stage in their development and never give up, we must also recognize that earlier help would have been better help.

The longer we wait, the more difficult it gets and the more burdensome it becomes to society. Counteracting deprivation, poor health, and limited stimulation is extremely costly. Compare, for example, the costs for the average child in Head Start—our major early intervention program for poor children—at approximately $6,666 per child, to Reading Recovery, a highly specialized remedial reading program in the primary grades, at $15,000 per child. The combined expenditures on remediation exceed over $2.1 billion each year. Early intervention programs are not only more economical and effective, but they can also help us fight failure and despair when life trajectories are more easily alterable.

We can begin by giving children the skills they need in order be successful in school. Economically disadvantaged children are every bit as eager to learn as their more economically advantaged peers are. But what they lack are the skills and knowledge necessary to do so. This deficit sets them on a trajectory of low academic achievement, with all the negative social and personal outcomes that are associated with poor school performance. We can prevent this negative spiral before it ever has time to begin by helping children develop necessary skills efficiently and effectively. Especially in the cases of children who have lived in highly disruptive settings, these early experiences will provide routines and structure that will help children better cope with the later demands of schooling at a critical time in their development.

Without help, some of our neediest children will beat the odds. Blessed with wonderful teachers and mentors, some will get through school relatively unscathed, earning decent livings and raising healthy children. Tragically, however, most will not. Most will struggle throughout their life, knowing full well that the odds are not stacked in their favor.

We can change this equation. As subsequent chapters will show, we can radically increase the chance that millions of ordinary children growing up in environments that threaten their healthy development will come into successful adulthood. Such gains won't come about by magic or by over-promising and under-delivering. They *will* come about by implementing policies that fund what works—research-based programs that have been shown beyond a shadow of a doubt to fundamentally change the odds for how we educate our most vulnerable children. And the next chapter describes how we can afford to do so.

CHAPTER 2

CHANGING THE ODDS BY FUNDING WHAT WORKS

Cynicism about the performance of government is a common if not always constructive refrain in today's conversations as much as when, years ago, Will Rogers exclaimed, "Thank God we don't get the government we pay for!" The toll is arguably highest, according to finance expert Mark Friedman and his associates,[1] among programs providing health, education, and social services. Confidence in government has eroded; the problems often appear too intractable and too expensive to fix.

But the problem is not funding. Since 1965, federal spending on K–12 education has ballooned from slightly more than $9 billion to nearly $68 billion. The problem is poor policy implementation. Federal programs, badly outdated, are not supporting disadvantaged children. Title I, enacted in 1965 to redress the educational disadvantages of poor children, has evolved into a complex, hybrid program that now includes every student enrolled in more than 16,000 schools, diluting any potential benefit for at-risk children. Thirty years and some $200 billion later, experts paint a dismal picture of incoherent, minimal, and weak programs, unsuccessful even on their own terms. The result is nothing short of tragic for America's children.

We can no longer defend an indefensible system that robs children of the time and opportunity needed to learn. Consensus agrees that government must change. Signaling efforts to restore public confidence, innovative agencies and districts have made a profound shift toward greater accountability and a focus on outcomes. Traditionally, public institutions were judged on inputs—what was bought, and how wisely money was spent—producing an audit trail that provided little information regarding a program's efficacy. Today, taxpayers demand to know whether public funds are accomplishing their intended outcomes—a focus on results. In education and human services, these results are defined in terms of measurable improvements in children's achievement—nothing less will do.

Results-based accountability represents a dynamic restructuring of funding using the best scientific principles available to implement policy in ways that increase the likelihood of disadvantaged children coming to school ready to learn and achieve. Focusing on results rewards programs that work, programs that have created a solid evidentiary record based on data, not anecdote.

The ramifications are nothing less than a major, transformative shift in how government works. At the very outset, results-based accountability highlights the enormous waste in federal spending. Today's education budget includes an extraordinary number of earmarks, pet projects by Congressmen and well-connected individuals diverting millions from what otherwise might be spent helping our most disadvantaged children. A focus on results unveils—perhaps for the first time—the sheer number of ineffective programs that are continually funded despite countless evaluations indicating little or no impact on achievement. By looking at results, it becomes clear that the public is often not getting what it is paying for, the result of poor program monitoring, helter-skelter implementation, and a tendency to spread the largess rather than focusing on those in greatest need.

Funding what works moves away from such excess to focus on programs targeted at raising children's achievement. Here, there is no shortage of exciting developments. In this chapter and those that follow, you'll read case studies about programs that will make it hard to understand why anyone would continue along the tortuous path of the last three decades with policies that have failed to produce any real gains for children.

We have an opportunity to turn government spending into a real force for changing the odds that disadvantaged children will learn successfully—not by spending more, but by spending better.

A Focus on Results

Effective programs have defined objectives designed to produce specified, measurable outcomes. Outcomes, or results, are bottom-line conditions of well-being that may include readiness for school, success in school, avoidance of trouble, successful employment, familial stability and self-sufficiency, and community productivity. Outcomes-based programs are required to spend public monies on services having a measurable impact on children's lives, monitoring how effectively and efficiently these programs work and striving continually to improve program results.

All this might not appear like rocket science, but a focus on results actually represents a massive change in the way human-service programs are used to measuring their performance. A focus on input—"number of clients served" or "amount of services provided"—has been the prevalent judge of effectiveness. A family literacy program, for example, used to be considered effective if it recruited many adults, provided a certain number of hours of instruction, held discussion groups, and gave parents a certain number of hours of child care. Whether or not the program helped parents get skilled jobs, and get off public assistance, or whether children came to school ready to learn, however, was regarded as either assumed or too distant a goal.

It is this misapplication—the focus on inputs—that captures much of what has gone wrong with the way we have traditionally measured programs. The number of clients served is not an output. It is an input, an action that should lead to a change in children's achievement—the output, what makes a real difference. Outputs, or results, answer three essential questions: What is the program trying to achieve? How is the program progressing? Have the desired results been achieved? These questions focus on results and represent a whole different frame of mind and a whole different approach to measuring effectiveness.

A closely related problem, noted extensively by economist Eric Hanushek of Stanford University,[2] involves treating dollars spent as inputs and measuring whatever the program happens to buy with those dollars as outputs. The problem is revealed when the relationship between resource uses and student performance is considered. In an innovative analysis, Hanushek aggregated data about the performance of schools over time against highly detailed school and classroom resource data. He found no consistent or systematic effect of resources on student achievement. Greater resources did not equal greater achievement. No wonder, then, the public's impatience with repeated calls for additional funding.

A result or outcome-based orientation clearly articulates the things that programs are designed to achieve. By themselves, however, expected outcomes don't provide a sufficient roadmap with which to assess whether or not program results are being accomplished. Indicators or benchmarks are necessary with which to measure progress along the way. Indicators are measures for which we have data, measures that help quantify the achievement of a desired result. They ask such questions as: "Are we on the right path? Do we need mid-course corrections? Is our intervention sufficiently powerful to ensure success? Indicators provide immediate and ongoing feedback to program leaders, who may then respond when programs go off-course.

Designing a system that focuses on results also requires fidelity measures, or quality control measures, to ensure that the promising model or program is being scaled up successfully, not diluted into ineffectiveness. Typical fidelity measures address compliance with standards, the quality of the staff, and the quality of the delivery that made the program successful in the first place. Measures of fidelity do not tap program implementation mindlessly, without recognizing the importance of adaptations in different settings, but they do require that certain features be in place if programs are to create results.

A focus on results, therefore, examines both means and ends. Results and indicators have to do with ends. Fidelity or quality control measures (to examine the integrity of the program) have to do with the means. The end we seek is not better services, but better results.

We can hold programs accountable for the best possible performance using an adaptation of a four-quadrant approach for measuring results-based budgeting.[3]

As shown by Figure 2.1 at the top level of the quadrant, we ask, "What is the intensity of the services we provide? How well are the services delivered?" Here, we use fidelity measures to address these questions. Indicators cross inputs with outputs to carefully detail progress toward outcomes. Measures of results, shown in the bottom quadrant, examine two types of evidence: quantifiable results, measured in improved child outcomes (e.g., achievement), and consequential validity. To be confident of results, we need evidence that children's lives have benefited from a program (e.g., fewer remedial services are now needed).

A results-based mentality helps to focus our attention on several key factors. It asks a number of questions: Have we put sufficient resources into programs to achieve desired results? If not, what resources are necessary to achieve similar results? Finally, if programs repeatedly produce disappointing outcomes, we may need to discontinue their funding.

The Government Performance and Results Act of 1993 (GPRA) was the first attempt to move in this direction to improve program effectiveness and public accountability by promoting a new focus on results, service quality, and so-called customer satisfaction. The law, which requires agencies to produce results and offer solutions to problems, aims to improve the government's management of programs, giving the public information regarding agencies' performance. It's a

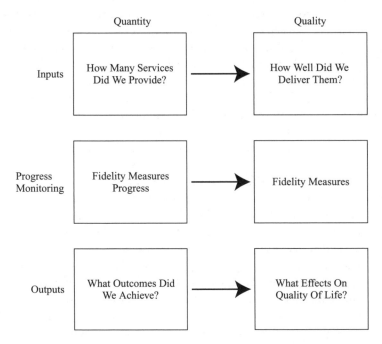

Figure 2.1.
Results-Based Accountability.

step in the right direction, even though, unfortunately, some agencies, according to a review by the Mercatus Center at George Mason University,[4] continue to ignore the results, using it more as a bureaucratic exercise than as an effort to make programs more effective.

What Constitutes Evidence of Results?

Funding what works clearly requires evidence. Agencies need data, not persuasive argument or testimonials, to determine what programs deserve public support. Drawing effectively on rigorous evidence is crucial for improving children's odds, moving us toward a more rational and systematic way of funding programs. Evaluative techniques, ranging from "gold standard" research techniques to promising practices using multiple forms of empirical evidence, are now available to definitively answer such questions as *Does the program work?* and *If so, under what set of conditions?*

Gold-Standard Evidence: The Randomized Controlled Trial

Life in America has been profoundly improved over the last 50 years by the use of medical practices demonstrated to be effective in randomized, controlled trials. These are studies that randomly assign individuals to an intervention group or to a control condition in order to measure the effects of a program. Practices proven in randomized controlled trials to be effective include vaccines for polio, measles, and hepatitis B and have brought about treatments that have dramatically improved survival rates of cancer and other illnesses.

Illustrating the importance of this methodological strategy, Stephan Raudenbush, one of sociology's most prominent methodologists and a professor at the University of Chicago,[5] likens the current effort to the early studies of the Salk vaccine in the 1940s and 1950s. These early studies seemed to show in essence that the vaccine wasn't effective. People who had the vaccine were almost as likely, or equally likely, to get polio as those who did not. Further, it showed a disturbing pattern that higher income families were more likely to get polio than were other socioeconomic groups, contradicting the prevailing hypothesis that polio and sanitation were related.

Subsequently, in 1954, scientists conducted a very important, huge, national randomized clinical trial of the vaccine. This was a double blind trial in which the treatment was disguised to both physicians and patients, with one group receiving a vaccine and the other a placebo of sugar water. The results were definitive. Use of the vaccine was far more effective than not, leading to further improvements and further clinical trials. The vaccine ultimately helped wipe out polio as a disease in America.

Striking parallels exist in education and social services. The first evaluation of the Head Start program, for example—what came to be known as the Westinghouse study—showed that Head Start had little effect on children's cognitive skills, regardless of whether they attended the program or not. Subsequent analyses revealed that the study was highly flawed because of large differences in the original sample, indicating that the Head Start children in the study were far poorer than non-Head Start children. Some argued that the results actually showed that the Head Start program might be highly effective because the children were doing better than otherwise expected. Others, however, claimed that the results showed that Head Start was ineffective. Both saw the same evidence, but the evidence was so weak that it couldn't really decide the question.

Left unchallenged, the Westinghouse study would have concluded erroneously that the program was ineffective. The study would have found that early intervention caused no substantial improvements in children's health, well-being, or cognitive outcomes. But, in fact, the instability of test scores was the result of other factors: the limited intervention period (some Head Starts were only summer programs), the differences in the selection of subjects (some were very needy; some were not), and still other factors.

The power of experimentation in random assignment can eliminate these types of confounding variables. Since then, researchers[6] have conducted better evaluations of Head Start to make sure that the children being compared are similar in their families' incomes and other social indicators. These studies, most recently reported in randomized trial estimates, indicate that Head Start has a positive, albeit modest, effect on children's language, cognitive abilities, and social behavior. With such evidence in hand, implementers may now examine ways to strengthen the program's effectiveness.

Our knowledge of what works has been deeply influenced by the results of randomized trials. Gathering many of these studies on one-to-one tutoring, Barbara Wasik and her colleagues,[7] for example, have definitively made the case that one-on-one tutoring by qualified tutors substantially improves students' reading proficiency. On an early Tuesday morning in Detroit, I watched as Wayne Yu sat at the library table with tutor Mary Snyder, attempting to read sentences. As he picked at his breakfast of eggs, he read, "She . . . st . . . ay . . . ed . . . at . . . the . . . ea . . . ch . . . ." "Not 'each,'" Snyder corrected softly. "You've got the 'b' sound at the beginning . . . try it again" "B . . . beach." "That's right. Great!" replied his tutor as Wayne beamed, one more sentence now in the bag. He finished the sentence, gulped down some chocolate milk, and ran off to class. Suddenly, he ran back, this time to retrieve his book. Proudly, he opened it up to finish one last sentence, "Will horse . . . shoe crabs be . . . b . . . ack next year? asks Billy," he read. It was a visible success story—the kind of story that happens when money is used to fund programs that work.

Or take the advances in classroom management techniques that result from randomized trials of the "Good Behavior Game," a low-cost intervention strategy for first-graders that rewards students for positive group behavior. Visiting a hardscrabble elementary school in a slowly gentrifying corner in this same city, I watched as the teacher kept order not by military precision but by playing a game rewarding children for staying on task. Students were divided into teams and a point given to a team for any inappropriate behavior displayed by one its members. "Hey, he didn't raise his hand," reported first-grader Madaline, as her teacher Samantha Burnell awarded her team a point. Gradually, the 10-minute game, played three times weekly, has become "a model for behavior all the time in class," says Burnell. And tracking these results over time in a randomized trial, Sheppard Kellam[8] has provided some powerful evidence to substantiate her claims, reporting a reduction of 30–60% in substance abuse, fewer school suspensions and conduct disorders, and a reduction of 25–60% in smoking and hard drug use, when compared to controls. "Learning how to be a student is not always intuitive," Burnell says. "Sometimes you've got to teach it."

Randomized controlled trials can also tell us what does not work. For example, despite continuing federal support, we now have convincing evidence from three clinical trials that Even Start—a federal program designed to improve family literacy (adults and children) has no effect on children's school readiness and no lasting effects on adult literacy.[9] According to results-based accountability, such research suggests that we should redirect our energies into new program development, funding only what works.

Descriptive Studies

As important as randomized controlled trials are, there are times when they may not be appropriate—or, in some cases, sufficient. There are terrifically important questions for policy, for example, that may not be causal. Have high school graduation rates changed over the past 10 years? Which children from which areas, and in which kinds of schools, are at highest risk of dropping out? Are there trends or changes in reading achievement for different groups of children over the last decade? We need surveys that are carefully designed to answer these questions.

But even when a question is causal, it may be impossible to do a randomized study to answer it. Consider another analogy with medicine: researchers have come to a strong consensus that smoking causes lung cancer even though we've certainly never had a clinical trial where we randomly assigned people to smoke two packs a day. We use multiple forms of evidence to come to these conclusions.

Randomized experiments can give us confidence in a program's general effectiveness. Yet, at the same time, these experiments sometime create artificial circumstances that limit our ability to generalize our findings to different settings. The randomized evidence might be crucial, but it must be supplemented to see whether a new program works in a less controlled setting. This often requires qualitative analyses that carefully study how expert practitioners in real settings implement the program under real conditions, as well as under what conditions it is effective.

Take, for example, a qualitative analysis we conducted to better understand how young second-language learners fared in pre-K classes whose class size was increased, by mandate, from 15 to 20, to cut costs. As the teacher orchestrated activity for 20 four-year-olds, I noticed how Ricardo, who had just arrived in the country, appeared almost invisible to his teachers. During music time, his eyes wandered off in another direction; during reading, he squirmed his way out of the circle. Throughout the day, he didn't say a word—whether to his teachers or to his peers—until his mother picked him up. Perhaps even more remarkably, not one of the teachers or aides spoke to him. This child—who needed all sorts of help in learning language, forming relationships, and understanding how things work in this country, received no special attention at all.

This kind of qualitative evidence helps us understand differential patterns of implementation. We cannot just say, "This shows that early care and education programs work." As scientists, we need to search for disconfirming evidence or for alternative explanations for why the program worked. We need to know what makes the program successful. We also need to look at whether some children are being left behind. These ingredients of implementation are critical for practitioners and policy-makers.

Empirically Validated Programs

Randomized controlled trials are expensive and not always feasible, especially in large community-based programs. It may not be possible to randomly assign individuals to a program that relies on including all community members. Many programs that look at the effectiveness of comprehensive community-based initiatives may be highly individualized to the particular needs of the community and impossible to transfer to other settings. Further, promising social programs are often complex efforts with multiple components that require constant mid-course corrections and adaptations to changing circumstances. Yet this is no rationale for merely asking the public to "trust" in the quality of the program or its effectiveness.

In our work, we have developed a method called the "formative experiment"[10] that gathers a rich set of clues and empirically validated evidence that can support promising practices. Conventional experiments try to control for the influences of situations and circumstances to ensure that an intervention is implemented uniformly. Formative experiments expect variations and deal with them while asking pertinent questions: What factors enhance or inhibit the intervention's effectiveness in achieving their goals? How can the intervention or its implementation be modified to better achieve that goal? Examining both goals and outcomes, they set out to find what it takes, in terms of materials, organization, and people, to reach the goal. My colleague David Reinking, professor at Clemson University, has defined the qualities of a formative experiment even further:[11]

- What are the goals of the intervention, and what data already exist that suggest its effectiveness?
- What factors enhance or inhibit the intervention's effectiveness?

- How can the intervention and its implementation be modified to achieve more effective outcomes?
- Have the outcomes been met?
- What unanticipated positive or negative effects does the intervention produce?

The point is to gather multiple indicators of evidence to determine what programs are worth supporting, which are not, and which need serious revision.

Instead formative experiments also allow us to pursue interesting modifications in the ways that programs are delivered, based on findings. For example, we know that a young mother's poverty, social isolation, and lack of education constitute major risk factors for children's immediate and later outcomes in life. Home-visiting programs—programs designed to help parents become more attached to their children—have shown relatively weak effects on child outcomes.

Even gold-standard randomized trial experiments, however, can't explain the reasons for these disappointing findings. In fact, the insights from these experiments are relatively modest. Formative experiments, however, begin to help us generate new hypotheses. They allow us to systematically examine why some home-visiting programs, such as Early Head Start, might be influential even as others, such as HIPPY (Home Instruction Program for Preschool Youngsters) and Hawaii Healthy Start, are not.[12] They help us realize that when you combine a home-visiting program with a mental health intervention, you have a more substantial outcome for both mothers and children.

For example, we conducted a formative study of a massive book flood on young children's developing awareness of print and of skills associated with school readiness.[13] Hundreds of books were delivered to child care centers in hopes that providers would read to children regularly. The intervention was based on solid research evidence that access to books improves the quality of teacher-talk and helps children to learn new vocabulary, among other benefits. As a formative experiment, however, we gathered highly detailed information—photographic analyses, observations, interviews—that began to reveal a very different scenario than expected. To the funders' dismay, the books were rarely unpacked and largely sat in corners, unused by the children.

Our interviews indicated that, among other barriers, child care workers had no place to put the books. Further, they doubted that children as young as two-and-a-half could listen attentively to someone reading a story to them. Using information from these data, program developers put in place new bookshelves and brought in coaches to teach providers how to read stories well to the children. These changes caused substantial improvements in children's school readiness skills.

Determining what factors enhance or inhibit an intervention's effectiveness in achieving a goal, and determining how the intervention or its implementation might be modified to better achieve that goal, are central to formative experiments. They not only fill a much-needed practical gap between randomized controlled trials and other experimental models but are also especially appropriate when studying how large delivery systems or comprehensive community-based initiatives may be contoured to a community or group. This approach, recognizing that all programs are likely to need tailoring to local circumstances, carefully details how and why such modifications are necessary in order to achieve results.

Case Studies

Randomized controlled trials and formative experiments rely on the use of comparison groups or controls that have not received the intervention to assess the added value of a particular intervention. But there are times when such comparisons are simply not possible. This is particularly true when studying large-scale community-based initiatives that target all the individuals in a certain geographic area or among a given group of people. For example, community-based initiatives might include a universal pre-kindergarten program designed to enroll all low-income children in the region, or perhaps a drop-out prevention program.

Still, we need evidence of results. We need to know whether the intervention consciously undertaken by the community-wide initiative generates change in outcomes.

As in virtually all community-based initiatives, the problem is establishing what would happen in the absence of the initiative. To make some type of adjustments, evaluators typically create a counterfactual by establishing some kind of comparison or benchmark against which to measure progress. We might look at the situation before and after the initiative is implemented in a given community, or we might compare communities having similar demographics but without the initiative. For example, in the case of universal prekindergarten, evaluators have compared children's school readiness-scores as they enter kindergarten before the initiative began, and then again after the program has been in place. In some cases, they might also compare states that have such initiatives with those that do not.

Or take the case of the summer slide. In this case, my colleague Donna Celano, professor at LaSalle University, and I wanted to better understand how time off in the summer affected disadvantaged children's skill development. Watching children interact in the library throughout the summer months in low- and middle-income neighborhoods, we came to realize the enormous differences in summer learning. Although Maeve, grandmother to four-year-old Justin, spent her time in a middle-class neighborhood library interacting continuously over books, reading *The Little Prince*, parts of *Winnie the Pooh*, and *Thomas the Tank Engine* in a single day's visit, in the low-income area, little Hilda's entreaties to her mom were answered in an un-library-like voice, with, "Put that book down. I don't want to read this," her mother preferring to play checkers with her son instead. Recording behaviors over the course of the summer, we noticed an average of 126 words per minute spoken to the middle-income child, but only 67 words to low-income children. The average number of words read by the child followed a similar pattern, with 1350 words read per child in the middle-income area to only 810 words read per child in the low-income area. Just imagine the achievement gap if early education programs were to shut down, converting early childhood years into an endless summer!

These kinds of case studies help explain patterns of behavior that would otherwise go unnoticed in larger, randomized trials. Furthermore, they often provide a more detailed description with which to better understand behaviors or interventions. Our findings, for example, both confirmed and further explained a landmark study of summer learning. Heyns[14] found that if opportunities for compulsory schooling did not exist, substantially greater inequality of outcomes associated with educational background would occur, and the children most dramatically affected would be precisely those with the fewest resources to fall back on.

Sometimes community-based initiatives may not show detectable effects in the short term. The well known Perry Preschool study, for example, in its earliest phases showed only modest effects. It was the long-term outcomes—improvement in employment, earnings, and delinquency—that is now most often talked about. Too often, community programs, in the flush of great enthusiasm, initially overreach, anticipating too great an immediate effect. Instead, careful evaluators should at the outset consider such questions as

- What is the final set of outcomes we hope to achieve? What would constitute the initiative's success or failure?
- Can we derive a set of intermediate goals related to our long-term outcomes?
- What is a reasonable timeline for achieving these outcomes?
- What are the costs and benefits of the initiative?

Community-based initiatives are, no doubt, difficult to evaluate. There are no sure-fire methods that may help to avoid a host of problems, making conclusions vulnerable to bias.

At the same time, we can't just dismiss programs as just too hard to evaluate, blindly following assertions that they work. We can no longer fund good intentions. Instead, evaluators must pull together a full set of data, looking at short- and long-term outcome measures to provide comprehensive information on the initiative. Systematic compilations of information begin to make a case based on evidence that the program is working. Together, these data help build a comprehensive, more complex body of information about strategies that are promising though not yet entirely proven. Program designers and program evaluators can make use of these findings to replicate and initiate more effective interventions that meet the needs of their communities. (See Appendix 2, *Where to Get Evidence.*)

To build a knowledge base of what works, we need to bring together insights from a diverse selection of evaluative techniques. Randomized trials have an enormous role to play in guiding decision-making about effective interventions.

At the same time, insights from empirically based studies, formative experiments, and case studies help us move the field away from oversimplified judgments about program success and failure. By combining insights from different kinds of inquiry, we build a more detailed and thorough understanding of plausible, promising, and proven practices.

Once again, we might return to a telling medical example. We might consider how the relationship between smoking and cancer was established. Initially, researchers recognized through clinical descriptions a relationship between smoking and cancer. They began to document its incidence by taking richly detailed case studies of people's health histories, including daily habits. Of course, it was impossible to perform an experiment, but they did proceed to conduct randomized experiments on animals. This information provided strong causal inference, but obviously no generalizability to humans.

Researchers followed these provocative findings by conducting non-experiments, quasi-experiments, and comparisons between smokers and nonsmokers, using the best possible survey methods and qualitative research. Putting this information together and looking at the weight of evidence, they ultimately made a compelling case that heavy smoking was causally related to lung cancer.

To understand what works, we need to create a continuous learning cycle of evidence, extending what we know and suggesting what types of mid-course corrections are needed to scale up interventions, as well as convincing evidence of outcomes. We must recognize that the technology of research methods will always be developmental and in need of improvement. We will need a large toolkit to determine what programs are worth supporting, which are not, and which need to be revised.

Without such a system, we will continue to fuel cynicism about government and about the performance of programs that help our most vulnerable children. Worse, we'll deserve such cynicism. With a focus on outcomes or results-based accountability, we will be able to build public confidence in government and community institutions and, more important, improve the lives of our most vulnerable children and their families, once again building on the assets in their communities.

Financing What Works

Anyone proposing to change the odds for children at risk by funding what works must be prepared to respond to the taxpayer's rightful skepticism or reluctance to invest in new social programs. Prior to reforming a system, it is essential to have a good understanding of current resources and of the conditions placed on their use.

Since President Lyndon Johnson's War on Poverty, we have relied on federal dollars to tackle issues having vital effects on children's well-being. The federal government, for example, helped end school desegregation, recognize the needs of handicapped and challenged children, and provide "least restrictive environments" in classrooms. Federal funds helped defray the costs of college, allowing even the poorest student to get a high-quality college degree. In these, and other, cases, federal funds have served as a safety net, a kind of "emergency response system," a means of filling in the gaps when critical national priorities arise that are beyond the means of individual states and local supports for education.

Current funding for early learning relies on these federal dollars. At the federal level, the largest single source of funding is Head Start, administered through a federal system to local agencies. The Child Care and Development Block Grant (CCDBG), which provides funding for state child care subsidy programs, represents a second large block, usually administered through welfare or human service departments in states. The third large segment is through the Temporary Assistance to Needy Families (TANF) program, also administered in states through welfare or human services departments and frequently used for family support programs as well as child care subsidies and cash payments for TANF recipients. A fourth source is 21st Century Learning Centers, which provide for extended day, after-school programs administered through the state educational services. Additional federal funding comes through Even Start and Title I funding, usually administered through the public school system and state departments of education.

Although spending on education has actually increased at an extremely rapid rate in recent years—about a 515% increase—funds for early learning have been essentially frozen. If you look at the lion's share of all federal efforts for poor children, you'll find that funds are focused on the years after, rather than during, these first years of life. Although 85% of a child's core brain structure is formed by age three, less than 4% of public investments in education and development have occurred during that time.

Table 2.1. Current Federal Funding Sources for School Readiness

Essential Service	Federal Funding Sources
Family education and support	Early Head Start
	Even Start
Early care and education	Child Care and Development Fund
	Temporary Assistance for Needy Families (TANF) (transfers)
	Child & Dependent Care tax credits
	IDEA, Parts B and C (Special Education Services)
	Head Start, Title I (less than 2% of funds are
	used for early care and education)
	Early Reading First
Supervision and guidance	21st Century Learning Centers (after-school programs)
Safe and supportive communities	Medicaid

According to a 12-state analysis by economist Charles Bruner of the Child and Family Policy Center,[15] on a per-child basis, public investments are nearly seven times greater during the school aged years ($5,410 per child) than during the early learning years ($740 per child). They are almost five times greater for college-age youth ($3,664) than they are for the youngest children. This means that for every dollar society invests in education and development of a school-aged child, society invests only 13.7 cents in its youngest children. Even worse, investments in the very earliest and most formative years of life, from infancy to toddlerhood, represent a modest 1% of the 0–5 funding.

These data suggest that the federal government, with its historic role in education as our country's safety net, has not worked as well as it should—or as it could—to help those children who are most susceptible to risk. At the same time, it provides an even greater impetus for us to make sure that we fund what works, ensuring that programs are structured in a way that creates a powerful, 360-degree learning environment for our most at-risk children.

Where Does Much of the Federal Money Go?

Given the near tripling of overall per pupil funding from the federal government since 1965, it may seem ironic that the funds targeted to preventing academic failure early on for high-risk children are so modest. The reasons, unfortunately, are often opaque to the typical taxpayer. Specifically, much of the funding that could go to alleviating problems is spent on (1) earmarks, which have escalated significantly in recent years, and in (2) ineffective programs that, despite attempts to eliminate them, continue to receive funding.

Earmarks

Although every President and Congress has pledged to support responsible budgeting, earmarks—special interest programs targeted to individual districts for politically motivated purposes—have continued to exact a heavy portion of the education funding. The 2005 budget, for example, was dubbed "the fattest legislative hog we have ever seen" by Taxpayers for Common Sense, containing over 11,000 earmarks worth $15 billion dollars. The practice by which members of Congress add to must-pass legislation diverting billions of dollars in spending projects to benefit recipients in their states and congressional districts actually reached epidemic proportions in the 2006 election.

Popularly known as "pork," earmarks in last year's budget included $450,000 for the Baseball Hall of Fame for "educational outreach using baseball to teach students through distance learning." The bill also included $25,000 for curriculum development for the study of mariachi music. Over $400 million on 1,175 local projects, taking up about 40 pages of small type in four lists in a massive conference report, gets regularly overlooked by the public. Not only do these small grants require an enormous bureaucracy to administer and oversee properly, they are not subject to oversight, or monitoring, or accountability measures.

Each year, the number of earmarks tucked away into appropriation bills has grown exponentially. Imagine the effect if Congress used these funds to help additional poor or disabled children receive educational services.

Ineffective Programs

As part of an effort to responsibly move toward results-based accountability, the Office of Management and Budget (OMB) initiated a review known as the Program Assessment Rating Tool (PART) to assess and improve program performance. Programs throughout the government receive scores for program purpose, design, strategic planning, program management and results, as well as an overall rating: "effective," "moderately effective," "adequate," "ineffective," or "results not demonstrated."

Of the 56 programs assessed since the tool was initiated in 2004, only 2 have been rated by these evaluations as "effective." Of the rest, 14 were "adequate," 5 "ineffective," and 35 "results not demonstrated" (see Appendix 4).

Ratings indicating that results have not been demonstrated typically involve problems such as the lack of long-term goals, annual performance measures, or reliable data. In some cases, program statutes often contribute by failing to give federal monitors the necessary regulatory tools to demonstrate success: clear and measurable objectives, strong accountability mechanisms or other means of ensuring participants focus on achieving results, or mechanisms for gathering high quality, reliable data on program outcomes.

Together, these programs waste over $9 billion in taxpayer dollars yearly. Even though evidence from independent evaluators[16] has repeatedly shown programs to be ineffective, they continue to be funded.

When we continue to support programs and activities that have not shown to be effective in producing outcomes for children and families, we undermine any arguments for the use of research in policy-making. If we are to focus on outcomes, we must abandon ineffective programs to adequately fund prevention and early intervention programs that work.

Getting Better Results

What will it take to reform the system? Seeking more resources has been the single most common refrain for improving poor children's achievement. How we might use these funds to better pursue programs and activities that achieve better outcomes has often been an afterthought. We need to turn this equation around.

A results-based approach demands that for every dollar spent, we should expect a decent return. Programs should represent high-quality investments. Our best programs should provide the largest social returns. Good returns mean putting our funds in programs where they are likely to matter the most. To get such results, we need to consider our priorities, concentrate our efforts, and reroute funds from failing programs to programs that work. No existing program or organization should be taken as a given.

Step 1: Set Priorities

We need to set priorities that address the sources of the problems that proposed policies are intended to solve. Policies to supplement the resources of families with children in the college-going years, for example, are far less effective than programs that can help to create healthy family environments in the early years, preparing children to go to college successfully. Similarly, programs that work to reduce the traumas of living in poverty in the adolescent years are far less efficient than when they are started early on before the problems ever began. No matter how worthy they are, job training, high school drop-out prevention, and alcohol abuse reduction programs cannot possibly remedy 20 years of poverty and its concomitants.

If our priorities are to reduce gaps in student achievement, improve test scores, and increase high school graduate rates, then we need to invest in programs in the early years. Calculating the average rate of return to investment in human capital, James Heckman[17] demonstrates the potential power of investing in the early years. Economists suggest that the real rate of return from investment in early education programs is about 6 to 11%—at least as great a return as an investment in the equity market. Compare these gains with remedial academic education or dropouts for disadvantaged youths aged 14 and 15, for example: programs that have some modest success alleviating problems yet are far less cost effective in their ability to reverse the early effects caused by damaging and disabling environments.

How can we re-right our course? Setting priorities means redistributing funds to the places where they will matter most: compensatory programs, grounded in best practices and able to produce results. Today, the massive inefficiencies in large funding programs such as Title I can be remedied by two key strategies: assisting states and local districts through nonregulatory guidance and consolidating existing programs so they can accomplish their goals more effectively. Let's take each in turn.

Nonregulatory Guidance

After the reauthorization of a law, federal policy-makers craft documents, additional regulations, and nonregulatory guidance to help guide states and local districts implement the new law. Although they do not carry the weight of law, nonregulatory guidance provides clarifications for how funds can be used in light of the law's regulations as well as intent, addressing questions such as, "May funds be used to provide additional tutoring?" "What role does the school district have in providing proper notification to parents?" "Can private schools access Title dollars?" These guidance documents hold significant sway on states, helping local policymakers make decisions about how, where, or on what funds should be spent. In a sense, it is the administration's attempt to nudge states and local school districts to use funds in the directions they believe to be most important.

Right now, even though large funding programs like Title I funds are authorized to fund educational activities for poor children from infancy through grade 12, only 2% of all these funds are devoted to children below five years old. About

400,000 are served, at an estimated cost of about $500 million—a drop in the bucket of a $12.7 billion program.

Federal and state staff, however, could provide stronger guidance and technical assistance from federal policymakers to support exemplary programs, get sound returns on investments, and target the needs of disadvantaged children. Urban school superintendents, including Arne Duncan in Chicago and Eric Smith in Charlotte-Mecklenburg, have used their Title I funds to create exceptional early childhood programs that demonstrate significant returns on investments. Somewhat controversially at the time, Eric Smith, then the superintendent of Charlotte, North Carolina, schools, placed 80% of his Title I allocations in early education to create Bright Beginnings. Rather than spreading funds across programs, this concentrated effort led to improved achievement scores, especially for minority children. The key breakthrough was focusing on results rather than on merely distributing resources.

Nonregulatory guidance doesn't mandate; it merely provides information on ways to encourage better implementation of funding decisions, helping states and local agencies make cause-and-effect connections between inputs and outcomes of improved performance. By and large, this will mean putting a larger percentage of funding in programs focusing on the early years, creating a ripple effect of improved efficiency for later interventions for the many children who will likely need additional help and assistance throughout grade school. Providing examples of successful uses of funds through nonregulatory guidance is absolutely cost-free and is in fact necessary if we want to see better returns on our funding investments.

Consolidation

Politicians love to reorganize—to put programs in different departments because it looks like they're taking action, saving money, or sporting some new innovation. More often than not, it causes new headaches and new reporting confusions, stalling performance rather than promoting it. A much more powerful alternative, ultimately better suited for the population it is intended, is consolidating funding streams for more powerful results.

Several years ago, the Government Accountability Office (GAO)[18] completed a report on early education and care that highlighted the large number of federal programs—69 in all—that provided or supported education and care for children under the age of five. Because of the sheer number of programs, as well as the fact that they were administered by no fewer than nine separate agencies or departments, the GAO quite reasonably suggested that the federal government might not be supporting early childhood education and care in the most efficient and effective way possible.

Although this administration has worked laudably trying to streamline and consolidate programs, there is much more to be done. Today, there are about 34 programs in the Department of Education that provide support for children under age five, and 13 more in the Department of Health and Human Services.

Many of these programs target children who are economically disadvantaged, have special needs, or are members of certain native populations, such as Native American Indians, Alaskans, and Hawaiians, with age criteria varying, eligibility criteria limiting, and tremendous overlapping among programs serving similar target populations. For example, an economically disadvantaged child may not be eligible for both child care subsidies and Head Start—two programs that target this type of children—all because of differences in income eligibility.

Duplicative programs waste valuable administrative resources. But, even more important, they confuse and limit those who may seek their services. They become barriers to using services. It should come as no surprise, then, according to the Heritage Foundation, that in 2004 alone,[19] states had to return as much as $4 billion to the federal government because of services not used. Program overlap can also increase the chances of unnecessary gaps in services. For example, children who have attended Even Start may not be eligible for child care assistance, making it difficult for parents who work or attend school full-time. Further, although many of these programs may provide or support education and care, less than half of these programs have this goal as their program purposes. Although the list of programs may therefore look comprehensive, mission fragmentation often means that very few services actually reach their intended audience.

In the past, the Departments of Education and Health and Human Services, at the federal and state level, have not worked well together. Program boundaries, territorial disputes, and communication breakdowns have benefited neither poor children nor their families. If we are serious about setting priorities—preventing learning difficulties rather than fruitlessly trying to remedy them later in life, agencies will have to coordinate programs across departments, integrate services when possible, and eliminate duplicative and ineffective programs.

There is no getting around it—no cheap fix actually works. Effective programs that provide stimulating environments for young children—for example—may cost at least $10,000 to $12,000 per child per year. High-quality parenting visitation programs may add an additional $5,000 annually to this total. This means that programs addressing the needs of children and their families are likely to cost about $15,000 per child/family.

Consequently, by setting priorities, we begin to concentrate funds to adopt programs that provide intensive services delivered by the highest-quality professionals. The data provide clear evidence: quality programs such as the Child-Parent Centers in Chicago and Bright Beginnings in North Carolina, described in later chapters, demonstrate a solid rate of return—on the order of 5 to 10 times larger than that of any low-intensity programs. Estimates of cost-savings for these and other high-quality well-implemented programs have been reported to exceed 10% and even to reach as high as 17–20% in their mean rate of return.

Step 2: Reroute Funds from Failing Programs

Accountability must be the centerpiece of quality control. Monitoring and technical assistance based on reliable performance data is critical for improving programs when it is possible and eliminating programs when it is not. Yet federal and state programs often lack the capacity for monitoring, data collection, and quick-response feedback systems. As a result, especially in programs where there may be significant turn-over, there is slippage in quality without any resulting sanctions. Money still flows, even though performance may be poor.

For example, in 1984, Congress passed the Single Audit Act, establishing a uniform entity-wide audit requirement for states and local governments receiving federal financial assistance. Designed to monitor programs, the audit examines programs comprehensively, therefore avoiding multiple audits by different agencies. These audits are designed to gather detailed information on the quality, management, and effectiveness of programs receiving massive amounts of funding. However, by the time this information ever reaches their constituent offices, months or even literally years of mismanagement might have taken place.

Furthermore, the federal bureaucracy in education is a poor candidate for helping struggling programs improve their practices. In my experience in government, for example, the program monitor team had limited experience in education. Most had been outside the educational system for over 25 years, and several team members were in their seventies—one had reached the ripe old age of 90. With minimal background on research or best practice, these monitoring teams were likely to follow audit trails more often than they were to follow measures of achievement. Know-how on travel, best restaurant deals, and great hotels around the country was high; strategies on improving programs was often nonexistent.

Some programs, as the P.A.R.T. scores demonstrate, are clearly not achieving results or may suffer from such major flaws in design or execution that they are unlikely to demonstrate results in the future or to improve over time. Some even do more harm than good.

In these cases, it makes sense to direct our energies and resources to more promising approaches. Although created with good intentions, none of these programs reflect the federal government's mission as an "emergency response system," filling gaps in state and local support for education when critical needs arise. Instead, they add incredible layers of administration for states and local school districts, translating more often than not into additional administrative staff instead of into services for children.

Consider just a couple of examples. Believe it or not, we continue to fund a partnership between the Long Beach Unified School District, Cal State University, Long Beach, and an agency called Dramatic Results. This trio runs a program on "how to use basketry to provide quality arts instruction, and how to integrate basketry into the academic curriculum to strengthen instruction in math." Yes, we use federal dollars to fund basket-weaving while millions of children go underserved.

Or take another acclaimed partnership, Stagebridge, a nationally known theater of seniors, and the Oakland Unified School District. Together, they team up to bring children "Story-bridge," a program designed to bring "storytelling, oral history, and intergenerational theater by senior citizens to at-risk, low income urban elementary students." The last I heard, they were bringing

Latino music to the children in an effort to build diversity in this already highly diverse district. Given that the state has had to take over Oakland schools in 2003, you would think a focus on achievement would be a bit more relevant.

We need to reroute these funds into programs that are working, that are demonstrating better returns for taxpayers' dollars. By funding what works, we begin to make a fundamental paradigm shift—moving away from funding many different programs to funding those that have shown solid evidence that they work to achieve outcomes for economically disadvantaged children. This will come about only if we set priorities, concentrate efforts to create strong programs, and reroute funds to successful programs. It is the only way that we can ensure that resources are used productively to provide high-quality, useful services to children who desperately need them.

Step 3: Create an Early Learning 360-Degree Learning Environment

If we're going to succeed in achieving results that all citizens care most about—increasing achievement and children's well-being, we must begin emphasizing programs that make the greatest difference in children's lives. Lessons of research and experience combine to explode the myth that a simple solution will work. It won't. Rather, we need to consolidate the myriad federal programs into targeted efforts that stand for one thing and one thing only—prevention of damaging outcomes for disadvantaged children.

What this means is that instead of pulling funds in many directions with dribs and drabs of dollars going into "Exchanges with Historic Whaling and Trading Partners" and other such pork, using public funds beyond even our wildest imagination, we need a 360-degree learning environment, such as that shown in Table 2.2, to ensure that children start school ready to learn and achieve. Based on what we know about the environmental conditions that damage young children so early on, only a 360-degree learning environment based on prevention will provide the targeted efforts necessary to give at-risk children what they need:

- Strong families: caring and competent parents who provide nurturance, stability, and consistency in their relationships with the child as well as sensitivity, love, availability, and unflagging commitment to the child's well-being, physical and mental health, and cognitive and social development

- Care and education: learning opportunities that help bolster and challenge the child's capabilities, experiences that encourage the child to explore and learn, helping him or her practice developing language, cognition, and interactions with adults and other children

- Supervision and mentoring: support from outside the child's immediate family and environment allowing him or her to explore new vistas, providing much-needed mentorship and guidance, as well as social organizations allowing the child to explore his or her unique talents and providing role models to expand the child's universe of knowledge and understanding

Table 2.2.   A 360-Degree Early Learning System for Children at Risk

Confident and competent parenting	Family support programs (parenting education, basic health and nutrition services)
Early care and education	Compensatory child care environments from birth to school age
	Comprehensive health services
	Ready schools
Supervision and guidance	After-school programs
	Mentoring
	Summer programs
Safe and supportive communities	Recreational programs and activities (libraries, museums, parks for families and young children, etc.)
	Community-based programs that build social networks and help revitalize neighborhoods

- Safe and supportive communities: safe conditions within the child's immediate environment, as well as supportive social institutions and neighborhood programs that may contribution positively to a child's language and his or her experience-rich environment

By consolidating our efforts to focus henceforth on the single priority of helping to prevent damaging outcomes for children at risk, we will be clearing more than a bit of the educational underbrush. We will be reorienting the federal role in education toward behavior as the emergency response system it has claimed to be.

A Great Bargain

Americans are a generous people. Contrary to the typical squabbling over taxes, a recent survey conducted by the premiere Educational Testing Service[20] indicates that more than 79% of adults would favor increases in their local taxes if these funds would translate to higher quality education. Recognizing the dire needs of the disadvantaged, three-quarters of these adults would even favor reallocating funds to other areas to help our most vulnerable children.

But Americans are also a pragmatic people. They want more for their education dollars. They want real accountability for results. A consistent theme in this same survey, reported by over 76% of adults, is that much of the money spent on education is typically wasted, providing no tangible changes in children's outcomes. As William Galston has explained, "People are getting very, very impatient. They are willing to do more. But they are not willing to invest more in the status quo."[21] Most Americans agree that solutions for improving education must exist that do not involve spending more money.

And they're right. Ever since President George H. W. Bush's vow to ensure that "all children will be ready to learn by the year 2000," a consensus has been forming throughout the United States: children's readiness for school must be a top national priority. In order to remain competitive and cultivate good citizenship, our children—particularly those who suffer from poverty and disadvantage—must be better prepared than they are now. This conviction is neither conservative nor liberal, neither Republican nor Democrat.

But although a bipartisan Congress has paid lip service to the needs of disadvantaged children, it has also embraced countless ineffective programs that are absolutely peripheral to this goal. A report announces that children can't write. Reacting to the latest study, the National Writing Project is born. Children aren't cooperating with one another. A new program in Character Education takes on a sudden new sense of urgency. And so it continues, until we have the bloated, unwieldy system of education that we have all come to know so well. Trickles of funds move in all different directions, diverting our priorities, diffusing our mission, and—most tragically—bankrupting our coffers.

Contrast this current approach with a new paradigm for funding—one that takes results and evidence as a key funding principle, setting our priorities to ensure a well-coordinated system supporting children and families. This paradigm shifts the equation from funding everything under the sun to funding priorities targeted at improving school readiness for disadvantaged children. Everything else, worthy though it may be, is peripheral and secondary.

By funding what works, we can change the odds for millions of children. In return, the public will get what it pays for—programs with a solid record of evidence and a good rate of return for every dollar invested. Instead of the billions wasted in worthless programs, redirecting our national priorities toward a new end and eliminating all incentives and practices that distract us from our mission is a great bargain. It is also a renewed commitment to ensuring that all children, especially those who have gotten a bad break through no fault of their own, get a quality education. And the good news is that these kinds of programs are actually working for children and their families in places all across America, demonstrating how seven essential research principles for funding what works can do just that.

CHAPTER 3

THE SEVEN ESSENTIALS FOR CHANGING THE ODDS

A tragic paradox has evolved in science and policy over the past several decades. On the one hand, there has been a virtual explosion of research in the neurobiological, behavioral, and social sciences on children's development. These scientific advances have generated a deep appreciation of the inseparable and highly interactive influences of genetics and environment, the central role of relationships as a source of either support or emotional detachment, and the powerful and essential capabilities—cognitive, emotional, and social—that develop in the earliest years of children's life. By accumulating this knowledge base, we have dramatically increased our capacity to help highly vulnerable children by means of interventions and planned supports.

Nevertheless, it is also astonishing how little of this knowledge has been used to change the prospects of the children growing up at greatest risk. Despite scientific gains from nearly a half a century of considerable research investment, we have rarely capitalized on this knowledge to constructively use it to improve policies and practices for disadvantaged children and their families. Even worse, there are striking inconsistencies between what we know and what we do. As transformations in social and economic circumstances place more families at high risk of adverse outcomes than ever before, however, no one can question the urgency of finding new ways to break the cycle of disadvantage.

The paradox between knowledge and action may spring from the multidisciplinary nature of intervention. Research on the developmental trajectory of children has typically cut across many traditional academic boundaries in both the physical and social sciences. Breaking through these silos, Jack Shonkoff and coeditor Deborah Phillips published a groundbreaking consensus report, "From Neurons to Neighborhoods,[1] in 2000 from the National Academy of Sciences. This important work has helped generate a new integrated science of child development, producing a compelling case for using our growing research capabilities to help children and their families.

The findings from this research are robust: scientific studies now indicate that we can prepare disadvantaged children for school success. In this chapter, I summarize this knowledge base in terms of key principles, acknowledging unresolved scientific, practical, and policy-related controversies. These principles can become the foundation for radically reducing the occurrence of adverse outcomes and dramatically increasing the odds for children at risk.

What Do We Know about Intervention for At-Risk Children?

If you guessed that one of the poorest areas in Philadelphia had test scores to match, you'd probably make a pretty sound bet. At McKinley, an elementary school in north Philadelphia, the demographics are highly predictable—83.8% of the children qualify for free or reduced-price lunch, most are ethnic minorities, 12.8% are non-Hispanic whites. In 2005, only 6.5% of the fourth-graders in this school—a dismaying 1 in 15—passed all three sections of the test: reading, writing, and math. By way of contrast, slightly five miles away, well-heeled Chestnut Hill, where almost no children qualify for subsidized lunches, saw upwards of 80% of students pass all three sections.

McKinley's demographics are precisely why the community has been targeted for early intervention—systematic and intentional efforts to provide supplemental services—hoping to turn at-risk children from these struggling homes into successful adults. Early intervention is designed to showcase the best possible care for very young children and their families, who are often besieged with major problems that sabotage their ability to nurture their children.

The "at risk" designation is usually associated with poverty, as we've seen, although it may include many other factors. Some programs, for example, may use a composite family risk index based on factors such as language and maternal education in addition to poverty criteria. Others may use child characteristics such as tested biological risks, prematurity, low birth weight, or medical conditions. Still others may include community risk factors such as inadequate services known to impact children and their families. In north Philadelphia, all these conditions are at work.

Despite variances in the formulas for identifying those at risk, the implications are the same. Disadvantaged children's trajectory is poor. They are likely to progress poorly in school, with concomitant risks associated with poor grades, retention, special education placement, school dropout, and, later, adult unemployment and inability to be self-sufficient.

Consequently, the long-prevailing question: *Can any intervention work?* Many have been profoundly skeptical that any educational interventions in any form can effectively alter the cumulative, negative toll that poverty and other risk circumstances take on the development of young children.

Our analysis in this chapter of key experimental studies will reveal an important discovery—one traditionally overlooked by policymakers and practitioners. Both quantitative research syntheses and traditional best-evidence reviews have found that programs *under certain circumstances* can produce meaningful gains in cognitive, social, and emotional development for high-risk children. But, *just as important,* in the absence of these conditions, educational interventions *do not* yield significant benefits, or benefits are modest, insufficient, and unsustainable.

In fact, you'll find remarkable consistencies in the cross-sectional analyses of the studies we review. Educational interventions that produce moderate-to-large effects on children's cognitive and social development are characterized by seven major scientific principles: (1) targeting, (2) developmental timing, (3) intensity, (4) professional training, (5) coordinated services, (6) compensatory instructional benefits, and (7) accountability.

Based on studies of children from economically impoverished families, children with combined environmental and biological risk factors, and children with disabilities identified during infancy, the evidence supporting these principles is described throughout this chapter. Together, they provide a road map for funding what works and for ensuring that the implementation of programs leads to sustainable benefits for children.

What Is the Scientific Evidence?

Interventions for high-risk children are complex. To be effective, they must compensate for many of the factors that place children at risk of poor outcomes: health, cognitive, and social. Simultaneously, they represent a tremendous challenge for researchers in designing rigorous field-based experiments to examine these interventions. They also raise a number of ethical issues. How do you isolate the treatment? Do you withhold treatment from eligible groups? Who is to receive the intervention? Who is to be denied?

Experimental evaluations, therefore, have had to rely on a number of inventive strategies that are outside traditional laboratory-like experiments. To create matched comparison groups or counterfactuals, for example, some studies match groups using various statistical techniques, relying on lag-time to compare an intervention to a similar population that live in areas where the program is not available. Sometimes they compare a treatment with another group who may be on a waiting list for an over-subscribed program. Other times, scientists might use the novelty of the intervention—preschool was not common for poor families in the 1960s—to compare it to similar populations that do not have such advantage.

These research designs provide important convergent evidence: They indicate strong, generalizable, causal inferences about the quality of interventions based on critical streams of related research rather than on the findings of single studies. Recognized for the quality of their experimental or quasi-experimental design, these evaluations address at least part of their interventions to child outcomes and school readiness, use reasonable samples sizes for statistical analyses, and are published by peer-reviewed journals or books. Four of the interventions have been subject to cost–benefit analyses.

As shown in Table 3.1, the interventions fall into two distinct patterns and program approaches.[2] The first set of programs (such as the Infant Health and

Table 3.1. Key Dimensions of Intervention Programs

Programs with a Strong Evidence Base

Program	Brief Description	Outcomes	Currently Operating?
Abecedarian[a]	Comprehensive early education program for young children at risk for developmental delays and school failure. Program operated in North Carolina from 1972–85, and involved full-day, full-year, center-based care, starting from infancy up to 6 years of age.	Positive results on children's IQ (short term) and achievement; declining enrollment in special education; grade retention.	No
Brookline Early Education Project (BEEP)[b]	Comprehensive school-based early intervention program for children aged from birth until kindergarten. Designed as a demonstration project, three levels of service to families ranging from extensive to minimal amounts were offered. Services included home visits and a prekindergarten program until entrance into kindergarten.	Positive results on children's social skills and academic skills. Limited-education families benefited most. Most intensive services had greatest effects.	Yes
Chicago Parent Child Centers[c]	Center-based preschool program for high-poverty children in Chicago since 1967. School-year program provides a structured part-day program for children ages 3 and 4, along with required family participation.	Positive results on children's achievement; declining enrollment in special education; reduction in crime and delinquency.	Yes
Early Training Project[d]	Implemented in Murfreesboro, Tennessee, the demonstration project was designed to improve the educability of young children from very low-income homes. The program consisted of a 10-week summer preschool for two or three summers prior to first grade, and weekly home visits during the remainder of the year.	Positive results on children's IQ (short-term) and achievement; declining enrollment in special education.	No

Note: The structure of this table is adapted from L. Karoly, M. Kilburn & J. Cannon, "Early Childhood Intervention" Santa Monica, CA: Rand.

Program	Description	Results	
Infant Health and Development Program[e]	Targeted intervention to infants born prematurely, the comprehensive intervention consisted of family support services tailored to reduce health and developmental problems. Program provided home visiting, parent group meetings, and a center-based child development program from the neonatal nursery until 36 months of age.	Positive results on children's IQ (short-term); no differences in grade repetition or special education.	No
The Milwaukee Project[f]	Beginning during the 1960s, the project focused on an intensive intervention from infancy through early childhood to minimize the statistical effect of heredity of high-risk children from mentally retarded mothers.	Positive results on children's IQ and school achievement (short-term); declining enrollment in special education.	No
Partnership Program[g]	Provides intensive and comprehensive home visitation by public health nurses to low-income, first-time-pregnant women and mothers of any age. The visits begin during pregnancy and continue through the child's second birthday. The program is intended to help women improve their care of infants and toddlers and their own development.	Positive short- and long-term advantages for both mothers and children. Fewer reported acts of child abuse, lower levels of criminal activity; fewer behavioral impairments caused by alcohol and drugs; fewer subsequent pregnancies and births; children had fewer arrests.	Yes
Perry Preschool Project[h]	Center-based early childhood education program . designed to promote children's intellectual, social, and emotional learning and development. The program, conducted from 1962–67, targeted 3- and 4-year-old children living in poverty with low IQs	Positive results on children's IQ (short-term) and achievement; declining enrollment in special education, higher employment rates; decreases in teen pregnancy; higher rates of marriage.	**No**

Programs with a Promising Evidence Base

Program	Description	Results	
Avance[i]	Established in the late 1970s to reduce the disproportionately high dropout rate among Mexican-American populations, the program provides a year-long parenting and parent education program, toy-making activities, home visits, and a child development program for children, birth through age 3.	Carnegie report findings show a decrease in high-school dropouts, increase in college enrollments, decrease in crime; slight increases in children's social skills and school readiness.	Yes

Table 3.1. Key Dimensions of Intervention Programs (*continued*)

Programs with a Promising Evidence Base

Program	Brief Description	Outcomes	Currently Operating?
Bright Beginnings[j]	Starting in 1996, a literacy-focused preschool program for low-income children in Charlotte-Mecklenburg, N.C. Program consists of a full-day program for 4-year-olds, parental involvement, community support and collaboration, professional development, and on-going research and evaluation.	Positive impacts on school performance; educationally most needy children were ready to learn in kindergarten; African American and other minority groups were more proficient in literacy and math than control groups; decreases in grade retention.	Yes
Early Head Start[k]	A federally funded community-based program that provides children and their families developmental services to low-income pregnant mothers with infants and toddlers up to age 3. Program includes home-visitng, child development, parent education nutrition and health care referrels, and family support.	Positive statistically significant impacts on children's cognitive development (age 3); positive impacts on language development; favorable impacts on social-emotional development; some progress on parents' efforts toward self-sufficiency.	Yes
Head Start[l]	A federally funded comprehensive, community-based preschool program initiated in 1960s to improve school readiness skills for 3- and 4-year-olds.	First-year findings from the Head Start impact study indicate small to moderate statistically significant positive impacts in pre-reading and vocabulary; but no significant impacts on oral language, phonological awareness, and math; no findings are available on social skills.	Yes

Oklahoma Pre-K[m]	Since 1998, the state of Oklahoma has provided a voluntary, half-day or full-day prekindergarten program to all 4-year-olds in participating school districts, credentialled teachers with a required ratio of 10 children per adult.	Positive impacts for Hispanics and blacks, whites and Native American children on letter knowledge, math, and spelling. No language measure was assessed.	Yes
Parent/Child Home Program[n]	Started in the late 1960s, the mother-child home program focuses on developing verbal interaction for families in high-risk groups. Intervention program begins when child is about 2 years old and centers around a parent education program using toys and books of high quality.	Positive short-term cognitive gains; gains on preliteracy skills and social-emotional competence.	Yes
Reach Out and Read[o]	A national program that promotes reading aloud to young at-risk children by using the pediatric office as a site for education and intervention. Doctors and nurses give new books to children at each well-child visit from 6 months to 5 years and accompany books with developmentally appropriate advice to parents on how to read to children.	Positive impacts on frequency of reading aloud to children, promoting positive attitudes about books, and stimulating vocabulary growth. Most effective for children at greatest risk	Yes

[a] F. Campbell and K. Taylor, "Early Childhood Programs That Work for Children from Economically Disadvantaged Families," *Young Children* 51 (1996), C.T. Ramey et al., "Persistent Effects of Early Intervention on High-Risk Children and Their Mothers," *Applied Developmental Science* 4 (2000).

[b] P. Hauser-Cram et al., *Early Education in the Public Schools* (San Francisco, CA: Jossey-Bass, 1991).

[c] A. Reynolds, *Success in Early Intervention* (Lincoln, NE: University of Nebraska Press, 2000); A. Reynolds et al., "Long-Term Effects of an Early Childhood Intervention on Educational Achievement and Juvenile Arrest: A 15 Year Follow-up of Low-Income Children in Public Schools," *Journal of the American Medical Association* 285 (2001).

[d] S. Gray, B. Ramsey, and R. Klaus, *From 3 to 20* (Baltimore, MD: University Park Press, 1982).

[e] J. Brooks-Gunn et al., "Early Intervention in Low-Birth-Weight Premature Infants: Results through Age 5 Years from the Infant Health and Development Program," *Journal of the American Medical Association* 272 (1994); Infant Health and Development Project (IHDP), "Enhancing the Outcomes of Low-Birth-Weight, Premature Infants: A Multisite, Randomized Trial," *Journal of the American Medical Association* 263 (1990).

[f] H. Garber, *The Milwaukee Project* (Washington, D.C.: American Association on Mental Retardation, 1988).

[g] D. Olds et al., "Prenatal and Infancy Home Visitation by Nurses: Recent Findings," *The Future of Children* 9 (1999); D. Olds et al., "Effects of Nurse Home-Visiting on Maternal Life Course and Child Development: Age 6 Follow-up Results of a Randomized Trial," Pediatrics 114 (2004).

Table 3.1. Key Dimensions of Intervention Programs (*continued*)

[h] L. Schweinhart, "The High/Scope Perry Preschool Study through Age 40: Summary, Conclusions, and Frequently Asked Questions" (Ypsilanti, MI: High/Scope Educational Research Foundation, 2004); D. P. Weikart, J. T. Bond, and J. T. McNeil, *The Ypsilanti Perry Preschool Project* (Ypsilanti, MI: High/Scope, 1978).

[i] R. St. Pierre, J. Layzer, and H. Barnes, "Two-Generation Programs: Design, Cost, and Short-Term Effectiveness," *The Future of Children* 5 (1995).

[j] E. Smith, B. Pellin, and S. Agruso, *Bright Beginnings: An Effective Literacy Focused Prekindergarten Program for Educationally Disadvantaged Four-Year-Old Children* (Arlington, VA: Educational Research Service, 2003).

[k] J. Love et al., "Making a Difference in the Lives of Infants and Toddlers and Their Families: The Impacts of Early Head Start. Executive Summary" (Washington, D.C.: Administration on Children, Youth, and Families, U.S. Department of Health and Human Services, 2002); H. Raikes et al., "Involvement in Early Head Start Home Visiting Services: Demographic Predictors and Relations to Child and Parent Outcomes," *Early Childhood Research Quarterly* 21 (2006).

[l] E. Boyer, *Ready to Learn* (Princeton, NJ: Carnegie Foundation for the Advancement of Teaching, 1991); Administration for Children and Families U.S. Department of Health and Human Services, "Head Start Impact Study: First Year Findings" (Washington, D.C.: 2005).

[m] W. Gormley et al., "The Effects of Universal Pre-K on Cognitive Development," *Developmental Psychology* 41, no. 6 (2005).

[n] P. Levenstein et al., "Long-Term Impact of a Verbal Interaction Program for at-Risk Toddlers: An Exploratory Study of High School Outcomes in a Replication of the Mother-Child Home Program," *Journal of Applied Developmental Psychology* 19 (1988).

[o] P. Levenstein, S. Levenstein, and D. Oliver, "First Grade School Readiness of Former Participants in a South Carolina Replication of the Parent-Child Home Program," *Journal of Applied Developmental Psychology* 23 (2002); R. Needlman et al., "Clinic-Based Intervention to Promote Literacy," *American Journal of Diseases of Children* 145 (1991), R. Needlman, P. Klass, and B. Zuckerman, "A Pediatric Approach to Early Literacy," in *Handbook of Early Literacy Research*, eds. D. Dickinson and S. B. Neuman (New York, NY: Guilford Press, 2006).

Development Program, and Early Head Start, highlighted in subsequent chapters) delivers services primarily to the parent via either home visits or parent education. These programs strengthen family resources to help parents provide greater nurturance, health, attachment, and stimulation to their children. The second set of programs emphasizes services to children through early care and education programs. Programs such as Perry Preschool, Abecedarian, Chicago Parent-Child Centers, mentioned in previous chapters, and programs such as Bright Beginnings and the Brookline Early Education Program (BEEP), emphasize early childhood education and school readiness. But make no mistake about it—they all involve parent education and parent support as critical features in their intervention.

Providing some of the strongest evidence to date, the story that these evaluations reveal is striking: once children receive responsive and consistent caregiving in settings that are safe and stimulating, they can make a substantial recovery from the devastations of poverty. They learn how to form healthy relationships with others, how to become eager to learn, and how to develop the skills and knowledge necessary to be able to finish school and earn a productive income.

But the subplot in this story is equally important. Looking "inside the black box" of these interventions, there is an extraordinary convergence in the qualities of these programs that made them so successful. The most effective interventions demonstrating sizable, robust, and educationally meaningful results follow seven essential principles.

What Works in Intervention Programs

Drawing on the literature from these high-quality evaluations, the evidence is compelling that the following principles are at work in shaping our most effective interventions:

1. Targeting

The children who are most likely to benefit from interventions are those who are at greatest risk. For both biologically and environmentally vulnerable populations of children, program impacts are greatest for the more disadvantaged families in these interventions. The consensus among the 15 programs profiled is striking: more substantial effects are reported for children in greatest jeopardy of poor outcomes.

For example, children whose mothers had the lowest IQ gained the most from the Abecedarian Project. Similarly, children with measured borderline mentally retarded IQ's in the Perry Preschool program showed more dramatic gains than did any others. In fact, each quality evaluation demonstrates larger benefits for children at greater risk than for those less needy.

Why is targeting so important? The first reason is purely mathematical. Children in the lowest quintiles, as seen in an analysis of the Early Childhood Longitudinal Study,[3] for example, have more ground to cover to reach reasonable benchmarks in

Programs with Strong Evidence Base	Principles						
	Targeting	Developmental Timing	Intensity	Professional Development	Coordinated Services	Compensatory Instruction	Accountability
1. Abecedarian							
2. Brookline Early Education Project							
3. Chicago Parent/ Child Centers							
4. Early Training Project							
5. Infant Health and Development Program							
6. The Milwaukee Project							
7. Nurse-Family Partnership Program							
8. Perry Preschool Project							

Legend:

■ Positive evidence of principles present   ▨ Mixed findings   □ No evidence found

Figure 3.1.
Programs with Strong Evidence Base.

reading, math, and general knowledge, as well as in basic social skills. There is greater potential, therefore, to grow. We also know that without help, the likelihood that these children will be left behind is in little doubt.

But there are other important reasons as well. Matching well-defined goals to the specific needs and resources of the children who are served, targeting supports a more individualized form of service delivery. Because targeted programs serve children who have the greatest needs, targeted programs are able to work with small numbers or even, when necessary, one-on-one. In these settings, teachers may develop diagnostic and prescriptive procedures that are more carefully calibrated to children's specific strengths and deficits. It is the closely matched diagnostic-to-prescriptive component of instruction that has made interventions, such as tutoring programs, so successful.

While conforming to overall program standards, Early Head Start—for example—works on the basis of parent and child individual needs. Weekly visits focus on helping families reach overall benchmarks, yet the way in which they do so is highly tailored to the most crucial needs of the family. In situations where parents may be struggling to survive, scripts won't work.

Targeted programs use federal funds as they were originally conceived: as an emergency safety net for children who are disadvantaged. In the Chicago-based Child-Parent Centers, for example, daily activities involve children in small groups of four or five in fast-paced, diagnostically prescribed activities that emphasize the perceptual skills and oral communication central to children's success in school. With a maximum class size of 17, teachers group children by skill level and provide the kinds of frequent and corrective feedback that focus persistently on task accomplishment. Such individualization would be impossible in typical classroom settings with their highly diverse ability groups.

Similarly, Brooklyn Early Education Program (BEEP) put together a design model targeted to the specific needs of their highly diverse language minority children, who were at risk for failure in their community. Because over 10% of the families in BEEP were Hispanic, a bilingual program was designed with the goal of language proficiency in both languages before ending kindergarten. During the first two years, a team of teachers made home visits. Then, in the toddler years, they worked closely with children in playgroup activities to support both languages. In prekindergarten, they involved children in small-group interventions using both languages for instruction. By the end of prekindergarten, significantly, all children were achieving above their age norms, and all Spanish-speaking children were readily conversant in both Spanish and English.

Most assuredly, had these at-risk children failed to receive these kinds of high-quality services, they would have come to school seriously behind their more advantaged peers. Despite all the tremendous resources in the federal funding of No Child Left Behind, nothing would have stopped their likely decline in acquiring skills necessary to keep up. Starting disadvantaged, they stay disadvantaged, or as the folk saying goes, "Them as has gets; them as don't don't."

Targeted programs allow us to serve these children without diluting program quality by spreading resources thin. Programs thwarted by inadequate resources and professional inertia have often worsened the situation for poor children. Only the highest-quality care will improve children's developmental outcomes.

But quality costs money. Given the few federal resources available for services to disadvantaged children, as well as the powerful evidence that intervention can play on their school readiness outcomes, targeted programs represent the wisest strategy for investing in children's future.

2. Developmental Timing

Developmental timing refers to the actual onset of intervention. Representing a more complex pattern than perhaps any other aspect of the evaluation literature, both the empirical data and clinical evidence indicate that interventions are most effective when they are timed to meet families' most pressing needs.

Clearly, early identification and timing of intervention are critically important for some conditions and particular circumstances. Helping first-time mothers negotiate the necessary health networks has been shown to increase the delivery of full-term, healthy babies. Helping parents connect with other essential services such as food programs (WIC) or health insurance (S-Chip) has significantly raised the chances that children will have regular sources of medical care and be better immunized.

These and other impacts of prenatal home visits in programs such as the Nurse-Family Partnership intervention and Early Head Start strongly correlated with enhanced health and safety outcomes in children's earliest months, demonstrating the principle of timing—helping strengthen families by breaking down barriers to meet their most immediate needs. Similarly, Avance, a multifaceted intervention targeted to parent health, education, and support for new Latina parents, has had its greatest effect in preventing early developmental concerns from becoming more serious problems later on. Evidence from over 10 local sites in Texas has shown the phenomenal recovery that infants display in attachment relationships once they receive more careful and loving attention, further revealing the importance of critical timing.

Other circumstances that call for early diagnosis and treatment are chronic health issues. Conducting early and periodic assessments of children to monitor their development, the Brookline Early Education Project (BEEP) helped to head off health problems for children shortly after birth until entry into kindergarten. These early diagnostic screenings were effective in reducing the adverse impacts of hearing loss, caused by chronic ear infections, on communication skills and cognitive abilities.

Weighing the costs and benefits in determining when to begin treatment, then, remains a critical policy challenge. However, quality evaluations of effective programs suggest several important guidelines:

- Programs that provide direct services to parents should begin as early as the prenatal period, or within a few weeks of birth.
- Programs that provide early and periodic screening, health, nutrition, and tactile/kinesthetic stimulation to children should also begin as early as possible. These programs have the potential to improve maternal and child health and can significantly reduce health costs.
- Programs that provide direct services to children in early care and education settings should begin before children enter formal schooling in the late toddler and early preschool years.

Return-on-investment analyses of the few programs that have been able to track costs and benefits related to children's use of remediation or compensatory programs (special education, juvenile justice, child welfare, health, and mental health) provide further substantiation for these guidelines.[4]

The most immediate return on investment is the parent-supported Nurse-Family Partnership program. For each dollar invested, the public return received an average return of $6.92. These returns were seen in reduced emergency room visits, welfare payments, and criminal justice costs. The greatest returns on investment for children, however, have been recorded for the Chicago Parent-Child Centers and the Perry School program in the *preschool* years, in contrast to the more costly Abecedarian project, which began in infancy. In other words, there were no direct returns for programs that provided direct service to children in early infancy in comparison to ones that began when children were toddlers or young preschoolers.

There is no doubt that the earlier children receive help, the better—in many cases. It is far more efficient to prevent reading difficulties early on than to wait until more serious problems later result in costly remediation. Nevertheless, the premature initiation of special services *too early on* can lead to inappropriate labeling or the removal of children from typical experiences, reducing the possibility of self-righting corrections or compensatory growth spurts. The identification of children as learning-disabled, for example, has literally skyrocketed in special education—not because there are more disabled kids, but because too many are being mislabeled.[5]

In addition, overidentification can lead to engaging children in developmentally inappropriate activities. Hoping to support children's learning early on, I have literally watched caregivers use flashcard drills with eighteen-month-olds still in their high chairs. Drilling alphabet skills to very young children when they are only beginning to explore what these symbol systems are can be costly in other ways as well, diminishing children's interest and motivation to read later on.

3. Intensity

The third essential relates to the intensity of support programs. The equation in this third essential is simple: more powerful treatments equal better effects. Change for highly vulnerable families is gradual, fragile, and often reversible, and disadvantaged children and their families typically need extensive support and specific knowledge to assume their new roles and responsibilities.

Operationally defined by a term usually used in medicine, called dosage, intensity typically refers to the amount of professional time—hours per day, days per week, weeks per year—spent with families or children. Programs that are more intensive produce larger positive effects than do interventions that are less intensive. Children and parents who participate most actively and regularly show the greatest overall progress.

But dosage—or the time devoted to the intervention—is only one characteristic of the intensity principle. The amount of time and duration of intervention varies dramatically across programs. Some preschool programs are part-day, some are full-day. Some programs, such as Nurse-Family Partnership, last several years; others, such as Avance, restrict participation to one intensive year. Therefore, it is important for policymakers to recognize that we cannot extrapolate on the basis of the evidence that longer programs are necessarily better programs or that there is a direct linear relationship between the length of a program and its potential benefits for children.

Rather, intensity relates to *how* the time is used in the program. Intensive programs are highly focused, using their time with children and parents as a limited resource. Program goals, for example, in the Brookline Early Education Program, are highly focused on children's cognition, language, and gross-motor, fine-motor, and visual-motor skills—critical skills related to school readiness. Using a diagnostic/prescriptive model of teaching, three teachers staffed the three-hour-daily classroom program in classes made up of 18 to 20 children. Teachers met with diagnostic specialists on a regular basis, working with individual children who might need additional attention.

Compare this approach with a large-scale experiment designed to enhance child development and help families achieve economic self-sufficiency. The Comprehensive Child Development Program (CCDP), begun in 1989,[6] was a 21-site demonstration program intended to provide continuous comprehensive, integrated services to low-income families from birth to age five. The program model mandated a wide range of services for children and for parents, as well as regular home visits and case management.

During the year, families received home visits every week or two in the early months, visits becoming less frequent over time. The majority of other services were 'brokered'—provided by other agencies outside of direct supervision. Perhaps not surprisingly, the research indicated that there were no effects on parenting or their problem-solving strategies, and no direct effects on children's school readiness factors, including cognitive and language development.

Similarly, Project Developmental Continuity, a large-scale effort to improve school readiness skills by following Head Start children into the elementary school, failed to promote children's achievement.[7] Working as a staff developer in this project, my role was to meet with teachers weekly, try to offer some quick solutions for helping a child's learning problems, and then visit the next teacher on my schedule—nine teachers in a day. With such large case-loads, services became diluted, and the intervention became weak and ineffective. This program, like CCDP, showed no improvements for teachers, children, or parents.

Once again, compare these ineffective programs with the more intensive Infant Health and Development Program. Targeting low-birth-weight infants in poor families, this program included regular home visits from birth to age three, a full-day, full-year center-based program for children beginning at age one and continuing through age three, parent group meetings every three months, and regular pediatric and developmental assessments. Families received an average of 67 home visits during a three-year intervention period, and children attended the center-based program an average of 267 days a year. The program reported positive effects of the intervention after three years on children's IQ and receptive language, and on parental reports of their children's behaviors.

Intensity can be examined by asking what specific interventions are being "added" to the child's regular early childhood program: how often, for how long, with how many other children, and with whom. If children are receiving daily additional (above and beyond) help of substantial time, on a one-to-one basis, or at most small group, with a highly trained professional, then children are likely to progress. However, if they receive services only infrequently, such as a visit once a month or a class one day a week for several hours, or if there are frequent interruptions in service, the program is likely to be inadequate for most needy children and families.

There are clear variations in the intensity of interventions. Programs such as the Milwaukee Project and the Early Training Project that work closely with parents and children in one-to-one settings, represent the most intensive programs. Others, such as Head Start, often part-day programs during the school year with larger teacher–child ratios than these other programs, and covering a wide array of services, are less intensive. Further, limitations in funding of Head Start often mean that children receive only one nine-month intervention, with parent involvement varying considerably across sites. Compared to the striking gains from the more intensive programs, Head Start's impact has been modest.

The lessons are clear. Given the consistencies throughout the research literature that intensive, highly stimulating programs to children can produce moderate-to-large effects on children's cognitive development in the early years, and given that low intensity programs produce less promising results, we can no longer afford to continue to waste enormous resources and public good will on programs that do not and will not work. Intensive programs, in which children and parents participate most actively, translate into competencies that can help boost the odds that children will achieve and thrive in school and beyond.

4. Professional Training

High-quality programs are not only defined by the services delivered but by the staff that delivers them. Working in challenging situations with families in highly distressed communities requires talent, skills, and commitment that only a highly trained staff, the fourth essential, can adequately provide. A convergence of research on early childhood pedagogy from the National Academies of Science[8] bears this out: programs that have shown demonstrable, significant, long-term, life-changing effects for our most needy populations have all involved professionals, not paraprofessionals or volunteers.

Specialized training is critical for working with at-risk children and families. Although volunteers try to do what's best for families, we need experts to deal with the many complicated issues that arise from poverty conditions. Take David Olds's Nurse-Family Partnership Program, for example. This intervention used highly trained nurses for his home-visiting program because of their formal training in women's and children's health, as well as their competence in managing the often complex clinical situations that would commonly arise with families. Rather than "I'll have someone get back to you," these nurses could easily field questions about the complications of pregnancy, the physical health of the infant and any emerging signs of health problems, and they could help families negotiate the often complex health care system for their child's continuing care. Equally important, these professionals were credible, and respected for their expertise by the families they served.

When the same program was tried in Denver,[9] using paraprofessionals instead of nurses, it was not nearly as effective. Turnover among paraprofessionals was high, and fewer visits among families were recorded, even though the paraprofessionals were supervised by clinical social workers at the time. Once again, with weaker interventions, as one might expect, the results were not as encouraging as in other projects. Although paraprofessionals were able to establish good relationships with families, they simply did not have the skills needed to respond effectively to family problems and to understand the nuances of children's health and developmental needs.

There is no substitute for the knowledge, ability, and commitment that define well-trained staff and professionals. Research demonstrates the clear linkage between well-trained qualified staff and child outcomes, particularly for children who are at risk for early developmental problems and later educational under-achievement. The extent to which these service providers have the knowledge, skills, and abilities to interact with their target population is fundamental to the success of the intervention.

How can you identify highly trained professionals? Not necessarily by their credentials. Certification and qualification are not always synonymous. Rather, highly trained staff are knowledgeable of their subject matter, whether it's health, early childhood services, or dealing with the unwieldy social service agencies. They are credible in the community and recognized as highly skilled and committed to the needs of the population they serve. Professionals in these programs are perceived by those whom they serve as people who care about and respect others—people who can be trusted.

Resource limitations and pressures to do "more with less" have led many interventions to substitute minimally trained staff for highly trained professionals. Summarizing evaluations from these best-studied programs, Deanna Gomby[10] portrays a sobering conclusion. Most often than not, these programs have struggled to enroll, engage, and retain families. Furthermore, assessing children's development using standardized tests has found no significant result on all or even a majority of the measures employed; in many cases, no positive effects were found at all. Weighing these results, researchers recognized that only extremely well-trained professionals can adequately serve families that face multiple complex issues.

The ultimate effect of any intervention is dependent on both staff expertise and the quality and continuity of the personal relationship established between the service provider and the family being served. These staff often become models to parents of effective ways of caring for and teaching children, and models to children of roles to which they can aspire. For example, mothers and children who received high ratings for active participation in the Nurse-Family Partnership frequently mentioned their high regard for their nurse provider. Some 13 years after the program, they were likely to experience fewer arrests and convictions, smoke fewer cigarettes per day, spend fewer days consuming alcohol, and be involved in less lifetime promiscuity.[11]

Quick-fix training programs with nonprofessional staff have been shown to be inadequate, disrespectful to the families and children they serve, and ultimately wasteful, because turnover and ongoing recruitment of new staff continually plagues these programs and reduces their potential effectiveness. Rather, we must recognize that nothing less than the most excellent service providers and teachers will do. Caring, competent, and flexible, these highly-trained individuals provide the quality of intervention that may best benefit our most at-risk families.

5. Coordinated Services

More often than not, families and children who are in the greatest need of early intervention struggle with persistent health problems, poor nutrition, and fractured family life. Collectively, these problems cannot possibly be solved with isolated fragments of help that focus in one particular area alone. Consequently, programs that help to coordinate a spectrum of services, the fifth essential, generally produce the most robust effects.

Intervention studies that have produced larger effects, such as the Infant Health and Development, Abecedarian, and Perry Preschool programs, have all used multipronged approaches, including the provision of ongoing health-related and social services to the families. This may include transportation, child care, and other services to meet their most urgent needs. These services provide social and emotional support on issues as diverse as food, housing, and employment, helping families attain their most immediate goals.

Head Start, clearly a leader in establishing comprehensive services, provided badly needed health, nutrition, and help from its very inception to families with a variety of concrete problems. In fact, one of its most important contributions has been an emphasis on the "whole child"—recognizing that the health, education, and well-being of young children are integrally connected, and that effective intervention is best accomplished through family and community involvement. Following Head Start's lead, a number of programs have adapted this model, demonstrating powerful, long-term effects on children's development later on.

The Child-Parent Center Program, for example, set in the most impoverished areas of Chicago and now running for over 30 years, provides a skills-based early childhood program along with comprehensive services for families that include health and social services and parent involvement. Community-based programs and health and nutritional specialists are located on-site, offering a wide array of programs to support family life.

Other programs, such as the Brookline Early Education Program, or Bright Beginnings, integrate a strong health and development component into the educational and family-support aspects of their programs. Recognizing that a child's chance of being successful in school is based on adequate hearing, vision, attentional abilities, nutrition and social–emotional control, children are monitored periodically throughout their programs to alleviate health or development impediments to learning.

Both the Chicago and Brookline programs are modeled on the Head Start approach—providing comprehensive services. In many ways they are ideal systems because they coordinate services under a central umbrella. But not all early intervention programs are able to organize these coordinated services. Some programs, such as Reach Out and Read and Bright Beginnings, rely on helping families by making referrals to other agencies.

The critical point here is that without some coordinated connection to health and social services, educational services alone are likely to be too isolated or may not address the needs of families struggling to survive. Interventions that provide a combination of services—parent support and early childhood services—are likely to be more powerful strategies for improving children's learning and later school adjustment. The effect that coordinated services may have on the children and families is quantifiable, reducing demands in the long run for public services and increasing tax revenue as a result of higher earnings.

The essential features of the principle of coordinated services include (1) providing health and developmental screening and monitoring to children, (2) supporting families through direct and indirect services, and (3) connecting family support with a strong educational intervention for children by means of information and parent education. The extent to which programs treat families with dignity and respect and are sensitive to their cultural and socioeconomic circumstances determines the degree to which services are used and are ultimately effective.

Successful programs that have changed the odds for children have reached beyond traditional professional boundaries, helping to coordinate health, social services, and education for families who must often deal with tremendous obstacles in their lives. These programs recognize that children learn best in situations when they are healthy and safe and in close, enduring relationships with family and kin.

6. Compensatory Instructional Benefits

In the early years, children rapidly develop the foundational capacities on which their subsequent development builds. In addition to their incredible growth in linguistic and cognitive gains, they develop critical dispositions for learning—motivation, curiosity, and problem-solving skills. All of these critical dimensions of development can be seriously compromised by social and economic disadvantage.

Consequently, children who come from disadvantaged circumstances will often lack rich opportunities to learn, not the ability or motivation to learn. Striking disparities in what they know and can do will be evident well before they enter kindergarten. They will need to catch up, and quickly. If we're serious about improving children's odds, then we must focus on enhancing background knowledge and conceptual understandings that are integral to academic learning. Interventions that provide compensatory instructional benefits, the sixth essential—will have greater effects on children's achievement compared to interventions that are weaker in focus.

The compensatory instructional benefits principle requires a critical examination of the curriculum—or what is taught in the intervention program. It cannot look like "business as usual." Rather, there are things that the economically disadvantaged child must learn in order not to fall behind. These knowledge deficits, if not addressed early on, can grow ever larger in the early elementary years to become insurmountable obstacles to later learning.

The intervention studies that have produced the greatest educational gains for children, such as the Abecedarian, Bright Beginnings, BEEP, and Milwaukee projects, all provided compensatory instructional benefits that deviated significantly from a typical preschool program. Typically, preschool programs try to provide a breadth of experiences through an accumulation of activities that seem to work well with children and that are compatible with certain principles of child development.

In compensatory programs, it is depth, not breadth, that matters most and that makes a significant difference for children's learning. Although each of these programs used a different curriculum, all had one thing in common: each program intensely focused on language development. Language is regarded not just as one among a number of skills to be taught and learned, but as a primary foundational skill from which all others derive. Language to describe, compare, analyze, deduce, inquire, and hypothesize is regarded as the central device that all inquiring individuals need if they are to gain and process information.

In the Abecedarian program, for example, special emphasis was placed on language development, caregivers and teachers being given intensive in-service training in such ways as to foster sociolinguistic competence in the children. The language program, made a regular feature of the entire day, focused on pragmatic features rather than on syntax and emphasized the contingent and interactive features of adult–child language. Four-year-olds were provided with individual sessions that focused on pre-phonics skills twice weekly for 45 weeks. Similarly, the early childhood stimulation program in the Milwaukee project intensely focused on language development. Participating in small groups, children engaged in verbal production exercises every day that emphasized language as a resource through which you can gain information, share ideas, and obtain help.

These programs recognized a key factor underlying intervention programs: time is the least available resource in educating disadvantaged children. Programs may comprise only 500 hours, a meager time allotment to overcome disadvantage that has accumulated over 20,000 hours.

Compensatory programs include these essential features: (1) Recognizing that children's progress must be accelerated, instruction has to be of higher quality and faster paced than it is for more advantaged children. (2) Programs must focus on specific learning goals that make high rates of progress possible. (3) Activities that make up programs must answer the following questions: How well does this type of experience lend itself to focused and rapid learning for acquiring and processing information? How well does this experience help children to master the cognitive uses of language—the ability to treat language more flexibly and to master the use of structural words and inflections necessary for the expression and manipulation for establishing logical relationships?

Spending federal dollars on programs that ignore children's significant difficulties in favor of programs that attempt to mimic the same kinds of experiences that average preschoolers might engage in merely intensifies the differences among children of different social classes. Although some might suggest that something is better than nothing, ultimately it is a poor investment for our multi-risk children, who need far greater help. Compensatory programs, through their intensity, focus, and accountability, eliminate the "miracle cure" in favor of data indicating powerful and lasting effects on achievement.

7. Accountability

Determining whether or not programs are accomplishing their goals demands greater accountability, the seventh and final essential. Programs that monitor progress, provide careful oversight, create clear expectations, and evaluate their own effects have shown dramatic results in changing the trajectories of disadvantaged children from failure to success. Bright Beginnings, for example, with its emphasis on oral language and prereading and math skills, uses a highly structured but diverse set of learning experiences to help children prepare to read. Lessons have goals, objectives, and procedures, as well as criteria with which to determine mastery. Using curriculum-based assessments on an ongoing basis, teachers monitor children's progress and provide corrective feedback until the criteria have been reached. There's no need for prayers at the end of the term: teachers know exactly the skills that have been achieved and the goals that remain still to be emphasized.

Accountability, to some, may have negative connotations, similar to being audited for taxes. But accountability is actually in the interest of program designers. Measures of accountability provide helpful information on the quality of the services (are they occurring with the intensity that was intended?), whether services are being rendered or not (what is the quality of the intervention?), and whether adjustments are needed to enhance the program's effects. Rather than continue to repeat the mistakes of the past, programs that use accountability mechanisms make use of a much-needed record for what works under what conditions, building a powerful knowledge base of effective intervention strategies that work for high-risk children and families.

Although each of the programs described in this chapter included a set of complex strategies to examine their impacts, accountability is much more comprehensive than evaluation, and it is much more thorough than just observing whether or not an intervention has taken place. As Chapter 2 described, it looks at issues such as fidelity to treatment—the faithfulness of the intervention to its original design. It provides quality assurance measures asking: Do the anticipated visits to parents in an Early Head Start program actually take place? Do they follow a specified format? Do they spend the expected amount of time in each home? What is the percentage of no-shows? Is their variability among programs across different sites? Together, all these details describe whether or not, or to what degree, families and children actually receive the quality of anticipated services.

Although many programs have pursued accountability mechanisms, the discussion of accountability became elevated to new heights when President George W. Bush made school accountability a centerpiece of his domestic policy platform with the No Child Left Behind Act of 2001. The act was controversial for many reasons; some assert that accountability policies can lead to the distortion of programs in undesirable ways, fostering gaming and unintended outcomes that have not improved, and will not improve, achievement. It is in this respect that the National Reporting System, requiring the testing of all Head Start children on language, pre-reading, and math skills, came under a tremendous firestorm of criticism for narrowing the program's goals to a reading and math skills-based intervention. Poor accountability mechanisms can, no doubt, unfairly penalize programs, and, quite literally, undervalue critical factors that have made them successful.

For accountability to make a difference in program improvement, then, it is imperative to use valid, reliable, and accessible tools. These measures should not be confined to the programs' cognitive effects alone. Rather, we need to measure the totality of child characteristics considered essential for successful school readiness, including social emotional skills and dispositions as well as self-regulatory skills. It is in everyone's interest, therefore, to ensure that accountability procedures accurately capture a rich and diverse set of indicators. Studies by Eric Hanushek and his colleagues,[12] for example, have shown that when these factors are in place, accountability can lead to larger and more sustainable achievement gains.

Accountability is often considered synonymous with assessment. However, accountability actually asks a different set of questions. Assessments or achievement tests measure children's learning gains—in areas such as reading, math, and science. Assessment asks the question: Are there gains in achievement? Accountability, on the other hand, asks the next set of questions: Are these gains sufficient to meet the standards of achievement that we hold for all children? Are children progressing at a fast enough pace to close the gap? If children at risk are making gains—yet these gains are only marginal—then the program is likely to be insufficient to improve performance.

Some scholars believe that accountability must include consequences—both sanctions and rewards.[13] However, as prominent political theorist Deborah Stone indicates,[14] rewards and punishments, or promises and threats, can be highly problematic and foster different kinds of political relationships. Positive rewards, such as productivity bonuses, wage increases, can create alliances and good will, but only if people are free to act on their own. Negative inducements, on the other hand, create a climate of conflict and, under some conditions, passive resistance. Further, negative rewards (such as in the case with No Child Left Behind where potential state takeovers of failing schools are possible) assume that the problem is intentional—the effects of intended consequences of purposeful actions.

Such "high-stakes" accountability mechanisms, I believe, are not in our best interests. Rather, accountability is about making the process of teaching and

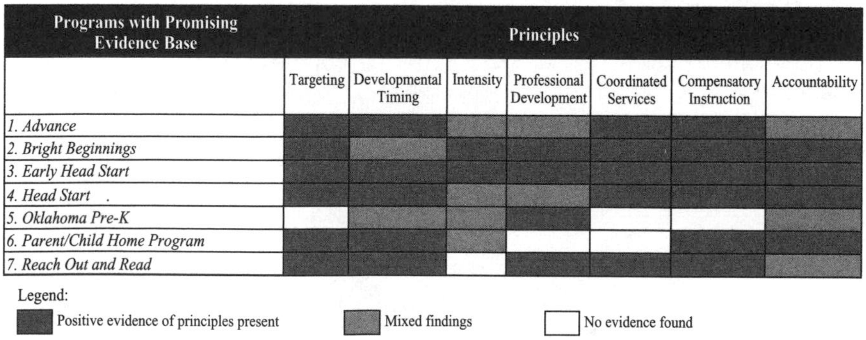

Programs with Promising Evidence Base	Principles						
	Targeting	Developmental Timing	Intensity	Professional Development	Coordinated Services	Compensatory Instruction	Accountability
1. Advance							
2. Bright Beginnings							
3. Early Head Start							
4. Head Start							
5. Oklahoma Pre-K							
6. Parent/Child Home Program							
7. Reach Out and Read							

Legend:
■ Positive evidence of principles present   ■ Mixed findings   □ No evidence found

Figure 3.2.
Programs with Promising Evidence Base.

learning a transparent and dynamic one, engaging everyone as a community in continuous improvement. It should not be used as a crude evaluation tool for teachers or children. Instead, accountability should be used to improve programs. It should encourage program developers to remain open to new ideas, continually asking: What can we do to make the program better? How can we enhance children's learning? What resources do we need to do our job better?

Accountability is about using data to make better decisions in pursuit of better results, knowing that children's earliest years are precious and cannot be replayed or simply revised.

What Can We Do to Improve Children's Lives?

At the applied level, evaluations of programs for economically disadvantaged children, early learning environments, and basic learning strategies provide us with a rich set of clues about what interventions may be critically important to improve children's development. Although literally hundred of variables have been correlated with child outcomes, I have condensed these empirical findings into a set of seven essential principles that may inform policy makers, practitioners, parents, and community leaders in their quest to improve children's lives, particularly those of children who live in the shadows.

Together, these essentials, representing a rigorous evidentiary base, indicate that high-quality early educational interventions can profoundly affect the developmental outcomes for disadvantaged children and their families. These essentials provide a road map, a set of strategies for policy makers, and community leaders to adopt practices that are effective, as well as to generate new programs that may replace those that are not achieving their objectives. These practical guidelines for enhancing children's daily environments can change the trajectory from *beating the odds* to *changing the odds*, turning highly predictive failure and despair to life-changing success and achievement.

There are people and programs who have capitalized on this knowledge base, successfully applying these principles in interventions spanning family support projects, child care, and after-school and community-based programs. Their stories are told in the following chapters. Together, they combine the lessons of research and practice to explode the myth that nothing works. They show what needs to be done as well as what can be done at a price we can afford.

CHAPTER 4

CHANGING THE ODDS BY HELPING TO STRENGTHEN FAMILIES

Human infants are remarkably helpless. Without care, they will die. But in relationships with nurturing, responsive adults, they will thrive and get off to a promising start. Their very transition from dependence to self-reliance and competence is deeply rooted in the context of close relationships with others, typically parents or those serving in parenting roles. The infant who learns that he can play peek-a-boo and make objects disappear and reappear acquires an understanding of stability in the world around him. The toddler who learns that she can playfully impose her own ideas by pretending situations is likely to develop feelings of competence and control. The preschooler who is regularly nourished with stories and books before going to bed is likely to enter kindergarten with a keen interest in reading. What children learn, how they react to people and events around them, and what they expect from themselves and others will be deeply affected by these relationships and by the environment in which they live.

Children's development depends on stability and security. They rely on the emotional support of their caregivers to understand, experience, and manage their own feelings. But families that have been damaged by poverty, depression, poor health, abuse, and neglect may not have the physical or psychological resources necessary to parent responsibly or effectively. These families will need support to overcome the tremendous hurdles they will face daily. They'll need help creating the kinds of daily routines and environments that enable them to provide healthy child–caregiver interactions and rich opportunities for learning.

We now understand better than ever before the basic connections between early family environments and damaging outcomes in adolescence and later life. We know that children whose memories are storehouses of deprivation and denial are robbed of the ability to dream about a better future. We know that children whose families were never able to convey to them a sense of being valued and cared for are in a poor position to cope with the world at large. In light of the consensus of data from the physical, behavioral, and social sciences, we can now predict with a fair degree of certainty the conditions that will determine whether children get off to a promising or highly problematic start in life. What's more, we are now able to identify the interventions that can put some of these risk factors out of play. Compelling evidence exists to show that applying what we know about beneficial parenting to intervention efforts can radically improve outcomes for children. Today, throughout this country, programs exist that are changing the odds for high-risk children, programs that have been demonstrated through rigorous evidence and ongoing research to have significant and enduring effects. These programs show that systematic intervention, following seven essentials support families early in children's life cycles, can improve children's lifetime prospects of becoming productive adults.

In this chapter, we focus on environmental hazards that jeopardize children's development, as well as the pervasive disparities in nurturance, health, and general family support for children in poverty. We'll see how these disparities influence children's school readiness. Then we'll take a look inside programs that are turning upside down the notion that these families are incorrigible, unable to responsibly parent, showing how supportive interventions for high-risk families can produce significant and enduring changes in parent behavior. Recognizing that the challenges are real—and even more daunting in light of the complex problems that face many at-risk families today, these programs will show that through painstaking attention to implementation and quality of service, we can effectively support parents and improve children's odds.

Environments That Jeopardize Children's Development

Four-year-old Anaya Jackson lives with her grandmother in a crumbling building among Philadelphia's Robert Wood Johnson projects. Last year, she was one of 3,228 children in this city diagnosed as having enough lead in her body to cause irreparable health problems. She is one of the children I visit at the Corner Clinic, an all-inclusive clinic in walking distance from the projects. According to a recent study, over 68% of these children in the clinic[1] have been diagnosed as having unsafe levels of lead in their blood, jeopardizing their futures.

Lead is an insidious poison. It quite literally damages the brain. It harms children's bodies. Children in poor communities such as this one are exposed to lead in peeling paint on buildings, in their drinking water (from lead solder in pipes), and in canned foods. Currently, an estimated 300,000 U.S. children[2]—22,000 in Anaya's state alone—will face lives of reduced intelligence and diminished futures because of its toxic effects. They'll arrive at the school door showing signs of hyperactivity, learning disabilities, and self-regulatory problems, conditions that are typically associated with living in contaminated neighborhoods.

But lead is only one of the known environmental hazards that wreak havoc on children's readiness for learning and well-being. Environments polluted by strong fumes, dust, mold, and smoke spark such chronic disorders as asthma, the leading cause of children's trips to the emergency room and also of hospitalization and absence from school. A teenage mother, describing her harrowing night at the emergency room with her eight-month-old baby, whose asthma has become so acute as to trigger regular hospitalizations, recounted her struggles to me: she tries to work two jobs—one on a night shift—while trying to take care of her sickly baby, which has blocked airways that cause her to wheeze and seem to struggle for breath. Asthma is one of the most chronic conditions among poor children, according to the National Health and Nutrition Examination Survey,[3] a study using nationally representative data, which reports that only 26% of children having two or more acute asthma attacks are likely to get the medication necessary to manage the condition.

Dr. Tanya Fleming at the clinic finds that she regularly confronts conditions that would have been routine had they only been treated early on—chronic conditions such as dental decay, allergies, and ear infections, all of which become difficult to resolve at more advanced stages. If left untreated, these normally resolving ear infections can develop into acute otitis media, a condition that can cause hearing loss.[4] Researchers estimate that at any given time, roughly 5% of two- to four-year-old children have hearing loss because of middle ear problems, seriously delaying their language at a crucial time in its development.

The environmental hazards that fill Anaya and her neighborhood friends' lives seriously impair their readiness for learning. It used to be that children's lives outside of school, the neighborhood they lived in, and the company they might keep were seen as separate from learning and reading and writing skills. But every parent and teacher knows that a small child, sick with an earache, may not be able to sit and listen to a story; in fact, the child may not be able to listen at all. Some chronically ill children who do not get the benefits of doctors in clinics, as Tanya Fleming does, will labor to achieve academically throughout their lives because of these hazardous environments.

Another killer in their midst is the enemy within: obesity. Not even this clinic seems to have solved the problems of the huge numbers of obese people in this poor community. Some researchers now proclaim that obesity is no longer the preserve of the unemployed and the disenfranchised but a societal issue, with the percentage of overweight children aged 6–11 quadrupling in the last 40 years from 4% to 16%.[5] Nevertheless, poor children from birth to age five are twice as likely as better-off children to be obese, about a third more likely to be anemic, and about 20% more likely to be deficient in vitamin A. But being overweight for these women and children isn't only about the failure on their part to buy fresh vegetables and fruits. It's really the story of food as a comfort and shelter in a barren emotional landscape in which all hope seems to have spiraled downward.

Sitting in the clinic, I see how extreme family distress can lead to confusion, incoherence, and instability in early childhood: the two-year-old who is slapped for playing with a toy, the baby who crawls to look at a book only to have it grabbed away as if it were toxic, the three-year-old who overhears her mother cursing about the child's father and about how she's got a "warrant after him" for past abuse. These are the experiences of early family life that create children who will feel hostile and alien later in life, lacking impulse control and finding even the most minor obstacles insurmountable.

It is said that a central feature of a baby's early relationships is best captured by the concept of attachment security,[6] which is built by creating close emotional bonds with regular caregivers, by knowing that needs will be met, and by depending on regular routines—mealtime, naptime, play. These early attachments become the foundation for developing confidence and constancy, creating deeply rooted relationships between babies and the caregivers who protect, nurture, and guide their development. In the rare situations in which infants do not have the opportunity to form an attachment with even one trusted adult, their development can deteriorate rapidly and dramatically.

When the process goes smoothly, the loving and predictable relationship between infant and caregiver seems natural and easy, but when the process is rough—which seems to happen all too frequently to young woman who are poor—the relationship may be disastrous. Beth, a social worker in protective services, recounts her year-long efforts with Darion, a child who was undernourished and failing to thrive. Born prematurely, Darion has Down Syndrome, a challenge to any young mother. Poorly educated, alone, and depressed, the mother doesn't respond to the child, repeatedly telling Beth during her visits, "I didn't want this baby." Recognizing that the source of the problem was not the mother's cruelty but her lack of understanding that she needed to feed the baby even if he didn't cry to be fed, Beth worked with the mother to schedule regular feeding times each day. Now, after seeing both mother and child forming a real bond, Beth recounts, "It's the first night I slept well in over a year. I knew he was going to be OK."

Providing sensitive, consistent, and responsive parenting of infants and toddlers is challenging for any family. The birth of a child disrupts routines, increases stress, affects the household budget, causes physical changes in the mother's body, and—in some cases—causes postpartum depression. Many a family must deal with these major changes while caring for a newborn—one whose needs come first day and night. It can be a challenging transition, to say the least, regardless of whether you're a first time mother or one with older children to care for as well. But all these changes can be further compounded by family dysfunction and poverty. Many women struggle with an idealistic image of motherhood, only to find that the day-to-day reality of life with a newborn falls far short of their preconceptions about what motherhood would be like.

Evidence abounds that poverty is associated with higher risk of depression,[7] which is almost two-and-a-half times more likely for poor, inner-city women than for their non-poor counterparts. Higher stress may be caused by a lack of resources or coping mechanisms within a landscape populated with multiple stressors. For some women, like Lauren, the combination of the aftereffects of a difficult pregnancy, internal emotions, and external pressures is overwhelming. The home visitor and I watch as the deeply depressed mother holds her baby like an object, making little to no eye contact, as the baby seems to search for her gaze. We turn to the grandmother for support, recognizing that if the infant does not have the opportunity to form an attachment with even one trusted adult, his development will likely suffer lasting damage. Deprived of affection and care and repeatedly disappointed, he'll eventually find it futile to expect aid or care from adults. Such a child may withdraw, shrinking back from building lasting relationships with others, feeling guilty and unworthy, and learning to distrust the surrounding world.

Those who study attachment, such as Professor Jay Belsky[8] and Megan Gunnar,[9] believe that children's first relationships, especially with parents or other primary caregivers, help to reduce their fear of novel or challenging situations, allowing them to explore ideas with confidence and self-efficacy. Responding contingently to children's wishes to venture out into the world, parents strengthen their awareness of their ability to influence events and others, simultaneously assuring them of a secure base if they venture a bit too far. When a mother is depressed, and her baby receives only negative or flat messages from her facial and vocal cues, he is unlikely to develop the confidence he needs to explore novel or challenging situations. Mothers, often fighting for survival both emotionally and economically, may act inconsistently with their infants, lavishing them at one point with attention but using force to discipline them at others. In fact, many studies document a relationship between maternal depression and both current and future child behavior problems, insecure attachment, and cognitive problems. Maternal depression, they find, can reduce test scores by as much as a third of a standard deviation among preschool children.

Efforts to better understand the relationship between maternal depression and children's outcomes has, not surprisingly, focused more closely on mother–child interactions. Contrary to the sensitive give-and-take in the way a healthy parent responds to her baby's cues, a depressed mother may show little emotion or energy or withdraw from her child entirely. She'll also express self-doubts about her ability to parent well and may blame her child's behavior for her own emotional trauma—"My baby's bad," a mother says, attempting to blame its fussiness on some inherent problem in the child.

The ways in which a mother talks to her child will have enormous consequences on the child's emerging capacities for communication and learning. Raised in a secure family arrangement, a child fairly effortlessly acquires the spoken language, the sounds, meanings, practices, and vocabulary necessary for learning in school and social contexts. But raised in a family mired in poverty where there may be pervasive maltreatment, or in a home in which the mother is abusing substances or is withdrawn and silent, a child soon begins to show signs of language impairment and cognitive deficits. At the local clinic, eighteen-month Emanuel tries to engage his mother in conversation, pointing to objects around the room. She looks away, ignores his attempts, and stares into space. Finally, with outstretched arms, he begins to whimper for her attention. She turns away from him, spurning his attention, as she tells me, "He has an attitude problem." Yet we know that children who learn to replace crying with playful babbling, making up pretend words, will spend more time in happier states and will be easier children for parents to manage in the long run. I want to tell her that he wouldn't have seemed so clingy if she had only engaged her son in language exchanges that acknowledged his attempts to communicate with her. Now 18 months old with no recognizable words yet in his expressive vocabulary, Emanuel is already at higher risk for linguistic and cognitive deficits.

More than likely, language delays such as Emanuel's will mean that he'll start school behind and stay noticeably behind in school as early as kindergarten. He'll represent a tremendous challenge to his teacher and to the school system. In one large longitudinal study, Jerry West and his colleagues found,[10] for example, that kindergarten children displayed vocabulary differences ranging from that of a two-year-old to that of a 10-year-old. These differences will have subtle (and not-so-subtle) consequences in how children fare in schools. It will affect how children are treated by their teachers, what friends they associate with, what kind of activities they'll engage in, and what their academic performance will be not only in their first three years but beyond.

In principle, of course, children such as Emanuel could catch up if given additional exposure to verbal input. A window of opportunity for language development does not shut down at a certain age. Rather, it has to do with the rate of catch-up that will be necessary to get him on the right track. As George Farkas and his colleagues describe it,[11] the amount of additional exposure to language a child will need to erase the gap is already huge by age three and only increases exponentially over time. With each passing year, the gap widens, eventually becoming insurmountable, for all practical purposes.

Consequently, when pervasive environmental hazards such as lead and toxins fill children's bodies; when chronic pain from untreated dental disease leads to problems eating, speaking, and learning; when maternal attention is focused inward instead of toward loving care and nurturance; normal development is seriously jeopardized. If infants are deprived of predictability—if caregivers are emotionally absent and their repeated attempts for affection go unrequited—a young child may simply conclude that it is futile to expect adults to be caring or helpful. Such children may withdraw to find more solitary sources of comfort, learning to distrust the surrounding world.

Poor housing, health, and nutrition, coupled with parents who may be distraught and dysfunctional, will indelibly mark children's character, confidence in developing relationships, and knowledge about their world. These are the experiences that will ultimately create untrusting adults who lack self-esteem and impulse-control, seeking immediate gratification, dropping out of high school, or failing to delay parenting. These are the experiences that create young adults who show little regard for others' feelings, becoming easy recruits into the world of drugs and the ranks of crime. Unsupported at a crucial stage in their lives, they are unlikely to develop the skills necessary to become self-supporting later on and will have few of the resources needed to lead productive lives.

What Can We Do About It?

Families will need help. Even those who might disparage certain lifestyles, the decisions some parents have made, and the unfortunate circumstances that may heighten tensions in these families' lives must remember that the victims are ultimately their children. We cannot afford to abandon them.

The good news is that we *can* improve parenting behaviors—not all, but enough to significantly benefit vulnerable children. There is now compelling evidence, collected and replicated through rigorous research, to suggest that successfully applying what is known about beneficial parenting to intervention efforts can improve children's outcomes. A fifteen-year follow-up study of the nurse-visitation program,[12] for example, found reduced arrests, convictions, numbers of sexual partners, and alcohol use, by 50–80%, when compared to controls. A seven-year evaluation across 17 different sites[13] found that the children of Early Head Start parents were nearly half as likely to exhibit antisocial behaviors as were those not participating in the program. The message of these studies is clear: high-quality parenting programs can promote more sensitive parenting, mitigating children's potential behavior problems and promoting more positive outcomes.

These changes are not easy, and the challenges are daunting. Many of these families have been rocketed by multiple stressors in their lives—poverty, hopelessness, depression, troubled relationships—and will need the most talented professionals and intensive services to deal with the serious life issues they face. What we do know, however, is that when programs meet these families needs "where they are," some stunning victories have been won.

Some of the strongest evidence comes from interventions that provide families with a range of supports. Educational support helps soon-to-be mothers such as those in small, semi-rural Appalachian regions learn to improve their lifecourses by graduating high school on time and getting jobs.[14] Preemptive care works with low-income, first-time mothers in Elmira, New York, to give birth to full-term babies who aren't already debilitated by excessive alcohol consumption, smoking, and drug use.[15] Social networks help postpartum mothers in great psychological distress receive the services they urgently need in order to control their emotional instability and prevent harm to their babies.[16]

The empirical evidence is strong, and it is replicated now in major medical journals, supported by the National Institutes of Health: graduates of family support programs show gains in employment ranging from 60 to 82%, have 43% fewer subsequent pregnancies, and are likely to delay pregnancies by at least a year longer than their control counterparts are. Beyond doubt, it shows that programs that help strengthen families can change the conditions in which children grow up, preventing damaging outcomes. This literature clearly highlights these conclusions:

- We can improve the sensitivity and reciprocity of care that parents give their infants and toddlers, also strengthening the security of their attachments.
- We can help mothers cope with the life issues in the world outside their family that drain their energies and remove their attention from their children's needs, helping them to parent more effectively.
- By improving parents' behavior management strategies, we can reduce children's aggressive and oppositional behaviors.
- Through relationship-based programs that involve emotional and psychological supports, we can improve parent–child interactions and enhance infant's security of attachment.
- We can reduce maternal smoking and substance abuse, subsequently reducing low-weight and premature births.
- We can help improve the safety of home environments and reduce hospital visits caused by injuries and the ingestion of poisons.
- Through intensive, targeted programs, we can teach low-income parents how to facilitate their young children's literacy skills, better preparing them for kindergarten.

Almost all parents wish for healthy and loving relationships with their children. But in times of family crisis and relentless stress, these early relationships may begin to fray badly. This research suggests that these tattered relationships can be repaired. We can support parents, helping them become better caregivers. Because of the irreplaceable importance of these early relationships for young children's development, it is vitally important that we do everything possible to enable parents to establish good relationships with their children from the start and, when things fail, help them find ways to reduce the stress that impinges on their ability and desire to be good parents.

Too often, however, we have failed to follow the seven essentials of programs that work. This has caused increasing pessimism about our ability to solve such problems. The pressure of unrealistic expectations—having to promise too much with too little—has undermined our once-confident belief that intervention can be effective. Strewn across this landscape of failure and disappointments, however, are programs all over the country that are following these essentials, helping families repair their lives to be the parents they have always wished they could be.

A Beacon of Hope

At County Estates, shabby rental trailer homes are separated by weedy lawns, uncared-for bushes, and streets with names that contrast sadly with the grim landscape, such as Peacock Lane and Bluebird Avenue. Aesthetically, however, the trailer park looks far less dismal than the brick jungles of downtown row-house projects designed to house factory workers in Flint, Michigan, during its heyday as one of the auto capitals of the country.

Socially and economically, this is a wounded community. Even now, some 20 years after the most notorious example of the 1970s collapse of the U.S. auto industry, documented in Michael Moore's film *Roger and Me*, the reverberations of this massive exodus can still be seen. Hospitals, mental health clinics, grocery stores, and small cottage industries, all designed to sustain factory workers, are now gone. Instead, prostitutes and drug pushers run rampant through the streets and trailer parks. Highlighting Flint's downward spiral, residents still talk about the six-year-old boy several years ago who brought a semi-automatic gun to a school and killed a six-year-old girl in their first-grade classroom. Of the 120,000 residents, 37% are living below the poverty line; only 29% of all households are married couples living together.

The day is bathed in sunshine when I visit County Estates with social worker Marva Williams. But the trailer where I meet Terry and her son Daniel is dark and dank. Entering it is like going through a tunnel—blankets and old towels cover the windows. Generations ago, Terry's family came from the Appalachians with little formal education and worked in the factories, received generous health care benefits, decent housing, and a genuine sense of community. Plant closings, however, left this city in culture shock. With family searching for work in the surrounding areas, Terry is alone most of each day as her husband Roy works two jobs to "get enough hours" to meet the family's needs.

Terry, 23, a large woman of about 300 pounds, has had a complex health history. About three years ago, after a very difficult pregnancy, she gave birth to a second child who was stillborn. She learned that she was pregnant again the following year—and that this baby, too, was in jeopardy. Deeply religious, with no health insurance and no family to turn to, she contacted the church, which in turn contacted the local school district for help.

The school put her in touch with a little known federal program called Early Head Start. Throughout Terry's harrowing pregnancy and subsequent months of trauma when her little son Daniel's life hung by a thread, Marva Williams of the Early Head Start program helped her to navigate the complex web of social services. Williams took her to the doctor on a regular basis, got her the services she desperately needed, and talked to her through the lonely and scary months of pregnancy. Now, as I watch Terry playing so effortlessly with Daniel and chatting with Marva as if they were at a coffee klatch together, it's a moment of triumph indeed—the celebration of Daniel's first birthday. With all these traumas behind them—premature birth, the fear of Down syndrome, 31 days in the hospital because of serious complications of blockages in the small and large intestine—here is Daniel today, looking healthy and content.

Coming at a time of increasing awareness of a "quiet crisis" facing families with infants and toddlers, Early Head Start began as a tiny gem of a program around 1994. Since then, it has taken root in many high-poverty communities across the country, helping young mothers traverse the complex and difficult transitional pathways from adulthood to good parenthood.

Early Head Start, however, is not to be confused with its well-known big brother, Head Start. Helping families years earlier than Head Start does, the two-generation program serves as a catalyst helping pregnant woman and low-income families with infants and toddlers get a good start in life. In the 1990s, through the inspiration of Associate Commissioner of the Head Start Bureau Helen Taylor; the commitment of the Secretary of Health and Human Services, Donna Shalala; and a top-notch group of experts in child development, health, and family services, Early Head Start created, tested, and developed a quality-control program that in only a few short years has grown to about 626 sites across the country.

What these experts realized is that pregnancy and those first moments of relationship-building and early attachments among parents and children are critical for children's development and later functioning. Building on what worked for Head Start and its comprehensive approach to child development and education services, they recognized that it was important to get these services to families early. But they had to meet families "where they were"—rather than according to a fixed model. They needed a flexible approach orchestrated around a set of program goals that effectively built relationships to provide child development services, family and community partnerships, and support staff for children and families. The how-to might change, but the goals must remain the same—strengthening families who need help and support—and now.

In Bendle/Carman-Ainsworth in Flint, Michigan, they have a philosophy: "Children come before deadlines; parents come before turf; families before paperwork; people before politics." Throughout my visits, it's clear that these words are not just empty slogans. "We work with families for the benefit of our youngest and most vulnerable," says Carolyn Rutledge, Early Head Start Director. "Our services don't just start in September and end in June."

Even before babies are even born, Early Head Start is at work. The program offers both center-based and home-based care. After an initial interview, a family might choose a center-based option with infant and toddler care or a home-based program of weekly home visits and at least two group socials per month for each family. A family may also choose a mixed approach, with some center-based services and home-based ones. Some families are ready for job training and work and find that the center structure is best for them; others, however, might need the comfort and trust that comes from the intimacy of home visits. Roy, Terry's husband, participated in all the home weekly visits the first year, according to Marva, "'to see if I was OK.' Now he seems comfortable not to be there all the time." Soon Marva will work with Terry to see whether she's ready to have Daniel visit the center twice a week. Regardless of setting, however, the goals will be the same: helping the child develop socially, emotionally, and cognitively and ending the isolation of families in poverty by providing valuable socialization that children and parents both crave and need.

It's not easy. Home visitors on many occasions have to rejoice in families making small steps toward recovery. Susan, a home visitor with a master's degree in social work, specializes in the medically complex cases. In her three years with the program, she has seen progress in nearly every one of her families, but in "baby steps," a term likely to infuriate anyone who holds test scores as the only evidence of change. "Very often these families don't just have single growth trajectory," she finds. "They'll go forward, then back, and then forward again. Sometimes even if they seem to 'graduate' from the home visiting situation to a combination program, after a while they might need to back into the combination or home-based program."

It's that kind of support and nonjudgmental help that seems to win families over. As Brenda, another home visitor, recounts, "Sometimes a parent will use outrageous behavior, foul language, and curse publicly," knowing full well that this behavior is socially unacceptable. They'll even talk about how they have successfully chased away many other well-intentioned helpers. But she steadfastly tells them, "We're one group that will not be scared away. We keep coming back."

The job, however, is not for the faint-hearted or easily frustrated. Illustrating one of these "baby steps," Mary recalls an experience with one of her most troubled mothers. Five times she made an appointment to visit the mother, but five times, the mother missed the appointment. After what seemed like months of missed opportunities and phone calls unreturned, one day the mother came to the center, asked to see Brenda, and said she was ready: "I knew you weren't going to give up on me like so many have in the past."

It's really all about teamwork on many different levels. Staff members engage in weekly reflection and consultation sessions to anchor their work and develop new goals with families. Working with an executive team of nurses, mental health professionals, nutritionists, social workers, and educators, the sessions provide a safe place for self-reflection, a place where home visitors can express the feelings that may arise from working closely with troubled infants and families. Together, they review cases, get feedback from their colleagues, and—perhaps most importantly—get emotional support and direction for themselves. As Beth describes, "we talk, we cry, we problem-solve together, knowing we have to get these feelings out somewhere." Believing passionately in a strengths-based consultation model, the Early Head Start program focuses on each family's social and emotional strengths, using them as a basis for discussing new strategies for families' individual growth and development.

And so it becomes clear to the team at Bendle/Carman-Ainsworth that Terry and Roy are ready to take some important next steps now that Daniel's fragile health has stabilized. Guided by a set of performance standards that anchors program goals and expectations, Marva targets Daniel's development—his cognitive and social needs. She focuses on the immediate environment, helping Terry make the limited space in the trailer safe for Daniel's increasing mobility. Then she moves to other goals: increasing Daniel's vocabulary and sensitivity to sounds and creating a more stimulating environment for his growing curiosity and independence.

By employing highly qualified professionals, home visits in Early Head Start do not use a formal script, unlike some other home-based programs that have relied on volunteers or less trained helpers. Relation-building is a key component to the program, demanding a more delicate balance between program goals and family needs. Home visits, then, may begin with a target focus, but they may evolve to help a family complete an application for assistance or take someone to the doctor if sorely needed. In contrast to a client–expert role, our visit to Terry begins like a conversation between friends. "How was Daniel's birthday party? Did all the relatives come?" They laugh about how—despite all the preparations—he misbehaved, putting his fingers in the cake and whining when he didn't get his way in front of the relatives. Marva commiserates and reassures Terry: "Yes, they get embarrassed and overwhelmed sometimes in such events." They compare notes about their children and their delightful foibles. It all seems so natural and fun.

With the fun come gently taught lessons, done in the name of intellectual, physical, and social development to prepare him for school, knowing that a child prepared is a child more likely to succeed. "We're going to focus on sound-learning toys, and we'll make a set the next time I come." Out come very simple hand-made toys, plastic bottles with different beans and colors. Daniel grabs at them playfully as Marva describes: "[H]ere he's getting the sounds, and he's manipulating objects, and look how great he's grasping and responding to what we're saying." Picking up on the child's cues, she labels objects; at the same time, she makes Terry keenly aware of key developmental patterns. "He'll probably start to point and babble, and want to know the names of things, and you'll want to label things for him." Throughout the conversation, she gently asks about whether he's had his health checks. "Did you get the lead results?" "Has his hearing been checked recently?" She brings out several more games, plays peek-a-boo with Daniel, and reads a soft-covered book, demonstrating and modeling behaviors that parents might do with their babies.

In this chatty, comfortable way, Marva discusses some very important issues such as washing Roy's clothes carefully to get off the lead before entering the house, and Daniel's occasional temper tantrums ("sometimes it's just because they're exhausted or fearful"). Before she leaves, Terry goes over concerns of the week that have been troubling her—"I wonder when it's time for him to get off the bottle"—to reassurance: "He'll probably taper off by himself." Marva ends the visit by saying, "You're doing an incredible job."

For families with troubled histories, outside help comes at a tremendous personal price. They lose their privacy and become dependent, subject to prying and scrutiny and the second-guessing of others. Every application for help—and there are many—asks them to reveal their most intimate details to strangers, indirectly sending a message that "poor people don't matter."

In Early Head Start, there is a belief that all families have a "right to privacy." In this relationship, built on mutual respect, families may reveal many of their troubles over time. But it is the commitment to helping parents achieve self-sufficiency, strengthening their capacity to enhance their children's development, that is at the heart of their relationship: There are no recriminations; no blame or sanctions if benchmarks aren't met—just support and help in dealing with all the conflicting pressures from outside. With these goals in mind, quite fittingly, most visits end with Marva asking each parent, "What are your dreams? What are your hopes for your child? Let's work together to make it happen."

Facing the most adverse of family circumstances, the Early Head Start program has not only defied the odds, it has changed them. Here in Bendle/Carman-Ainsworth, children who come from multi-risk environments are scoring equal to or above district and state averages on the state tests some four or five years later. Their results only mirror the findings of a national evaluation conducted by Mathematica[17] of more than 1,000 families in the first years of its existence. Overall impacts within the first year were modest, with effect sizes in the 10–20 range, but considerably larger for the more needy families, with some effect sizes in the 20–50% range, representing almost a half a year's growth compared to controls. In just a few short years, Early Head Start has helped to improve

- Higher scores on standardized tests of infant and toddler development, including reports of larger vocabularies and the ability to speak in more complex sentences
- Better developmental functioning, reducing the risk of poor cognitive outcomes later on
- Greater parent involvement in supporting and stimulating cognitive development, language, and literacy
- More frequent reading aloud by parents to their children daily and at bedtime
- Greater security and attachment
- Milder disciplinary techniques such as distraction, explanation, or conversation rather than spanking
- Lower levels of family conflict and stress

Hailing these results, previous HHS Assistant Secretary for Children and Families, Olivia Golden suggests, "There will be more to learn, but we now know that the Early Head Start blueprint of an early, intensive program can yield significant results and brighter outcomes for children." By taking into account families' broader life circumstances, Early Head Start enables mothers to become more attuned to their children's needs to feel healthy, secure, loved, nurtured, and stimulated to learn. Over the course of two or more years together, through intensive and continuing relationships, this program will help to improve children's outcomes by improving children's care. Hundreds of programs throughout the country, many of them different in structure, are helping to strengthen families so desperately in need of outside support.

Early Head Start has rightly earned its reputation as a beacon of hope[18] for our nation's most vulnerable children.

A Helping Hand

Less than 50 miles from Flint, you'll find even a sadder city. Once an economic giant, home to the world's three largest automobile companies, Ford, GM, and Chrysler, Detroit is now almost a ghost town—isolated, fragmented, and nearly bankrupt.

"Cattle could graze in the vast swaths of depopulated neighborhoods," quips commentator George Will,[19] describing a city in apparent irreversible decline. Twelve thousand homes lie abandoned around Detroit, a byproduct of the decades of layoffs at the city's auto plants and white flight to the suburbs. Despite scores of attempts by government and civic leaders to set the city straight, this once proud automobile capitol of the world seems trapped in a vicious cycle of urban decay.

Detroit has lost more than half its population since its heyday in the 1950s. It is still losing about 10,000 people a year. Suffering from a vanishing middle class, the people who remain are mostly black—83%—and mostly poor, with 30% of the population living well below the poverty line, according to the most recent census. More than 70% of the children are born out of wedlock.

The schools are bad. The roads are filled with potholes. Crime is high, and so are taxes. And when it comes to threats in the neighborhoods, Audrey Taylor, a nurse of 40 years with whom I travel, isn't sure which is worse—the rats or lead poisoning. Suburbanites who once lived here are known to take the bodies of their relatives out of cemeteries because they're afraid to come to the city. "There are more than 150–250 being moved a year," reports Stephan Vogel,[20] dean of the school of architecture at the University of Detroit. "Detroit has become an icon of urban decline."

Among Detroit's most tragic problems are the stark differences in white and black infant mortality rates; the rates for black infants are near those of a Third World country. In 2003, for example, the latest year for which figures are available, 18 black babies of every 1,000 born in this city died before their first birthday. The rate for white babies in Detroit was 5–7 per 1,000. "Infant mortality is the yardstick" of how a nation cares for its people, says Bob Marks, a general manager of community health services in the health administration department.

Three problems are known to contribute to the early death of babies: low birth weight, (birth at less than five-and-a-half pounds), prematurity (birth before 37 weeks of pregnancy), and unsafe sleeping environments.

Birth weight "is the most powerful predictor of a baby's survival," reports Delores Smith, a Wayne State University School of Medicine nurse with Healthy Start, a program intended to reduce perinatal health disparities in Detroit children. Statistics show that black women in Detroit are more likely to receive inadequate prenatal care than are women of any other race. Black babies are born at low birth weights three times as frequently as are babies of any other racial and ethnic group, she says. "When I get up and put on my work boots, the work is about prematurity and the ravages on society," reported Dr. Theodore Jones, vice president of medical affairs at the Hutzel Woman's Hospital, and a high-risk specialist.

The solution is to get women into care before birth: to help moms get food and essentials through the federally-funded WIC program and health care for themselves and their children through the state's Medicaid program. For family support, it is also important to have nurses specially trained in prenatal care, such as Audrey Taylor, to visit and help care for high-risk moms before and after birth.

Begun in 1977 as a research-demonstration program in Elmira, New York, the Nurse-Home Visitation program, (now known as the Nurse-Family Partnership) brainchild of psychologist Dr. David Olds, was designed to meet this need. Rather than wait for mothers to come to them, nurses visited 90 mothers and their families in their homes during pregnancy and 99 more during the next two years of the children's lives. Sixty-one percent of the women in the first study were at or below the federal poverty guidelines. Almost half of the mothers were teenagers. Sixty-two percent of them were unmarried. And all were having their first babies.

David Olds believed that helping these women get off to a good start during their first pregnancies and care of their first child would allow these skills to carry over to subsequent children. Nurses specially trained in home-based care regularly visited the soon-to-be moms starting early on, generally before the end of the second trimester, and continued throughout the next two years after the baby was born. Each mother was visited by the same nurse each time. As Olds reported in an NPR interview,[21] "For many of the young mothers, they hadn't had someone who was consistently there for them. And this relationship, many of the young mothers tell us, was a lifeline. It was a lifesaver for them and their child."

What started out as a good idea in Elmira has since yielded some concrete results. In a fifteen-year follow-up of the first children born into the program, there was less drinking, less drug use, and less crime—59% fewer arrests than of children from similar backgrounds whose mothers did not get the training.[22] "Improving health, improving care, helping families become more economically self-sufficient improves children's outcomes," reports nurse Becky Roberts. Two subsequent studies in Memphis and Denver yielded even more encouraging findings: nurse-visited children were better prepared to enter school. They had better language development. They had better cognitive development—and to hear from some of the children from the initial study, they turned out well. In a CBS interview,[23] Julie Petros, one of the first moms drafted into the program and a teenage mother, proudly reports, "Tom was high-risk." He ended up graduating second in his high school class of 300 and went on to be a 3.8 GPA student at Rensselaer Polytechnic Institute in Troy, N.Y., one of the top technical colleges in the country.

Since the initial demonstration project, the Nurse-Family partnership (www.nursefamilypartnership.org) has evolved and expanded to a vibrant network of local sites expanding across 23 states and currently serving over 20,000 families per year. Helping women improve the outcomes of pregnancy, child health and development, and maternal life course, the program uses a "person–process–context" model that draws heavily upon research in self-efficacy, attachment, and human ecology. Nurse home visitors support young, low-income, first-time mothers as they

- Set small, achievable goals for behavioral change that, if accomplished, strengthen their confidence in coping with similar problems in the future.
- Develop supports from families and friends and the use of community services.
- Plan for the future (including planning subsequent pregnancies).
- Increase their levels of responsivity to their children and promote greater interaction through smiling, hugging, and signaling.

Home visits are considered essential in developing these close, therapeutic alliances with mothers and other family members. As Audrey reports, "We're on their own turf—it breaks down barriers." Many low-income mothers are reluctant to use office-based care, having experienced discrimination or at least felt discriminated against, or having been given poor care. By visiting the home, nurses are able to get a deeper appreciation for the physical and social environment and can work with the mother to improve the environment for the child's development.

Audrey reports that housing conditions, for example, can be so poor that parents are reluctant to put their babies on the floor because of cockroaches and rats. It's also not uncommon for young mothers to be in households where there is criminal activity, such as drug dealing. By observing the environment first-hand, nurses can better see the conditions mothers are contending with, enabling them to help the mothers make better choices for themselves.

On another visit, I am meeting Margaret, 18, who has had multiple complications, both during and after her pregnancy. During the birth, she had cardiac arrest. To make matters worse, as she was being delivered by a c-section, a blood clot in her lung was discovered. Now, suffering from severe depression, pain, and occasional fever, she is in a family dispute with her mother, who wants her to take charge of her baby.

Audrey sits quietly at the table: "How's everything going? What's up, hon?" Margaret breaks down, saying, "Everything's making me cry; I'm even thinking of giving him away. I can't get him to stop crying." Audrey replies, "It's a lot to expect full recovery or movement. The healing takes place, but it's gradual, and you've got to manage your medication."

Her mother joins and tells us, "I don't think it's depression. Margaret is spoiled, and she just doesn't want to do anything around here. That's why I'm angry. I expect progress, and progress is not what I see." She turns to Margaret: "Sign the baby over to me and that will be that."

All the theory in the world can't begin to help overcome the painful realities and the emotional distress among these family members and others in similar challenging situations. This is where the training, the professionalism, and the years of developing healing alliances with families begin to become so transparent. Over the next hour, I watch how Audrey negotiates between the family members, helping Margaret set some goals such as taking her medication and making a bottle for the baby, trying to get her to take some baby steps. "What goal do you think is the most important to achieve right now?" she asks Margaret. "Can you change the dressing on your incision? It's Thursday now, should we say Saturday? I'll come by and check on Saturday."

As a nurse, Audrey brings an extraordinary set of skills to the program not only in her knowledge of medicine but also in her ability to establish therapeutic relationships with families and connect them with other key resources in their community that are able to help. It is such skills that seem to set the Nurse-Family Partnership program apart from the many other preventative health programs. Audrey's training—20 years in community health—helps to address the comprehensive needs of the family, focusing particularly on the mother's health and ability to care for her child. As you watch, you can see that her ability to competently address the family's concerns about the difficult complications of pregnancy, labor, and delivery, as well as the physical health of the newborn, gives her enormous credibility and persuasive power in the eyes of the family members. Her knowledge about how to prevent additional health problems and her ability to wade through the complex network of the health care and health insurance systems are an enormous asset to these at-risk families.

Even with all this experience, however, Audrey will be expected to take additional training courses throughout her involvement in the program to keep up with the latest research findings in the field. (A hallmark of the program is its continued use of research to improve services.) She'll also receive regular clinical supervision from a supervising nurse to ensure that the program is being implemented with fidelity to the intervention model. Data will be collected regularly to improve partnerships. The program designers leave nothing to chance, always seeking to strengthen the program in ways that best serve their families.

Each full-time nurse in the program carries a caseload of 25 families. Although they'll have a structured set of visit-by-visit guidelines and goals, these experienced nurses adapt as needed to meet the individual needs of families. In my visit, for example, Audrey had intended to help Margaret make eye contact with her baby, Malik, to encourage a beginning attachment. But Margaret's depression, poor health, and family crises quickly changed these plans. Instead, she spends time reviewing her medicines, reviewing the next goal, and encouraging Margaret to take just a few baby steps. After a seventy-five-minute, emotionally wrenching visit, Audrey and Margaret hug one another long and hard, followed by what becomes evidence of a baby step. Showing attention to her baby for the very first time, Margaret demonstrates her deep desire to be a good mother with the remarkable words, "What should I do with his cradle cap?"

Audrey will be there, helping Margaret take those baby steps in the direction toward self-sufficiency, for the next two years. She'll provide support and guidance to the family while Margaret is learning the parental role. She'll work to develop Margaret's skills, resources, and intentions to help her become a responsible parent. To the extent that she can, she will help Margaret plan for the future to develop the life skills necessary to make choices about family planning and economic independence.

It's not always easy. Close by, in Pontiac, an equally grim city also in distress, Beth McClure, an Oakland Country Health division nurse with about 2 years in the program and about 20 in public health, struggles to maintain connections with her families. Beth's clients are at a different point in their program—they've had their babies and are making their way toward independence. Jennifer, a young woman with levels of lead so high that they have deposited permanently in her brain, is trying to finish school, but chaos in the home, tremendous learning disabilities, and transportation issues make it difficult for her to stay in school while continuing to care for her young son Victor, who is now one year old. Beth tries to "get into their world" to find ways to connect their interest in helping their child with the long-term goals of finishing school and becoming economically stable. In this case, during a respite in the school day, Beth teaches Jennifer how to knit a new hat for Victor as a way to encourage her to come to school for her weekly visit.

Keke, another client who is now at the verge of becoming independent, no longer keeps many of her visits. Although Beth tries to find ways to reconnect with her, she admits that "on a scale of 1 to 10, a trip to the mall is an 8 and I'm about a 3." But Beth always has a backup plan. Refusing to give up, she'll speed-dial through a list of family and friends' telephone contacts to make sure that Keke is on the right track. Throughout this program, the nurse home visitors will see their clients 14 times during pregnancy, 28 times during infancy, and 22 times during the child's toddler years—64 visits—speaking volumes for the intensity of the program.

Accountability is a key component of the program. Every site, whether Detroit, Pontiac, or Memphis, enters its data into a national information database that tracks the extent and scope of services that families receive, as well as their relative status on selected indicators of maternal and child health and development. These indicators are examined monthly to identify vulnerabilities in the local process, testing strategies to improve program performance and ensuring continuous quality improvement activities within and across sites. These data now contain findings from over 5,500 participants that the program is continuing to track throughout their child's second birthday.

And what they show is nothing short of extraordinary. Independent studies weighing the cost benefits based on three randomized trials of implementing the program demonstrate a return of $2 to $4 dollars for every $1 invested.[24] These figures translate into long-term benefits, according to the Washington State Institute for Public Policy,[25] of over $17,000 per family. In Louisiana alone, the program reduced the incidence of premature births by 52%.

Among the consistent effects demonstrated in the voluminous literature, Olds and his colleagues have found dramatic gains for nurse-visited mothers compared to controls:

- Significantly improved prenatal health for mothers
- Delayed subsequent pregnancies
- Increased maternal employment

The mothers' children enjoyed benefits, too:

- Fewer childhood injuries
- Higher IQs and language scores
- Fewer behavioral problems in the borderline or clinical stage
- Better academic and behavioral adjustment to elementary school

But these analyses also indicate another important trend: the functional and economic benefits of the Nurse-Family Partnership program have been, by far, greatest for the *families at greatest risk*. Tremendous cost savings accrue to the higher-risk group; among families at lower risk, however, the financial return for the program is far less. Plainly, this means that the program has been most successful when targeting families who need the help most. Interpreting the pattern of results and cost benefits, the program helps to avert many of the most devastating outcomes for this at-risk population.

Efforts to replicate these findings with paraprofessionals have only highlighted the importance of the nurse as professional. In a randomized trial comparing the benefits of nurse-visited mothers versus paraprofessional-visited mothers, Olds and his team reported that although paraprofessional-visited mothers began to experience the benefits from the program two years after the program ended, their children didn't benefit significantly from their control group counterparts. Nurse-visited mothers and children, however, continued to benefit from the program two years after it ended.[26] Interviews with clients indicated that paraprofessionals did not enjoy legitimacy in the eyes of these families during pregnancy and infancy. It eliminated one of the key features of the program—the highly trained nurse, rated by the public as having the highest honesty and ethical standards of all professionals.

Families facing serious life issues—poverty, hopelessness, depression, and troubled relationships—are likely to need more intensive services and more highly trained staff who are specifically qualified to work with multiproblem families. Thirty years of research studies and successful implementation in 23 states indicate that the Nurse-Family Partnership program has earned its "blue chip" status, providing a helping hand to thousands of young mothers and their children.

A Child's First Teacher

Everyone feels overwhelmed at the birth of a new baby. But for immigrant mothers who may speak another language and have to cope with overwhelming poverty and a complex and often unavailable social service system, things are even more intimidating. Limited resources and an absence of connections and social networks that can help in parenting a child may become social dynamite—children who come to school limited in language skills, sound supervision, and motivation to learn. How to help these children and their mothers is a question that can be overwhelming, too—so much so that it may induce paralysis even among the best-meaning.

To visit the parent–child education program in San Antonio called Avance—Spanish "to make headway" or "to progress"—where hundreds of immigrant mothers are learning English and parenting skills, is to begin to see an answer. Meeting young parents "where they are"—in the community, housing projects, local centers, and churches—Avance was established to reduce the disproportionately high dropout rate among the Mexican American community.

A child of the barrios herself, first leader Gloria Rodriquez began Avance in 1973 to provide family support and education services to Latino families who were at risk and economically impoverished. Having grown up in poverty, she knew the importance of a strong and supportive family and community. "My father died when I was two, leaving my mother with five daughters," she explained. "But my mother was strong and had deep faith. My grandfather came to live us and help bring us up. So we were poor but rich with kin and had many wonderful people in our lives." Rodriquez recognized that the single most important factor that allowed her mother to cope was the family. It was the family that was the center of support in the education of all the children.

Her work with Avance began with a painful truth—despite her efforts as a first grade teacher, she found that the school system had more or less given up on her bilingual children, labeling them as "retards," "slow," "vegetables," or, with even more finality, "uneducable." Because they were all Hispanics, she assumed that the children's problems lay in learning English. Yet it turned out that this was not so: the children's language was also as limited in Spanish as it was in English. Although she worked her best to help all children prepare for the second grade, it was clear that this language and knowledge deficit would continue to haunt these children throughout their schooling, placing them at serious risk of school failure. She needed to reach families earlier on, helping them understand the importance of early education.

Frustrated with trying to change education within the system, she went outside the system—to the families in San Antonio. Going door-to-door, she recruited 50 women to attend a parenting class, drawing the attention of the Zale Foundation in Dallas, which had tried to set up such a program in a housing project. Through these efforts, as she describes it, she found her purpose in life.

On the day I visit Avance in Hope 6, a family center in the heart of a renovated housing project, the women are busy making "concept balls," an educational toy designed to teach their children basic concepts of texture, color, and sound. Based on the research of Phyllis Levenstein,[27] these toy-making sessions look more like a quilting bee: non-didactic, playful promotion of verbal interactions with their children, also emphasizing other parenting skills. As the parents work and sew together, the instructor goes over the concept words that children will need to use: words related to spatial relations, adjectives, and verbs; questions that will spark interesting interactions. Wonderfully animated, the parents speak in Spanish, chatting about their children. Part of the instructor's effort is to end their isolation, helping these immigrant families build a supportive social network. Several mothers have formed close friendships and are helping to support each other in caring for their children.

Meanwhile, their children, anywhere from a few weeks to three years old, are nearby getting physical care and intellectual stimulation in the child care center. Big, bold pictures are everywhere, with board books galore and lots of soft features throughout the rooms that help increase cognitive and emotional development. Taught by certified teachers, the children are learning prereading skills, conversing in English as they make playdough letters. Another provider plays peek-a-boo with an infant, who giggles with delight.

Everything in the program is embedded in the "Rodriquez philosophy" of family—services are comprehensive in scope, targeted to instill in parents the value of education for their children and for themselves—all to improve parents' ability to get on their feet, providing a quality learning environment for their children. Today, after making toys, they'll learn about other community resources, such as the library and summer programs for their children. They'll also spend an hour learning how to prepare nutritious snacks. Bilingual parent–educators will make periodic home visits to help mothers apply their new knowledge and steer them to other resources they need.

"Given that the Hispanic population is the fastest growing in the country and has the highest dropout rate (most of these families have less than a seventh-grade education), we know we need to provide comprehensive services to these families," says Rodriquez.

The program never turns a mother away. Transportation is always provided for parents who are likely to come at least once a week for classes in parenting and English. Parents also get access to a wide range of social services for their children.

"You slowly see these mothers begin to change," reports Mercedes Perez de Colon, the research director for the foundation. "In the beginning, they come to class often looking quite slovenly, not caring about themselves or their children's grooming. By graduation some nine months later, you'll see them incredibly well-dressed, healthy looking, with their hair and make-up in the very latest style. They see that things can be different, that there's hope, and that what they do affects the development of their child."

Parents attend 32 sessions throughout the year and will graduate if they attend 75% of all the activities. On the day I visit, over 100 women are getting ready for the big event, and the place is bustling with excitement and activity. Many of these parents will return to Avance. They will act as volunteers in the program or will receive further training as paraprofessionals to recruit next year's class. In Mercedes's eyes, these graduates are critical for continuing to connect with the community. They knock on doors, and they bring enormous credibility to the project in the community, "speaking the language and the feelings of these mothers in distress."

After graduating from the nine-month "core program," some will go on to work on their GEDs and even apply for admission to college. "If we can make families strong," says Rodriquez, "we can make whole communities strong, and this will have an impact on the whole country."

Her message is working. Today Avance reaches out to 18 districts in Texas, Los Angeles, and Puerto Rico, affecting the lives of thousands of families a year. Results of a Carnegie Corporation report[28] suggest highly promising qualitative results: mothers in the program are providing more stimulating and emotionally encouraging environments for their children than are mothers who do not attend the program; they are also less restrictive and use fewer negative punishing behaviors. The study also found that these caregivers provide greater variety in children's daily routines and are more involved in children's education. More recently, a 2004–2005 survey of the Avance children in the Dallas Intermediate School District[29] showed the benefits of these changes in behaviors on children's achievement, as indicated by a recent report card:

- 100% of Avance prekindergarten children scored excellent or satisfactory on their pre-reading skills.
- By second grade, Avance children reported a B+ average in math, science, and language arts.
- By third grade, Avance children had an A– average in math and science and a B+ average in language arts.

Following the initial group of families some 17 years later,[30] the results are impressive: 73% of Avance parents significantly increased their annual household income, 57% completed their GED, 43% attended college, and 94% of their children completed high school (somewhat less than half went on to attend college).

The sustained success of the program is further supported through a talented team of researchers and curriculum developers who continue to ensure fidelity to the philosophy and approach, regularly reporting to an active executive board to track the program's progress. Says Garcia, the new president, "[W]e build a social support network, we connect them with services, we give information on child growth and development, we establish memorable experiences at the time, we deal with issues in their community. Instead of solving problems the wrong way—with more prisons and more police—we help families solve problems the right way—through education."

There has never been greater need for education. Persistent poverty is pervasive for Hispanics, reaching over 76% of populations in Texas and New Mexico. Recognizing that the best way to capitalize on immigrant parents' educational drive for their children is to partner with them, Avance is sharing its expertise in new areas, moving beyond services in family literacy to capacity-building in community development. Under new leadership, Sylvia Garcia, a twenty-eight-year veteran of the program, Avance is building close relationships with state legislatures to increase levels of family services, creating laboratory sites that will use the expertise of what they've learned to benefit communities. And the news is promising. A recent study of Avance mothers found that despite their own low levels of education, over 91% reported ambitious attitudes and goals of achievement for their children.[31]

Reweaving the social tapestry, Avance is helping Latino families in these underserved communities become advocates and role models for their children. By providing a critical support network—reaching out to families in a manner respectful of their dignity and culture—they are helping parents recognize their enormous influence as their child's first teacher. And in doing so, Avance is truly unlocking their potential.

Effective Interventions That Strengthen Families

Together, these programs weave a story of how we can help strengthen families even when tremendous odds are stacked against them. Built on solid empirical evidence, the successes of these programs converge around the seven essential principles described in Chapter 3.

Although different in emphasis, the programs are all about relationship-building. They recognize that families experiencing incomparable levels of economic hardship may have differing needs and desires for assistance. Far from one-size-fits-all, they focus on the importance of a customized intervention carefully matched to the needs and resources of the children and families served. They use insights and skills from multiple disciplines, such as psychiatry, education, and child development, to establish an atmosphere of trust, respect, and confidence in their dealings with families. Exhibiting front-line flexibility and perseverance, professionals work over the months to create therapeutic alliances. As a result, these programs have enhanced independent family functioning and significantly improved the quality of the caregiving that children are likely to receive.

What can we learn from these programs about tailoring specific services to children and families in different circumstances and with different needs? What do these programs tell us about the thresholds of program intensity and levels of parent engagement that are necessary for measurable impact, in particular for our most troubled families? What have we learned about the developmental timing and duration of different interventions?

Successful programs that are changing the odds for high-risk families, producing significant effects on children's cognitive and social development, *begin early on* and offer a broad array of services. Although no compelling data support the notion of an *absolute* critical period for effective interventions, we know that the earlier we start, the better families are likely to get on the road to success.

This is not to suggest a zero-sum game that sets the importance of the early years of children's development against the later adolescent years. Rather, it emphasizes that beginnings of life help to establish a set of capabilities and expectations about how things and people will behave that will definitely affect subsequent experiences. Relying on the emotional support of their caregivers, young children are particularly vulnerable when parent–child relationships are insecure or otherwise troubled. Helping families build quality experiences early on to enable their children to become independent later on is one of the most critical elements of good caregiving.

Successful programs offer *comprehensive services*, providing connections to a multitude of services and networks to enhance children's development. They typically help our most disadvantaged families find a broad array of health-related and social services, meeting families' most urgent needs. Programs find ways of providing comprehensive services, helping families qualify for WIC nutrition program or finding access to "gently used furniture" or "toys for tots" for the holiday season. These programs recognize that services and supports to parents who need help with their lives will also help these adults make good use of services for their children.

This understanding builds on the research base from demonstration projects that have produced notable effects that have been sustained over many years. In each case, these programs recognize that social, emotional, and concrete help (food, diapers, or anything else that might seem to a family to be an insurmountable obstacle) may have to be provided so that a family can make use of other parts of the intervention, from advice on parenting to the discussion of future job aspirations. The most successful interventions strive to help improve parents' sensitivity to their children, taking into account mothers' broader needs and life circumstances.

Successful programs employ highly trained professionals who can respond to the multiple needs of families in distress. These professionals are not only highly skilled and committed to the families but also perceived by those whom they serve as models and authorities whom they can trust. With these professionals' support, parents begin to believe in themselves. They become able to responsibly keep their scheduled doctor's appointments, attend parent meetings on a regular basis, and participate in programs for their children—basic skills that will be critical for children's development.

In these programs, professionals will often respond to severe but often unarticulated fears and needs of the families, helping them read and respond to questions on an application for WIC assistance, visiting a health clinic where they feel undervalued and diminished, wielding their way across the complex Medicaid system. Crossing the traditional boundaries of their job descriptions, these professionals will often help families walk through the process. They'll provide transportation. They'll accompany the family to the clinic to help describe problematic symptoms of a child's illness to the doctor. They'll read and go over the instructions on the prescription labels, acting as ombudsmen between families and outside community. These skilled and highly committed professionals have the depth of training necessary to help families make significant steps toward their goals.

Successful programs provide powerful intervention, evidenced by the intensity and amount of professional time spent with families or children throughout the program (e.g., hours per day, days per week, weeks per year). Program intensity clearly matters. The Early Head Start program, for example, generally stays involved in mothers' lives from pregnancy to preschool; the nurse-practitioner program, two or more years; and Avance, an intensive nine months for the core program, followed by additional supports for families through age three. It seems that only the most intensive services are sufficient to benefit those children at greatest risk—the lowest and intermediate intensities have repeatedly proven to have no measurable consequences.

In short, programs that succeed in stopping the negative spiral of poverty in which children and their families find themselves are integrally connected to the seven essential features for implementing social policies that work. They begin early, helping families through comprehensive services, involving highly skilled professionals, and are intensive. Each of these programs is highly targeted to the population that needs help the most; in fact, when any of these programs has attempted to stray from its key targeted audience, it has been much less effective. Rather, these programs have refused to become diluted, maintaining their quality through continuous assessment and ongoing refinements, holding themselves accountable at every turn. Together, these programs are powerful demonstrations of changing the odds for our nation's most disadvantaged children.

But it's not until you see what programs can do—what is possible—that all these words and images come vividly alive. Visiting a housing project in the heart of the barrio, I watch as a mother learns how to swaddle her infant daughter. "That's it," her parent-educator coach, says: "You can do it. Wrap her just like you were making a burrito." Tentatively, the mother folds one side of her daughter's blanket, then the middle, then nervously tucks in the remaining side. Cradling her daughter in her arms, the baby coos, responding to the warmth of her mother's contact, her gaze, her broad and genuine smile. As if sharing a secret, the mother's and parent–educator's eyes seem to nonverbally communicate. Two months ago, I later learn, this child had been "failing to thrive." Today, she is being held by a loving, more confident mother, learning to trust her world.

As Florence Nightingale once said, "Results shown are the only test."

CHAPTER 5

CHANGING THE ODDS THROUGH HIGH-QUALITY EARLY CARE AND EDUCATION

When Bobbi Ann McCaughey gave birth to septuplets in the late 1990s, her church provided around-the-clock care for the newborns. Several months later, like the majority of women, she was dependent on child care. But although seven babies can be a handful for a couple and friends, that's not too many for one child care worker to take on, according to what's on the books in many states. The job of caring for babies, keeping them fed and dry, nurtured and stimulated, is entrusted to people with little training and not much more than a criminal background check. And for a 10-hour work shift, they're likely to make about $80.

The state of American child care is in crisis. With rare exceptions, high-quality, reliable, affordable child care is out of reach for all but the affluent. According to a 1995 national study conducted by the University of Colorado Economics Department, nearly half of the 400 centers serving infants and toddlers administered such poor-quality care that the health, safety, and development of the children were jeopardized. Babies and toddlers cared for in private homes or by relatives fared even worse. These qualities are gauged by reviewing staff-to-child ratios, employee pay, training and turnover rates, and lack of adult–child interaction.

Today, millions of children are spending precious hours in a maze of unstable, substandard places that compromise their chances of starting school ready to learn. Child care in America is poor to mediocre, with approximately only one in every seven providers meeting standards of quality that promote healthy development, and almost half of infant and toddler programs not meeting even minimal standards.

A visit to Heavenly Hall might capture it all. Entering a decrepit building, one presumably on Philadelphia's then-Mayor John Street's tear-down list, I follow the hand-written signs to a basement. Children are held in playpens in the darkened, dank room while two elderly women watch a program on a black and white TV. One child is picked up at a time, changed, fed, and then returned to the playpen shortly after. Silence permeates the day's activities, with no conversation other than what comes from the television program. Centers such as this, with safety problems, poor sanitation practices, unresponsive caregivers, and a dearth of stimulating toys and materials, are serving millions of children.

The absence of high-quality child care weighs heavily on all families. But for working poor families, the situation is more dire. With limited personal resources or subsidies, parents resort to unstable arrangements, compounding the consequences of growing up poor. And tragically it is these children, the children who live in poverty, who have the most to lose from poor care and the most to gain from good care. Although associations are seldom large,[1] we know that the positive effects of high-quality childhood care for children from the very poorest home environments can endure long into the adult years. When we ignore children's child care experiences, we jeopardize *their* chances to become self-sufficient and we jeopardize *our* chances to change the odds.

If the nation's provisions for child care in the past have been negligent and chaotic, things have only taken a turn for the worse in recent years. The need for high-quality day care has become more acute since the influx of former welfare recipients to the work force. Today, behind closed doors, children are warehoused in unsafe, unlicensed storefronts, church basements, and windowless, claustrophobic rooms by poorly trained workers who are barely making enough to buy groceries for their own families. Children spend large amounts of time—sometimes as much as 12 or more hours daily—in these caverns of care where they become so starved for nurturance, attention, and stimulation that they can concentrate on little else.

It should come as little surprise, then, that these children come to school unready to learn. They don't know their full names, or that a pencil is something to write with. They can't pay attention, and they don't know how to defer gratification. They use food to fill their cravings for affection. Experts Valerie Lee and David Burkam[2] estimate that before even entering kindergarten, cognitive scores for low-income children are likely to average 60% lower than those in the highest socioeconomic groups.

Communities are making valiant efforts to pool resources, trying to offer a patchwork of services at times and places that may fit families' needs, hoping to contribute to or at least not detract from children's development. Agencies are coming up with every trick in the book to try to cobble together programs from a variety of disparate sources to create a network of child development settings, from family child care homes, to centers, to Head Start programs. Government policymakers, on the recommendation of the Government Accountability Office, are trying to stitch together a more coherent set of guidelines, knowing that federal subsidies alone can come from 90 different programs located in 11 federal agencies and 20 different offices.

But children can't wait for policymakers to untangle the morass of fragmented and contradictory policies to solve the child care problem. We need to do something now. Overlooked in this search for a more rational national child care policy are lessons of stunning successes in providing high-quality care and education for disadvantaged children. Following seven essentials, you'll see that child care can be a significant source of nurturance, friendships, and early learning in programs that are serving thousands of children. As the evidence will show, these programs demonstrate that scaling up need not be a formula for dilution of high-quality child care services.

The Exploding Need for Child Care

Working is no longer a choice for many women. In 1996 the welfare reform act known as the Personal Responsibility and Work Opportunity Reconciliation Act (PRWORA) created a sea of change in welfare, changing it from an entitlement to a cash assistance program. Its ramifications changed the landscape of early care and education in unprecedented ways. Prior to the 1996 legislation, states were prohibited from requiring single parents caring for infants to participate in job-training or work-related activities. Now, states have broad discretion not to automatically exempt from work parents of children less than a year old. Single mothers in most states are now required to work 30 or more hours a week. Before welfare reform, only about 20% of families receiving welfare were either in job training or employed—or about 4.9 million families (monthly average) on the rolls. By 1998, fewer than 3.2 million families were on the rolls.[3]

For all its controversy, welfare reform neither boosted self-sufficiency nor led to the draconian fears of its harshest critics. It might have ended "welfare as we know it," as President Clinton claimed, but it did not substantially transform family income. No-income families merely became low-income families, still struggling to make ends meet. During the first three months after leaving welfare, average monthly wages, according to studies in eight states, went from $733 to $900.[4] It created a new, financially vulnerable class—one that is working poor—left to pay the spiraling costs of health care and housing needed to raise healthy children.

Scrambling for child care, mothers could take advantage of the newly expanded and consolidated federal subsidy in the Child Care and Development Block Grant (CCDBG), as well as those funds transferred from the block grant Temporary Assistance for Needy Families (TANF). Federal and state spending on child care rose dramatically to over $8 billion by 2002. Gaining access and maintaining subsidy assistance, however, represented a challenge for families also trying to meet the employment demands. Given the wherewithal to figure out how to get them, these subsidies could be used to enroll children in preschools and center-based care.

But what was not anticipated was the size of the demand. There wasn't a sufficient supply of providers in local communities. Given the nature of low-wage work, with its nonstandard hours, rotating shifts, and weekend and evening hours, mothers entering the job market needed to find available help quickly, someone to rely on, who could speak their language—someone they could trust to care for their children. Covering the hours, many turned to relatives and friends, who offered greater flexibility to provide child care for odd-hour, ever-changing shifts.

Known as family, friend, and neighbor care, some of these arrangements worked to the benefit of children. But many did not, leading to highly unstable, sometimes harmful situations. Stories abound of children unprotected for hours at a time, infants left alone in crib while caregivers ran errands, children suffocating in cars while family members partied at clubs, babies crying for hours, seeking love and attention. Stories such as these not only led to parents' fear of leaving their child in someone else's care, but actually diminished their efforts to enter the workforce.

Stories of lives permanently imperiled, as this young child's was—a one-year-old recovering after being shot in the leg while being watched by the mother's boyfriend—were found far too often in local papers:

> When the police arrived, they found the 33-year-old man and his children, a 2-year-old girl, and a 3-year-old boy, with the mother's 1-year-old child. The 1-year-old, who has a different father, was suffering from a gunshot wound to his upper leg. The child's mother was at work at the time of the shooting, having left the children in the care of the man. The man had heard about a fight down the street at a party store and left the children alone in the apartment, knowing there was a loaded handgun under a couch cushion. When he returned, he told the police, the 3-year-old had shot the youngest child.[5]

Conditions such as these, in which children are victimized directly by neglect or abuse, or indirectly by repeated exposure to violence, are life-threatening. These children become adults with learning and memory problems and stress-related physical and mental illnesses, burdening our society and themselves for the rest of their lives. And unfortunately poor children are disproportionately those who are cared for in these highly unstable informal arrangements.

When free options such as family members or generous neighbors are not available, most working mothers "settle" for the best arrangement they can afford. Too often, such care doesn't even begin to meet minimal quality standards. Visiting a job-training center for single mothers with an accompanying child care center "exempt" from licensing requirements, I found two adults caring for 26 infants—according to the authorities there, the facility could house up to 60 children. When I asked about the deplorable situation, the local director said, "If just a fraction of single mothers drop off their infants, it brings down an already fragile system."

And the system is extraordinarily fragile. Bruce Fuller, project director of the Growing Up in Poverty study,[6] found precious few child care slots in communities for poor parents when compared to those available to more well endowed families. When having to rely on friends, family, and relations for long hours at a time where children's very safety may be at issue, it is not surprising to find that instability in family life has sharply increased. Lacking a safety net of care for their children, and having limited options for child care, only fuels higher rates of erratic employment and further instability.

Rewarding Work

The irony is that in good care, children benefit when parents work. Moving off welfare and into work with incomes above the poverty threshold is associated with parent well-being and better child outcomes. Children see the value of employment in combating poverty. They learn important lessons about self-sufficiency and hard work. They become exposed to a richer educational environment. They try harder not to repeat patterns that led to their parents' dependence on federal assistance, such as dropping out of school, drug dependence, and teen pregnancy. It is to everybody's advantage to support policies that help make work pay.

Affordable, flexible, and high-quality child care helps reward work. Strikingly, the research suggests that when previously welfare-dependent families are able to find high-quality child care centers instead of having to make informal arrangements with kith, kin, or others, their children come better prepared for school.[7] "Kids who have been exposed to center-based care are between three and four months ahead developmentally of kids who have remained in home-based settings all the time," reported Bruce Fuller in his welfare-to-work multiyear study. The study found that as participating mothers went to work, many more used their subsidies to enter their children into center-based programs rather than remaining at home with kith or kin. Children in these high-quality centers displayed stronger learning trajectories—cognitive abilities, language, and school readiness skills—associations that remained robust over time.

"This is very good news for those poor families who are able to access centers and preschools," reported the researchers. "If mothers in our study are able to secure spaces, the quality of care is quite high." In areas such as verbal interaction between providers and children, the supply of play and learning materials, and the condition of the facilities, centers were found to score relatively high on a widely used rating scale for early childhood programs.

These findings are not just confined to one project. An analysis of the Next Generation Project,[8] a study based on 13 welfare and antipoverty programs, providing information on over 30,000 low-income single-parent families, tells a similar story. Center-based care, in contrast to informal kith-and-kin programs, can positively affect children's school achievement. When child care assistance policies expand access to center-based care arrangements, parents appear to use them; in turn, children's cognitive and social behavior improves. Similarly, in a separate study sponsored by the National Institute for Child Health and Human Development,[9] researchers found that children who regularly attended center-based programs showed stronger cognitive growth in such areas as language skills and familiarity with print materials than children who were placed in some type of informal child care arrangement.

Making access to high-quality center-based care all the more imperative, the latest welfare reform bill, signed in 2006, demands that states ramp up their programs to ensure that parents do countable activities each week, such as going to work, getting training, or looking for jobs. But if the first wave of welfare reform policies is indicative of this next generation of reform, the long-term successes for helping families get a fresh start—finding jobs and sticking with it—will depend on the availability, affordability, and quality of child care. Helping families find good center-based child care not only supports work but ultimately promotes children's early development.

When children are given consistent, sensitive, and stimulating care, they are not harmed but helped when mothers return to work. High-quality child care— care that provides the social involvement of adults with children and language interactions—can work to benefit children's cognitive development, especially for children who come from low-income families. Evidence associating quality of care and early cognitive and language outcomes is striking in its consistency. According to the NICHD Early Child Care Research Network, the impact of high-quality care has been found to continue well into the school years, with the strongest effects for children who have the fewest resources and the greatest stress.[10] Children at special risk, growing up in persistent and concentrated poverty—children being raised by a single parent and children of school-aged mothers—can find good child care not just a lift but a lifeline for themselves and their parents.

Consensus about the Characteristics of High-Quality Child Care

Academics often spend a lifetime arguing on one side of an issue or another. But when it comes to characteristics of quality child care, there is striking consistency. Volumes of scholarly and popular materials converge on the same set of ingredients. High-quality care essentially boils down to the quality of the relationships between child care providers or teachers and children. For children to thrive, they need caregivers who give them generous amounts of attention, affection, and stability. They also need safe and stimulating environments in which to engage in warm and stimulating interactions with others. Just like parents, caregivers in child care settings need to be a source of comfort and strength to young children, involved with and sensitive to their developmental needs and able to encourage verbal communication, creating a climate for learning that supports and controls behaviors without being overly restrictive.

In a three-year study during which 17 experts appointed by the National Research Counsel reviewed studies from many different research methods— qualitative and quantitative, observational and experimental—the following pedagogical principles were confirmed. A high-quality program must have

- Stimulating experiences and learning activities that respond to children's interests
- Resources that actively build children's language, vocabulary, and conceptual knowledge

- Different levels of guidance to meet the needs of individual children
- Opportunities for sustained and in-depth learning
- A "masterful" orchestration of pacing and management (i.e., activity, behavior, and resources) that provides for children's choice and teacher-assisted learning
- A collaborative and supportive relationship with families
- A highly competent staff with a staff–child ratio small enough that children at each developmental age get the personal attention they need in order to thrive
- A safe environment that meets all licensing standards and regulations

These characteristics, all of which are extraordinarily important, might be considered as a foundation for high-quality care. Yet, as important as they are, high-risk children—our most vulnerable children of the shadows—need more than just an extra boost toward learning. They need more than a two-and-a-half-hour program filled with fun learning activities and more than competent staff. They need a high-quality program that essentially compensates for the benefits they have not had.

Compensatory programs share four features: they are longer, more focused on instruction, smaller in size (with highly qualified teachers), and accountable for results.

Time. Compensatory programs recognize that time is the least available resource to children who have been disadvantaged by chaos, defeat, unpredictability, and despair. If economically disadvantaged children are to catch up with their peers in language skills, concepts, and developing world knowledge, time is the most crucial commodity. To make any sort of significant impact, we need to seriously extend the time devoted to learning experiences in prekindergarten.

A number of obvious ways exist to extend learning time. Programs for children most in need should begin at an earlier age—during the toddler years—and should include full-day, full-year services for the children and their families. But extending learning time can also be accomplished by a very cost-efficient means: programs need to pay attention to compressing more teaching into the time available, providing intentional learning experiences expressly targeted toward highly predictive outcomes for school success.

To illustrate my point, in a recent visit to a locally funded prekindergarten classroom specifically targeted to low-income children, I clocked the amount of time devoted to instruction. I counted 20 minutes, total, within a three-hour day. The day was not filled with instruction but with transition (late arrivals, early dismissals, breakfast, snack, lunch, brushing teeth, toileting, getting ready for outdoor play, getting back from outdoor play, cleaning up, and so on). The classroom was not an unpleasant environment for young children; in fact, it struck me as a rather typical program. The children were well cared for, certainly well-fed, and seemed to enjoy themselves.

But such programs are not going to begin to close the gap between these low-income children and their more advantaged peers. As pleasant as the program might be, these experiences waste children's valuable time, using resources unwisely.

Contrast this visit with another I paid to a community-based center in a highly distressed community. Stafford County Head Start deliberately emphasizes teaching and learning. Using the highly constructive curriculum from High/Scope, teachers are engaging children in learning about important concepts of sound and vibration by playing with toilet rolls and long strings to make their own telephones. The room buzzes with conversation, not just between the teacher and children, but the children among themselves, who are busily using their telephones. Throughout the morning, I hear words like "transmit" and "electrical connections," as the teacher involves children in understanding concepts and the technologies of sound. For children who need more one-on-one, a speech therapist is on-site. She will work on helping children use these new words in meaningful contexts, knowing that the words are a central device for acquiring and processing more information as the lessons proceed. Off in a corner, another teacher with checklist in hand is examining how each child is progressing. Nothing is left to chance.

To make an impact, these teachers know that their program will need every precious minute to promote learning. By diagnosing children's learning, they will be able to better tailor children's instruction. Increasing the amount of "time on task" and making sure every minute counts will be essential for changing the odds.

More focused on instruction. Compensatory programs concentrate more on developmentally appropriate learning that is highly focused on outcomes. These programs recognize that what children lack is not the ability to learn but the opportunity. Compensatory programs have a clear mission: they recognize that instead of offering a smorgasbord of activities, children will need higher-quality, faster-paced instruction that accelerates learning.

Working on such a plan, I visited two centers in Miami's voluntary prekindergarten program that couldn't have been more different. The Biltmore Playhouse program was every bit as elegant as its name attests: a Reggio Emilia school, the prekindergarten is located on three acres of land with fruit trees and greens lining every line of sight. The short days are spent on investigations that the teachers, parents, and children all engage in together; in fact, the day I'm there, they are planning a snow weekend, with truckloads of snow being laid around the school, brought and paid for by the parents' association.

But on the other side of Miami, the Miami that lives in the shadows, children were busily engaged in a YMCA preschool. This school as well was joyous, yet the day was scheduled very differently. Here, children coming from the very poorest sections of the city were sitting in a circle, playing language games and laughing at the silly rhymes. Quite structured, the teacher monitored children's progress on a clipboard close by, making sure that each child had been given the opportunity to respond.

Everything about the place—the class environment, even the menus—seemed intentionally focused on learning and language, with concepts revisited through the full-day program in storybook reading, play, songs, computer activities, and snack time. As I enter, the children are noisily playing post office, writing letters to each other and speaking English and Spanish. Nearby, the infants are playing in rooms that have bright pictures, mats for crawling, and soft objects for stimulation. The center provides full services, treating long-neglected illnesses and helping families get the nutritional and social services they need. Each child will get his or her immunizations right here in the center.

These programs illustrate what we know about early care and education at different levels of intensity. The results are strikingly consistent with those from earlier interventions and demonstrations of effective programs: although children of more highly educated families can benefit from all kinds of high-quality programs, children from at-risk families benefit only from the more intensive interventions, which include an aggressive outreach and attention to their school readiness needs.

These programs don't divide the children's time into a smattering of activities in many areas. They are highly focused, proactive, and targeted to the goals of helping these children learn the language, skills, and dispositions necessary to enter school successfully.

Smaller in size with highly qualified teachers. Compensatory programs need highly qualified teachers who spend time with each child. There's just no getting around it. We cannot underestimate the individual attention that children will need to begin to feel confident about themselves as learners—to question, listen, and persevere. Many of these children already carry significant handicaps in these early years—low-self-esteem, a weak sense of efficacy, a feeling of failure—that deeply affects everything they attempt to do. We need to help these children become motivated to learn, believing in their own power to learn and in their ability to be successful.

This requires our best teachers, teachers who know each child well—what makes them laugh, what brings them joy, what touches their heart. We need teachers who smile when they enter the classroom door, who regard the disparities in children's learning not as a problem but as a challenge to overcome—magical teachers such as Theresa and Heather, who work in a community-based child care program in the District of Columbia with a gaggle of two-and-a-half-year-olds.

The eight children, about half of them Spanish-speakers, are in circle time, eagerly awaiting their lesson to begin. Today, their teacher Theresa has brought in a saxophone. The children are enraptured. First, each child gets to touch it. She asks them to listen to its sounds, using interesting words to comment on the tones. She sings a song and demonstrates the hand motions to go along with it, performing it first in English and then in Spanish. The children then do it together, asking her to sing it again and again.

Later, in this same program, I watch Heather brilliantly tell them a story, using little objects, a lion, a net, and a mouse as props to help her Spanish speakers understand her meaning. The story must go on for 20 minutes, but there is not a motion or a sound in the room. The children are listening to her voice, her words, with their eyes glued on the objects. Afterwards, they talk about the story, and predictably ask her to "do it gin."

Such magical moments for children don't just happen. They require teachers who are incredibly dedicated and skilled in knowing how to reach young children. They require an environment that helps teachers teach—it is futile to believe that we can reduce the disparities between privilege and poverty in classroom settings filled with 20 or more little three- and four-year-olds. Although it's clear that high-quality teachers and high-quality environments matter for all, they matter most for vulnerable children—those who lack confidence and fear failure. In a follow-up to the landmark Cost, Quality and Outcome project, a longitudinal study in more than 400 centers across six states,[11] researchers found that it was the relationships that teachers established in these small group early care and education settings that mattered most. Children who had closer relationships with their child care teachers exhibited better classroom behavior and social skills, fewer problem behaviors, and better achievement, sustained through second grade.

Accountability. Not without its critics, the No Child Left Behind Act created a sweeping change in the way we view programs. Several years ago, after a young teacher was observed by her supervisor, I remember her asking, "How did I do?" Teaching was defined by teachers' performance, the quality of their lesson plans, their creativity, and their ability to hold children's attention. Today, we look at children's progress. We look at children's growth in cognitive and academic achievement, their ability to solve problems, their growing curiosity, and their dispositions to learn, knowing full well that if we fail to develop the very best programs for our high-risk children early on, we had better be prepared for the consequences later.

Here's an example of the kinds of changes I've seen as teachers move toward a more accountable system. When visiting a preschool, evaluators used to look at the children's schedule—the amount of time they spent reading, playing, and engaged in physical and fine-motor development. Now, when visiting a parent–child center in the heart of Chicago, you are likely to find teachers talking about children's progress. Ask Mr. Paul—as he is known by his preschoolers—about how things are going. Directing me to his file cabinet, he picks up a child's folder and carefully reviews the data he has regarding the child's readiness skills, social–emotional development, and enthusiasm for learning. He shows me examples of the child's artwork and his emerging concepts of print and describes the skills he needs to work on next.

Knowing how to pace instruction and how to support children's progress requires these kinds of detailed records. It's about making informed decisions and a plan of action. From this perspective, teaching and progress-monitoring are complementary processes, informing one another and helping teachers tailor instruction to children's needs.

A Bright Beginning

Visiting Double Oaks Pre-K center in Charlotte-Mecklenburg, North Carolina's largest school district, would be a treat for anyone interested in observing four-year-olds who are focused, happy, and energetically playing with purpose. I'm visiting to hear the remarkable story of Bright Beginnings, a program for at-risk preschoolers. My purpose is to learn how a dynamic leader successfully convinced an entire school board that a high-quality pre-K could make a difference for poor children.

I arrive at Double Oaks just in time to see a group of three- and four-olds playing at the writing table during "choice" time. Four-year-old Destiny waits patiently while two classmates show off their writing and reading skills to me and my host. After DeMond and Tracy finish, Destiny begins to read from a book off the library shelf, asking for help on only one big word. When she finishes, she glances shyly at her friend DeMond, who enthusiastically exclaims, "Her is a star!"

Destiny wasn't the only star I saw on that day at the Bright Beginnings program. School officials would say that all of the youngsters in the program are shining stars. And they believe that success stories such as those of Destiny, Tracy, and DeMond can be duplicated in school districts not only in North Carolina but all across the country. "This can work in schools anywhere," said Barb Pellin, one of the originators of the program. "We just need to help them understand how to do it."

Launched in 1997, Bright Beginnings was the brainchild of Eric Smith, Charlotte-Mecklenburg's dynamic superintendent, who had just come to North Carolina's largest school district at a troubling time. Charlotte-Mecklenburg's success in merging city and suburban schools, way back in 1959, a model of an integrated school system that helped grow Charlotte into a major-league city, was becoming increasingly strained by a recent influx of more than 30,000 into its schools. These newcomers supported community schools, not busing, leading Arthur Griffin, a former school board member who served for 18 years, to remark, "Now you had a real debate about the value of diversity."

Fearing 'white flight,' Smith and his school board needed to solve a problem that continues to plague every urban district in this country: how to provide an equal education for the disadvantaged while also sustaining vital middle-class support. Moving from mandated to voluntary integration, Charlotte-Mecklenburg struggled, like all major cities, to maintain a racial balance.

Smith's answer was to create a gold-standard education program that supported high achievement for all students. To meet his goal of having 85% of all third-graders performing at or above grade level, the district needed a strong and effective early education program to ensure that its most needy children were ready for kindergarten. The existing prekindergarten program, though pleasant, had minimal effects on school readiness. Seen as a step-child to the more important elementary school years, teachers had limited resources or direction, and taught their own curriculum with little accountability or support. Clearly the district needed a new approach.

Bright Beginnings became just what its name says: a child-centered, literacy-rich curriculum and learning environment that builds strong foundational skills needed by these children when they enter kindergarten. Turning what had been a typical child development program into a literacy-focused program for four-year-olds seemed tantamount to placing young children in a stress-inducing environment. Might the pressures to read and write overtax children and damage them beyond repair? Yet, working with a committed staff of teachers, principals, and curriculum developers, he managed to figure out a way to integrate instruction in ways that didn't look like an academic program.

Although the children may come from economically disadvantaged homes, they have plenty of advantages when they arrive at school. There are about 18 or 19 children with a certified teacher and an aide. There are literacy facilitators, social workers, a paid parent/family coordinator, and other resources, such as computers and other technology. To be admitted, a child has to have a measurable educational need. Using a specially developed screening instrument, and starting with the lowest scores, children are selected by ascending scores until all available seats are filled, about 3,200 all together.

Although the mood at Double Oaks is relaxed and friendly, the educational day is structured nearly down to the minute. The children move from task to task, unaware that their teachers are working on instilling specific readiness skills in them. In the "Play and Learn Centers," children go from the manipulatives center to dramatic play, working on different skills under a common theme. They may be working on sorting or using their words to compare and contrast objects.

On the morning I visited, the theme of the day was "Going Places." In one classroom, teacher Michelle Kennedy was reading the book *Oh, the Places You'll Go!* to a group of 16 children. She asked the children what they saw in the picture. "Houses and trees and the road," one little girl responded. "A church!" a little boy piped in.

A couple of doors down, children were playing games in an imaginary world of travel. James Hutton, five, wrote the words on a makeshift sign for the "Snack Shop" at the bus station. On the other side of the classroom, Shakeara was playing with toy airplanes. "One takes off," she said, showing the tiny airplane taxing down its imaginary runway before taking off. "Now there are two left."

In Anna Patterson's class, the children sat in a circle and played a game in which they matched a small toy with the item from a storybook she was reading. They then found the name of the toy on the whiteboard. Four-year-old Javonia couldn't resist raising her hand every time her teacher asked for the answer. When it was finally her turn, she ran to the board to find the word "jeep" to match the little green vehicle she held in her hand.

When Anna started teaching prekindergarten some 16 years ago, there was great concern about the "hurried" child, a belief that learning to read and write would drive children to detraction and anti-social behavior, which discouraged Anna from teaching them the alphabet or how to count. But as the understanding of early childhood development has evolved, educators have learned that teaching methods can be tailored to four-year-olds' short attention spans and natural curiosity. Anna's classroom today is full of words—words labeling the "loft" and the "sand table," as well as blocks and other toys that help children learn to work with their hands and their brains.

Routines in the classroom play a big role for children who have little routine and stability in their lives. Days follow a fairly fast-paced schedule. Each day is organized around Literacy Circles. Teachers use these circle times for explicit instruction, focusing on the theme of each day, such as "Working Together," and teaching skills through reading aloud and writing songs, rhymes, and finger plays. After the 15–20-minute lesson, children plan what they'll do next among 12 different learning centers that have been carefully stocked with learning activities. They'll reconvene later on in a circle to talk about what they've learned and to put their ideas together down on paper, using their developmental spellings so that teachers can figure out whether they're learning their letters and sounds. Next, they'll settle down after their active outside play time in a third literacy circle to sing and listen to a story. Moving toward the close of their day, they'll assemble in one more circle to review, summarize, share, and celebrate what they've learned throughout the day.

Although these children might come into school not knowing how to hold a book or that reading goes from left-to-right and top-to-bottom, they leave the program knowing all this and much more. "What we found is that the Bright Beginnings kids not only kept what they learned, but scored better in many cases than kids with preschool," said Pellin, who directed the program. "Remember, these are kids who would have come to us with little or no preparation for kindergarten."

After a year of Bright Beginnings, over 66% of the children score at or above grade level on year-end literacy and math tests given to them as first-graders. "We have kindergarten teachers calling and saying, I can tell who our Bright Beginnings children are without even looking at their records," Pellin claimed. "It's just amazing."

The administrator's unbridled enthusiasm is understandable. Consider these statistics:[12]

- A significantly higher percentage of Bright Beginnings students score at or above average in reading skills both at the end of kindergarten and first grade, in comparison to a group of nonparticipants.

- A higher percentage of participating African American first graders are at or above grade level.

- Among children on free and reduced lunch, Bright Beginnings youngsters performed better than those of similar economic status.

- Compared to more advantaged kids, the gap has significantly narrowed to within five percentage points at kindergarten and nine in first grade.

Using sophisticated cost–analysis procedures,[13] school officials have reported near-term benefits such as declines in retentions, child care costs, and disciplinary problems, estimating about $2.47 in savings for each $1.00 expended.

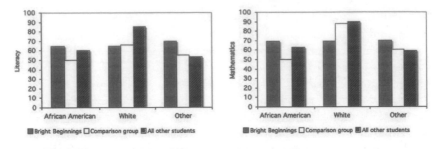

Total Number: 7,885 (Bright Beginnings=1,492; Comparison group=209; All other students=6,184)

Source: Bright Beginnings: An Effective Literacy-Focused PreK Program for Educationally Disadvantaged Four-Year-Old Children. Smith, Eric J.; Pellin, Barbara J.; Agruso, Susan A. Educational Research Service, 2003.

Figure 5.1.
Gains for Minority Students Resulting from Bright Beginnings

Because the program is still young (less than 10 years old), longer-term bene-fits, averaging approximately $13.74 for every dollar—including the more speculative reductions in crime costs to victims—must await future confirma-tion. But if you ask teachers in the system, they're more likely to report the intangibles: children are more focused, able to listen, motivated, and ready to learn.

Drawing heavily from the Bright Beginnings program, authorities in Clover, South Carolina, found that it's really the structure of the program that makes it work. As a targeted, compensatory pre-K program, Bright Beginnings offers about twice as many hours of child-centered instruction with a stronger language development and literacy component than Head Start classrooms. Children attend a full six-and-a-half hours a day, with additional options for extended day programs, all designed to build a strong foundation of basic literacy skills needed by these children when they enter kindergarten.

What these program developers recognized was that to enact such a rigorous curriculum, teachers needed not only to be certified, but to be specialists in the years from birth through kindergarten. Teaching young children to acquire the self-regulatory skills—to develop rich and complex language and the vocab-ulary skills necessary to close the gap—is incredibly demanding. Charlotte-Mecklenburg also provided a technical assistance team, including a social worker, nurse, and parent educator, all to provide ongoing support for teachers and com-prehensive services to their diverse children and families.

For these services, the Charlotte-Mecklenberg program exacts something in return. Parents are required to sign a formal agreement to serve as full partners in their children's learning experiences. Working with a family advocate, this includes home visits, parent meetings, and a pledge to read at least 100 books over the year with each child. Building on what the children learned each day, the goal of program developers was to continually work toward intensifying the intervention, recognizing that there's not a moment to waste if they are to help close the reading and learning gaps.

Leaving nothing to chance, Smith and his team member accountability director, Susan Agruso, smartly created an air-tight case to document the effects of his program and what focused learning strategies, talented teachers, and a community organized to provide the skills could do for children who needed a better start. They created a precise audit trail of assessments, observations, and constant progress monitoring so that community leaders couldn't claim ignorance about what was needed to help prepare at-risk children to work at grade level. Bright Beginnings had shown them how.

Not only have Bright Beginnings' graduates entered kindergarten on par with their peers—in some cases, even outperforming their peers—but they have sustained that progress as students have gone on to the first and second grades. Showing evidence of the program's continuing positive impact on student learning, African Americans, Hispanics, and students receiving free and reduced lunches who had been Bright Beginnings participants were more proficient in literacy and mathematics than were their demographic and economic peers. Further, the out-migration rate of children from Charlotte-Mecklenburg schools during the three years slowed substantially compared to that of all other students.

Smith left about a year after I first visited the program. Returning later, I worried whether the program could sustain the loss of its dynamic leader, as well as his right-hand assistant superintendent, champion, and spokesperson, Barb Pellin, who has since retired. Programs have been known to decline or die a slow death after their chief sponsors have gone.

Yet the program was thriving and producing the kinds of outcomes we all yearn for: at-risk four-year-olds from the most economically disadvantaged sectors were outperforming their peers and performing at or above grade level, offering more evidence that sustained high achievement is possible for all students regardless of their economic status or race, so long as resources are put to bear on problems and communities maintain commitment and focus.

Smith's ploy to ensure financial stability, a critical linchpin in any program, was convincing his colleagues that a good start for poor children could lead to a great finish for all. Unlike other school districts across the country, instead of spreading his Title I funds throughout the system, he concentrated them, putting 83% of all Title I funds into the program. That gave Bright Beginnings its strong fiscal base.

He also bundled funding from a score of different resources. He used state funding from initiatives including Smart Start and More at Four, federal resources from Head Start and Even Start, and district funding—all to support the program. Together, this helped him build a coherent program regardless of funding stream. No longer were children involved in a smattering of supportive services, some receiving aid from one program and others from another. Rather, through agreements forged between agencies, all needy children received the Bright Beginnings program.

Bartering across programs, the partnership also brought important health services into the picture, building a "circle of strength," as Barb Pellin describes it, by linking available services to children and helping with minor illnesses and conditions such as ear infections, which—if unrecognized and not promptly treated—might have led to later damaging outcomes. Children received regular health assessments and immunizations, their teachers knowing full well the connections between good health and good learning.

Today, thanks to these efforts, thousands of children in the Charlotte-Mecklenburg school district who needed a better start are getting just that. But the Bright Beginnings story isn't just about a local preschool and a thoughtful leader. What Eric Smith, Barb Pellin, and their colleagues devised was actually a set of principles that could be put in place in schools all over the country. Challenging the status quo, these leaders figured out how to effectively prepare economically disadvantaged children to meet the challenges necessary to enter kindergarten. They used the research and vigorously supported further, ongoing research to develop, implement, and get results from the program. They refused to cut corners. They demanded excellence. And although this story underscores the challenges of galvanizing a community to target its resources, it more than overwhelmingly reaped its rewards: Bright Beginnings is getting kids off to a good start, helping them read at grade level by third grade.

Beyond the Hothouse: The Challenges of Scaling Up

If you asked the locals at a New Jersey diner what two topics rile them the most, you'd most likely hear about property taxes and Abbott schools. And you'd find that the two issues actually become one, with Abbott schools at the eye of the economic maelstrom.

When the New Jersey Supreme Court handed down the ruling in a series of lawsuits from *Abbott v. Burke* in 1998, requiring the state to do right by its poorest school districts and provide its most impoverished children a "thorough and efficient" education, pockets were flush with economic prosperity, and school reform was a hot topic. Most in the state had come to recognize the stark comparisons between urban districts still ravaged from the riots of the 1960s—with inadequate and unsafe facilities and lack of preschool and kindergarten readiness for children—and suburban districts, where children were flourishing. In light of these conditions, it made sense to try to level the playing field and remediate these conditions, hoping to foster an equitable situation that might benefit all children.

But the Abbott rulings went beyond all expectations. The New Jersey Supreme Court required the state to equalize spending between those city systems. Spiraling into what many have called the country's most expansive legal case involving the adequacy of public education, it required the state to play Robin Hood. New Jersey's wealthiest suburbs were ordered to yield hundreds of millions of additional dollars to address the deficiencies in New Jersey's 31 poorest districts, about 22% of the state's 1.3 million school children. Over 40,000 preschoolers alone were to be the targets of these reform efforts.

Never had a court written—or a state been required to fill—a prescription for reform of anything approaching this magnitude. In essence, the court mandated reform at the top, requiring the commitment from those at the bottom.

What's more, the mandates didn't end with changes in school financing. They set out a highly detailed and prescriptive blueprint mandating that schools adopt whole-school reform models, full-day kindergarten and preschool, broad social service programs, enhanced school security and technology, high school dropout programs, and smaller class sizes, as well as a major facilities program to overhaul sub-par buildings.

Eight years into the state's bid to put poor districts on an equal footing with the wealthier, you'll find a house divided. If you mention urban education, many taxpayers will laugh bitterly. They've paid billions of dollars to fund failing schools around the state, and they don't believe they've gotten their money's worth. Others argue that if you scratch the surface of resistance to urban education, you'll find those who believe that troubled urban schools are essentially a lost cause.

One thing seems clear: anyone who would expect demonstration programs or reform models to scale up quickly into massive, large-scale reforms might be in for some surprises. As reality set in, some believed that the Abbott program lost its target focus and went completely out of control, becoming what Assembly-man Bill Baroni Jr. described as a "bootstrap program to solve every problem in urban New Jersey."

At least, one group, however, steadfastly kept its course throughout the entire controversy. Early childhood experts, headed by Ellen Frede, then-assistant to the commissioner for early childhood education, seized on the Abbott decision to remake early education into a high-quality program as a cornerstone to education for its most economically disadvantaged children throughout the state.

If you go to the city of Vineland, a sprawling medium-sized town of 57,000 lying in the southeast corner of New Jersey, you'll find one of the many recipients of Abbott's largesse. Low-rise public housing projects and trailer parks dot the landscape in sharp contrast to its hyper-posh neighbors on the New Jersey shore, with their massive homes and manicured lawns. "If you want to understand why New Jersey desperately needed the Abbott decision to help our poorest districts, just look at this," remarked my host Nancee Bleistine, "It's like a tale of two cities."

Vineland, like many towns in the Northeast, has seen many changes in the past few decades. Although many light industry and manufacturing jobs have moved elsewhere, agriculture in the surrounding fields remains strong. In recent years, an influx of Hispanic families has arrived to work as migrant farmers. Today the town's main street, Landis Avenue, reflects the mixed heritage of its residents, who are largely Hispanic, poor white, and African American. Although the handsome city buildings and parks still stand, the local deli is now a Mexican restaurant, and the one-time Presbyterian Church is now Baptist.

We're here to visit the IMPACT (Innovative Model for Preschool and Community Teaming) center, which lies on the outskirts of town. It's a joint venture of many local agencies, including health and human services and education. Nearly all of the agencies have a presence at this facility, spread out among a series of modern one-story brick buildings, each containing different services: an infant-to-two-year-old program, a preschool for three- to five-year-olds, family literacy services, adult education classes, a health center, parent education programs, guidance counselors and social workers, and a teen drop-out prevention program for pregnant and parenting teens.

Kim, the thirty-fiveish center director, is actually an employee of the hospital, although she works among employees from other agencies. "What we have here is a quiet crisis. Rural poverty—families isolated, uneducated, who lack any kind of health services." The goal of IMPACT has been to link family, school, health care, and community services in one facility. As Kim says, "the center is unique in that we provide so many services for families. We get some children in here as early as six weeks old and we provide services until they are adults."

Although rural children might enjoy some advantages in comparison to their nonrural counterparts, such as safer neighborhoods, statistics[14] find that they may have fewer advantages in getting an early start in education. Rural children are only about half as likely as nonrural to live with both biological parents or have a family member with a high school degree or more. Early care and education are often of poor quality or highly unstable, with fewer than 15% of these children having any access to preschool. By kindergarten, according to a national study,[15] a startling 15% are expected to be placed in special education.

Giving hope to the rural poor as well as those in urban districts, the Abbott decision brought over 10 classrooms for three- to five-year-olds to this area. Nancee Belistine, the early childhood supervisor, shows us Room 3, which is just about as fine as they come. The clean, bright room with modern, child-sized furnishings reflects the added funds and requirements of an Abbott center: abundant books, ample supplies, computers, science centers, kitchen, and work and block areas.

As we enter, the 15 children and 2 teachers are just finishing up greeting time. The children's ethnic backgrounds reflect the local demographics: a mixture of smiling Hispanic, African American, and Caucasian faces. Angela, the teacher, is holding up a picture of a child and asking "Savannah, did you have milk for breakfast?" "Yes," says Savannah. "Then go put your picture in the 'yes' column," Angela instructs her. With some help, Savannah is able to place her picture with the "yeses" on a chart attached to the wall. Angela repeats the process with Tiffany, Lizbeth, and Jose; each child fixes his picture in the appropriate column. Although some children are quite able to recognize their name and picture, others need a little more help from Angela or from Paula, the special education teacher. "Looks like the yeses win," one child says after each had taken their turn. "Yes, that's right, Tiffany!" Angela says, "More of you had milk for breakfast than those who didn't."

While scenes like this would be hardly out of the ordinary in the most posh areas, what sets it apart are certified teachers and special education teachers working together in the classroom, with a maximum class size of 15, along with rigorous standards and accountability. According to Marie Adair, supervisor of curriculum, this type of intensive education has reaped amazing changes in the district's children, particularly in the areas of language development, conceptual understanding, and skills such as cooperating and sharing. "They're now coming to first grade with a given set of skills that previous first graders didn't have."

Just down the road, in an even more hard-pressed rural area, Anna Bermudez, a private preschool teacher at Curiosity Corner, is now also part of the Abbott network. The court rulings allowed—and the Department of Education ensured—that a large network of private preschools such as Curiosity Corner would be able to provide similar services to in-district schools. Last year, Anna learned the grimmest realities of what preschool can mean for poor kids in these isolated areas. A little girl's mother was murdered.

"She was scared, frightened to talk to anyone about it. Sometimes she'd come in and say, 'I miss my mama.' I wouldn't know what to say. I'd just hug her and try to comfort her as best as I could."

The child's older sister was deeply involved in making sure her needs were met, but Anna thought it was the daily routine of preschool that seemed to keep the child together.

"I think she needed something she could depend on—some consistency in her life," said Bermudez. "Winter can be so isolating here. Here they get stability. Routine."

With very little commotion, we watch the daily routine unfold as the children move quickly and quietly to tables in groups of four for "planning time." Knowing first-hand the serious home difficulties children face, the teachers work on routines, or what they call "self-regulatory behaviors." "A newborn infant, rocking in the arms of a loving parent, feels warm, calm, protected, and safe. But in stress-inducing environments, a child's capacity for self-regulation doesn't develop normally, making him at risk for many problems—from persistent tantrums to impulsiveness to difficulty regulating his own sleep and diet," says Anna.

What helps release children's stress response systems is developing repeated exposures to controllable challenges. With repetition comes mastery—what "his brain initially interprets as potentially threatening is now familiar and tolerable. Over time, he becomes capable of tolerating more stress," she finds.

Children's planning time involves writing their names on paper and drawing the activity center that they'll move to next. Some children are quite adept at this: they quickly print their name and start to draw themselves doing an activity in one of the classroom's centers. Others need more assistance.

Anna asks, "Xavier, write your name at the top of the paper." With some difficulty, Xavier prints his name. "Now what's your plan, Xavier?" "To go to the house area," he replies. "And do what?" "I'll make a pizza with Jose." Marie follows, "Ok, now draw yourself working in the house area with Jose." She moves on to help another child while Xavier works on a rather minimalist drawing of himself and Jose making pizza. Marie comes back to help him. "Now write the words, Xavier." Xavier makes 10 dashes under his drawing, "That's right, Xavier, there are 10 lines there, let's count, "I will go to the house area to make pizza." She writes the words on Xavier's dashes. She also writes the words "pizza," "me," and "Jose" and reviews these with him. When they've finished, Xavier happily skips off on his pizza-making mission.

For a child like Xavier, who has suffered chaos and disruption in his family, the structure, predictability, and repetition of these routines has brought comfort and control. Such planning is known to develop executive functioning, leading to changes in the front lobe of the brain. "He seems much less reactive and impulsive" than when he first came here. "Despite what it looks like, we are really teaching him some of the basic tools of the mind," she laughs.

The degree of attention and nurturing that children like Xavier need has often been beyond the capacity of a preschool. But a "master teacher" who helps to oversee and give advice to teachers is yet another part of the Abbott professional network. With her help, Marie has developed strategies to make the environment less overwhelming for children who need more support and comfort.

A far cry from rural Jersey, some three hours north, is an Abbott district that has seemed immune to the countless reforms that have come its way. Newark could be the poster child for the Abbott decision, with dismal test scores, high school dropouts, and more than 70% of its 40,000 children poor enough to qualify for subsidized government meals. Yet in a rented former church in a South Ward neighborhood rife with abandoned homes, graffiti, and hopelessness, as darkness was falling, we see yet another aspect of the Abbott reforms. A dozen parents, with their children in tow, are learning what they need to do in order to keep from perpetuating what they themselves have often come from: an environment too often distracted by drugs, violence, or creditors.

On one evening, a parent volunteer who attended public schools in Newark and sent her children through them did most of the talking. "We know we haven't had perfect lives," she said at one point—describing how her mother used to chase her drug-addicted father from the house while she and her sister tried to study—"but we've got to make things better for our kids."

Mindful of the hour, she speeds through a regimen of advice, encouraging parents to get and stay more involved in their children's education. It is a delicate mission: admonishing parents for their past inattention while at the same time asking them to become more attentive to the basics, such as checking homework or turning off the TV at study time. She talks about keeping a watchful eye on the children, even if it means picking through their book bags, pestering them for details about their lives, or letting their friends hang around the house.

These parent meetings began three years ago[16] and are small-scale affairs held in the evening or on weekend mornings for a dozen or more parents at a time. It's part of a small operation that has been trying to galvanize parent volunteers, funded by private grants to work alongside the "parent liaisons" paid by the

Abbott funds. The parent education initiative represents an important grassroots acknowledgement that things won't improve for the district unless parents are actively engaged in the struggle.

According to locals in the public schools, parent involvement and volunteering has been slow going, catching on in only a few places. In one school, for example, the parent liaison actually paid to have a washer and dryer installed for parent use—on the condition they visited their child's teacher while in the building. Yet it is exactly these small-scale efforts that may ultimately decide whether test scores in Newark and other impoverished cities through the state ever rise to acceptable levels, and whether dropout rates fall to anywhere near those in more affluent suburbs.

Putting all these pieces in place in a stretch of eight years could overtax anyone's imagination—or any one system, for that matter. Certified teachers in every classroom; comparable teacher salaries for public schools and private providers; maximum class size of 15; minimum square footage requirements in classrooms; professional development for teachers; curriculum coaches (with degrees in early childhood); rigorous standards, curriculum, and assessments; added specialists for special education and for English-language learners; wrap-around and summer services; health and nutritional services; parent liaisons and community involvement—all looking like someone's wish list after many years of neglect—these all fall within Abbott's rulings.

But the billion-dollar question that looms in everyone's mind is this: after spending billions of dollars to right the inequities of funding and help over 40,000 children get off to a better start, is the experiment working?

Tracking test scores, the Early Learning Improvement Consortium in its 2005 analysis[17] clearly indicated progress, even though the gains were relatively modest. Children reached kindergarten with better language and literacy skills. The quality of preschool programs was up. The percentage of classrooms scoring in the good-to-excellent range in quality increased from 13% in 2003 to nearly 40% in 2005. More children received services of greater intensity. Gains in the average receptive vocabulary scores showed a difference of nearly four months from the year before. The evidence showed signs of forward movement.

Still, the scores are dismally low. Focusing on the overall effects of the remedies of Abbott, although about three-quarters of the school's fourth-graders show significant leaps forward in passing the language section, up from half in 2003, math scores continue to be disappointing, even though they're up about 25%, compared to 7% in 2003.

These results have more than fueled the fires of discontent among New Jerseyans. Pointing to the fact that almost eight years of near-parity spending for rich and poor districts have done little to close the performance gap between them, some question whether the Supreme Court's package of remedies and continuous involvement might ever do the job. Calling it a "flop," these skeptics see it as the wrong path to improve the lot of urban school children.

Hardly. In fact, what New Jersey has accomplished in less than 10 years is just short of a miracle. Enrolling over 40,000 three- and four-year-olds in public and private preschool programs with significant improvements in language and literacy skills represents a hard-won and heroic accomplishment. Still to come are even higher goals for these districts. Before heading back to her faculty position at the College of New Jersey, then-assistant commissioner Frede has put in place a plan for continuous improvement, a cycle that begins with high-quality standards and required child outcomes, essentially creating an iterative process for gathering evidence about progress and improving instruction—an ambitious accountability system for public reporting. The National Institute of Early Educational Research, funded by the Pew Foundation, will continue to issue yearly report cards and reliably track child outcomes.

But the delicate calculus for whether or not these reforms ultimately benefit the poorest of the poor children in New Jersey, unfortunately, has turned into another story—one about the efficacy of Robin Hood funding. Court-mandated remedies most likely eroded public support because of the way the cost basis was determined—linking it to spending in the wealthiest districts, rather than calculating what it actually might cost to provide services. And in true New Jersey fashion, reforms have gone from discussions about equity to a pitched battle over money, creating high-stakes winners and losers.

The losers, unfortunately, could be the children. Tracking progress, in 1999, Abbott districts had scored an average of 24 points lower on the state's Elementary School Proficiency Assessment than non-Abbott districts, according to extensive research conducted by Bari Erlichson, professor of political science at Rutgers University's Bloustein School. With the help of Abbott reforms, the gap narrowed to 15 points. Perhaps even more striking, 66% of Abbott students scored in the lowest possible category in the language section of the 1999 ESPA. That percentage has dropped to only 37%, reducing the difference between Abbott and non-Abbott districts from 37% to an astonishing 21% in these years.

Ten years ago, three-quarters of fourth graders failed reading and writing on New Jersey's state tests. Last year, close to three-quarters passed. What had once been a system in turmoil, consigning poor urban and rural children to a shoddy education—violating their constitutional rights—is now showing significant progress. Today, children in these communities are entering schools better able to learn, with parents who are more involved in their educational development. Children are becoming more self-sufficient and gaining greater confidence in their ability to learn.

Those who wish to reach into the constitution to claw out the sentence about a "thorough and efficient education"—the legal basis for the Abbott ruling—hoping to scale back reform, had better consider how programs are reaching the untapped potentials of children such as Savannah, Xavier, Jose, and Tiffany. What we now know is that when these children are systematically helped to achieve, when they are provided with exceptionally well-trained teachers—when families become partners in their children's learning experiences—the results are measurable, substantial and evident later in school success.

Mission: Learning—Transforming the Ghetto of American Childcare

Although preschool programs can succeed masterfully in preventing or at least ameliorating the effects of risk factors, they will not be enough to change the odds. For vulnerable children—especially those who live in the shadows—a high-quality child care program will be every bit as crucial as the preschool experience.

Child care has been the neglected stepchild of early learning, often relegated to custodial care with poorly trained, poorly paid, and overworked staff. But although almost everyone agrees that something must be done, there has been little agreement on what to do about it—until, that is, it becomes a serious problem confronting a very important workforce: none other than the armed services of America.

Just about everyone agrees that the 1980s military child care system was a disaster, a "ghetto" of American child care. The litany of woes included poor-quality services and educational activities at child care centers, too few (and badly trained) adults trying to look after too many children, high employee turnover because of low pay and bad working conditions, long waiting lists, and high fees for parents. Isolated but disturbing incidents of abuse also surfaced at centers.

With the switch to an all-volunteer force, the military became a microcosm of American society. Today, the modern armed forces comprise women, men, two-career couples, and single moms and dads. By 1989, when the Department of Defense decided that inadequate child care was jeopardizing military workforce performance and affecting recruitment and retention, the number of women on activity duty had jumped almost 10% in little over a decade. Close to half of military personnel had spouses in the workforce, and there were 55,000 single parents in uniform and 55,000 dual-military couples. In what sounds all too familiar to those concerned with the state of child care across the country today, there were too few slots for the military's growing population of children. Facilities were plagued with lead-based paint peeling from ceilings and walls, roofs leaked, caregivers supervised as many as 15 babies and toddlers at a time, and entire staffs turned over three times a year.

Prodded by the General Accounting Office (GAO) reports and Congressional hearings exposing horrific charges that workers had molested children, Congress got into the act, passing the Military Child Care Act of 1989[18]—mandating improvements in military child care—and the military turned its system around. "We're asking our service personnel to put their lives on the line for what we're telling them is the national security interest of our country," said one official. "We owe it to them to have some sense of comfort that their families left behind will be looked after."

In a remarkable turnaround almost overnight, child care became a priority in the government. Creating a network of child care centers, child care in family homes, and before- and after-school programs, the system nearly tripled the number of child care slots. At the same time, it established and rigorously enforced training requirements, safety, health standards, and child-to-staff ratios. It also raised wages for experienced caregivers and provided substantial subsidies to ensure that child care was affordable to low-income families.

Darlene White, center director at the Ft. Dix army base in rural New Jersey, witnessed the transition, having seen both the worst and the best of the child care programs serving the offspring of military personnel over her 25 years. The worst included a cold stark, abysmal center with only a well-worn Fisher-Price toy farm and a single tricycle with poorly trained staff members whom she remembers as "bodies standing there." That was in the early 1980s, when White began working in child care programs for the U.S. Army.

Early on this July morning at the Child Development Center, mothers and fathers come to drop their children off, some in camouflage and face paint fresh from early-morning maneuvers. The CDC houses more than 13 classrooms and offers care for children six weeks to six years old. Most of the children attend full-time programs, but hourly care is also provided in a separate classroom to military families who need just occasional help.

The rooms are filled with learning opportunities. Toys are plentiful. Simple labels are all over so that children get constant exposure to letters, words, and their meaning. A library corner has 20 new books. There are dolls of different ethnicities and camouflage helmets for fantasy play.

Aside from the rather foreboding entrance to the Center, lined with video cameras to monitor all rooms, perhaps the only whiff of militaristic rigor can be found in the center's activity schedule which reads like this: "1430 hours 1500 hours: wake up/personal hygiene; 1500–1530: Child choice in Activity Centers Group 1" and so forth. Teachers follow lesson plans, all with themes that build on literacy and other skills. Yet the teaching is rarely as rigid or rote in its method as memorizing the ABCs.

Instead, you'll see children learning about their world in almost a camp-like atmosphere filled with children's choices and activities. About 100 yards away from the Child Development Center is a beautiful pond, ringed by pine trees, barbecue pits, and a playground. We meet Miss Sally, a young nineteen-year-old teacher, who is helping four-year-old Keana and her class learn to fish. "Now throw the line in the water. Now, wait," says Miss Sally, and the children get very quiet. A mere five seconds later, the line begins to wriggle. "Oh, you've got one!" she says, helping Keana pull up the six inch sunny. Squealing with delight, the children gather round to look at the fish in the bucket. "Oh look at him!" "I'm going to touch it" Oooh, he feels so slimy!" says one. "Oooh, I like him. I'm going to call him Hershey! Hi, Hershey!" says another.

One boy, Tom arrives in the middle of the activity, accompanied by his father. Tom's dad stays for a while, talks about fishing, and helps another boy get his pole in the water. All the while, Tom hangs quietly by his dad. When Miss Sally hands Tom the pole, he turns toward his dad. "No, you can do that yourself," his dad replies. "I have to get back to work now." Tom looks a bit sad, biting his lip. "Come, I'll help you with that," Miss Sally says, and soon Tom, too, has a fish and is admiring it in the bucket with the others.

Military life can affect children deeply. Families face tremendous financial hardships caused by low salaries and financial burdens caused when parents are deployed to all parts of the globe. The separation of families is a constant strain. In many cases, both parents are deployed and the child is left in the care of a grandparent, other relative, or friend. Many families deal with the stress of having a loved one in combat or waiting to be called up to combat. "All of these problems come to child care each day, and we expect our staff to respond to them."

Addressing these hardships, the Child Development Center has developed a family atmosphere, says Val, the curriculum coordinator. "We try and take care of each other." Today, she is observing nineteen-year-old Brenda as she handles three-year-old Deseree, who has been crying and whining for a few minutes. Deseree, it turns out, is now being cared for by her grandparents in the absence of her mother, who is serving overseas. Val takes the new teacher aside and whispers some suggestions. Brenda offers the little girl some soap bubbles and a wand, and soon both are busily blowing bubbles in the breeze.

David, age four, seems also to be having a needy day. From time to time, he complains to his teacher about the other children: "He took my bucket!" "She threw sand at me!" Later, he can be seen stealing a bucket from another little girl. "Hey, David," his teacher says. "Come here and show me your shirt." David proudly shows his shirt, which boasts a number of military trucks. "Aren't they like the trucks your Dad brought to show our class?" "Yeah my dad brought all the Army trucks and lined them up there on the grass, and my whole class saw them." He sits with her for a few minutes and recalls the time his Dad, who is now away on a training exercise, entertained the whole class.

Sensitivity to the children's needs, according to Darlene White, is perhaps the biggest change in the quality of the center's care. Before the Military Child Care Act, the center was "just a place to hang out while mom went to work." There was no expectation for learning. Now, staffers must understand the interests of children and learn to observe and document their progress. Today, over 95% of the centers are accredited by the National Association of the Education of Young Children, receiving the highest of marks.

Amanda, 19 years old and recently hired, is typical of the staff here at the Center. After high school graduation, she attended a four-year college but found she "just wasn't ready" and came home mid-year. Taking a job as a teacher at Ft. Dix, she's required to take a 13-step training program over 18 months. The training consists of reading materials, being tested on the material, and then being observed by the training/curriculum specialist to see how well she is incorporating the material.

Amanda has worked diligently on her training, having already completed three modules. She's allowed time to read and study the modules during the school day, but she finds she likes to bring the materials home and study on her own. "The training is persistent here," she says, "But I've learned so much, even in three weeks."

As we visit the Center, we see other teachers sitting in the conference room studying during playground time or rest time. "Everything is about learning here," says one teacher. "For example, I just couldn't believe they wanted the children to pour their own milk. I had one little boy who was pouring but didn't realize he had to stop. It was going all over the place. But since I know it's important for him to learn, I put my hand over his and helped guide him."

Turnover rates of staff, once 300%, are now less than 30%. Although many attribute these changes to increases in salary, ranging from about $7 an hour to $10 an hour—compared to $5–6 an hour in the private sector—of equal importance, says Amanda, is that "I feel treated like a professional with valuable skills."

The training teachers receive represents only one layer of quality assurance. Accountability virtually pervades the entire system. Inside each room, surveillance cameras placed in the ceiling tiles of the classrooms, piped into video monitors at the front desk, provide comfort for parents who might experience separation anxiety or want to know that their children are adjusting well. Video recorded interactions between caregivers and children might smack of Big Brother, but here they are used for additional training purposes, providing constant guarantees for parents that their children are thriving and developing critical social and cognitive skills.

Another layer of accountability is provided by teams of specialists who, through unannounced inspections of military centers and homes every year, check curriculum, staff–child relationships, and physical conditions. If a center fails one of its four-times-yearly inspections, it has 90 days to fix the problem or it's closed. "We consider this a safe haven for children," White said. "We do mind our children well."

You might say that all this is easy to do with an annual budget of more than $352 million and a military hierarchy that functions based on the chain of command, but here's the shocker: calculating center-based child care costs for families who use it, on average, 50 hours a week, the RAND Corporation[19] found that the system costs 25% *less* than what civilians—whose average use is 38 hours a week—would normally pay. To keep center-based child care fees affordable for parents, the military uses a sliding fee scale based on income. It makes up the difference in cost by bundling subsidies. As a result, even though the cost to the military of providing center-based care is slightly higher than comparable civilian care, and even though military families typically use care for longer hours and for younger children, the cost to parents is lower. The military's example shows how a systematic approach to resources and subsidies can save money, unlike of the current hodgepodge of programs we now have.

The military's experience is instructive in another way as well. Whereas many states have tackled child care demand by focusing on quantity, the military emphasized high quality, even though this slowed progress on supply. Their rationale was simple: to develop a system that could promote children's healthy development and learning for the benefits that it could deliver over the longer term, they need to pay attention to the details. "We were told, 'We're going to give you money. Prove to us that money works,'" said Darlene White.

Studying the military child care system, the National Women's Law Center [20] suggests that there's a lesson for politicians amid burgeoning scandals of poor-quality child care programs across the country, if they're serious enough and realistic enough to apprehend it: "One of the most important things they did overall was to approach child care systemically and look at all the pieces needed to improve the child care system," says Nancy Duff Campbell, the author of "Be All That We Can Be: Lessons from the Military for Improving Our Nation's Child Care System."[21] Basic standards—health and safety, small staff–child ratios, continuous professional training, standard curriculum, and accountability—helped ensure a high-quality system. The Law Center's findings indicate that when you commit the resources necessary to get the job done, the system will pay for itself in the stability of the workforce and the healthy development of children.

Analyzing the effects on child outcomes, the RAND study found that of the 80 installations, at least 75% responded that quality of care had significantly improved. Although methodological considerations precluded a detailed assessment on child outcomes, qualitative reports among kindergarten teachers indicated that children were better prepared academically. They knew songs, shapes, numbers, days of the week, and colors and were able to listen and learn.

What the military model demonstrates so powerfully is that high quality need not be cost-prohibitive. In fact, low-quality child care costs money. In the absence of a coordinated system, child care has been kept afloat by a series of hidden costs—caregivers bear the costs by forgoing decent wages and benefits; employers bear the costs of an unstable workforce; parents bear the psychological costs of placing their children in inadequate arrangements. And—perhaps most tragically of all—children bear the long-term social, emotional, and cognitive costs of being warehoused in unsafe, unstimulating, and unhealthy environments.

Some argue that the remarkable transformation of the military child care program is truly a Cinderella story. Others would claim that it was just a matter of serious attention and focused hard work. A better explanation is that it demonstrates how changes in priorities can affect a generation of children, turning their surroundings from a ghetto into a gold mine of learning and opportunity. It exemplifies how a mediocre or poor child care system can be raised to a level of quality on a massive scale to become a model for the nation and perhaps even the world—so long as funds are committed to it and someone is in charge to say: *Do it.*

Lessons of Successful Early Care and Education Programs

If young children were only sporadically or briefly exposed to child care, we might not care much about its quality or its association with developmental outcomes. But this is not the case. Child care today is an enduring fixture, starting often within the first few months of life, for many hours each day, and continuing up to school entry and beyond. Child care affects the very quality of children's day-to-day life and profoundly influences their developmental trajectories and long-term outcomes.

Quality matters for all children, but especially for those who are poor. It is these children who have the most to lose from poor programs and the most to gain from good-quality ones. By the age of three, these children will already lag measurably behind their middle class peers in their ability to reason, use language, and believe in their own efficacy. Only the very highest-quality programs, having consistent, sensitive, and stimulating care, can possibly transcend these circumstances to protect and promote children's development. Subject to poor quality, children who are surrounded by chaos, defeat, and unpredictability— the ill effects of living in poverty—will only further succumb to the social and economic stresses in society.

We now have overwhelming evidence that we can change the odds for literally thousands of these children. Programs that are successful recognize the inseparable connections between the care and education of children. They understand that we simply can't educate children without caring for them, and we can't care for them well without educating them.

Successful programs in this chapter demonstrate that it is possible to do both—to transform preschool education and child care into systems that provide high-quality care at affordable costs for children and families who need it. These transformations don't need to take a decade: Just look at the short turnaround times in each of our cases here. Bright Beginnings, the Abbott schools, and the military program started delivering high-quality education in less than five years.

The basic principles are simple:

Successful programs that reach out and help our most disadvantaged children are all about quality. They recognize that at the heart of any program is the quality of the relationship between the caregiver and the child. In programs that succeed, high-quality caregiving is never left to chance. In fact, no credential or previous training is assumed to be sufficient. For example, training is a constant, not a variable, in the military preschool programs. Caregivers are expected to teach according to standards, and supervisors are there to ensure that they do. Similarly, master teachers circulate among the Abbott teachers to make sure that the curriculum is targeted to the highest standards set by the program and communicated to parents as they work together to relentlessly focus on outcomes.

Successful programs that help our most vulnerable children are more intensive, comprehensive, and provide greater individualization for learning. Smaller teacher–child ratios in Bright Beginnings and the Abbott schools, for example, help establish a closer bond between teachers and children, creating a climate that encourages learning. When individual learning goals are established that are challenging but achievable, children begin to believe that they can successfully achieve. These programs eschew a one-size-fits-all approach, understanding that the ravages of poverty and disadvantage can cause severe damage to children's learning. These programs work because they use every available resource and activity to foster children's disposition to learn and improve their skills.

Successful programs for children whose life courses have been threatened by socioeconomic disadvantage and family disruption are well organized, with well-defined objectives that include well-designed evaluations. Bright Beginnings, for example, developed its own assessment plan specially focused on its literacy-based curriculum. These assessments are compared with standardized measures to calibrate how closely the curriculum is aligned to overall school readiness skills. Abbott schools have indicators and progress-monitoring tools, as well as comprehensive assessment highlighting not only high-quality practices, but outcomes. The military program uncompromisingly bases its goals on standards and results. These programs literally create a circle of accountability across all aspects of program implementation. They include rigorous progress-monitoring strategies to tap children's growth, knowing that social and emotional development is just as important as linguistic and cognitive competence. These programs use their findings to better tailor instruction to children's needs. Through self-assessment and the analysis of the intervention's impact, these programs ramp up through quality improvements, growing stronger over time.

In short, programs that succeed in changing outcomes for high-risk children may be different in type and structure but similar in the seven essentials of what makes them work. They begin early and target their efforts to low-income children. They provide comprehensive services with high-quality professionals. Resisting dilution, they scale up but don't scale down on quality, giving children the kind of intensive compensatory education services that they need to survive. Knowing that they must be accountable, these programs focus on indicators and benchmarks, monitoring their progress along the way as they march uncompromisingly toward better outcomes for children.

Visiting a military child care program at the Andrews Air Force Base, I watch a teacher as she works with her three- and four-year-olds, making binoculars to focus on "what to see" outside. I learn that they're about to go on a scientific expedition, looking for bird migrations and nests in the trees. The center is wonderfully stocked with books—with titles emphasizing their current projects—and cognitively stimulating materials, including a magnifying glass and microscope. Off in a small area, another teacher is quietly assessing a child's ability to sort in patterns: first by number, then by number and color. These children and their teachers expect success. They expect to learn. And who would deny that they deserve to?

CHAPTER 6

CHANGING THE ODDS THROUGH COMMUNITY-BASED PROGRAMS

To be a parent in the northeast section of Philadelphia known as Kensington is to live in fear. For some, it's mild fear, just the extra pulse of tension, the kind that is present when a father leads his son past abandoned row-houses to the storefront preschool or when a mother steers her daughter clear of rancid garbage piled up under "No Dumping" signs. For others, it's the nightly terror of gunfire and frequent shootings heard outside their children's bedroom windows. The cruel hardness of life threatens to sweep their children away in its undertow, something beyond what any parent can control or even alter.

Single moms and their kids are everywhere, but Kensington is not built for children. Parks are almost nonexistent. None of them are free of crack addicts or bands of young criminals. During the day, you'll find parts of the neighborhood at work at storefronts under the train trestle. After dark, residents can't get pizzas delivered. They can't drive around the corner to a major grocery store. There's no 7-Eleven. No local Wawa Food Market, either. John Davies, who lives near a crack house off of Front Street and has chronicled neighborhood crime for 20 years, calls his local bodega "the murder mart."

Bad neighborhoods are bad for children. They shape their opportunities. Neighborhoods like Kensington will place enormous constraints on children's life. Living in a bad neighborhood will affect their social circle, the school they attend, and the freedom they will have. The morning after the third person in two weeks was killed by gunfire, Tanya Martin wouldn't let her daughter move beyond her sightline. Before they leave their apartment each morning she always prays silently, "God protect us and shield us from guns, danger, and harm."

She has good reason to be afraid. Children in poor neighborhoods are "more likely to suffer from every imaginable childhood malady," reports Susan Mayer,

Dean and professor at the University of Chicago's Harris School of Public Policy, and are "more apt to die young from accidents, low-birth weight, and violence."[1] Disputing the idea of an inborn capacity to succeed against the odds, Alan Scrofe points out at an American Academy of Sciences meeting, "There aren't kids who can make it all right no matter what. If life throws you enough slings and arrows, you will fail."[2]

The collective landscape of neighborhoods for the predominately very poor has dramatically deteriorated over the last four decades. Inner-city neighborhoods have suffered massive desertions resulting from the closing of factories beginning in the 1960s and also the residential mobility among the more advantaged. What's left, according to sociologist William Julius Wilson,[3] are homogenously impoverished neighborhoods that provide neither resources nor positive role models for children and adolescents. Caught in the wake of this demographic tsunami are the children, surrounded by murder and mayhem, dilapidated housing, garbage, crime, inadequate health care, and a pervasive sense of hopelessness.

Fewer than one in five families live in urban areas characterized by this extreme and concentrated poverty. The multitude of problems faced by inhabitants of these neighborhoods, however—joblessness, substance abuse, crime, violence, and poor schools—presents a serious challenge to us all. These communities affect our quality of life—our economy, our sense of well-being and safety, and our deep sense of humanity. Helping these communities build on their assets and strengths to end family isolation, then, must be part of the solution in changing the odds.

Why Neighborhoods and Community Conditions Matter for Young Children

Despite the booming economy of the 1990s, high-poverty urban settings have grown substantially in recent years. According to the most recent census,[4] the number of children living in severely distressed neighborhoods increased from 4.7 million in 1990 to 5.6 million in 2000—an 18% increase. These neighborhoods, heavily concentrated in metropolitan areas, reflect census tracts with high percentages of poverty, female-headed families, high school dropouts, and joblessness, creating a critical threshold, a tipping point of devastation and discouragement.

Poverty is not just an urban problem. In 1999, for example, 48 of the 50 U.S. counties with the highest poverty rates were located in rural areas—especially in parts of Appalachia, the Rio Grande Valley, the Mississippi Delta, and the Northern Great Plains. Like their urban counterparts, these families often face tremendous isolation, as well as challenges in access to social and economic pathways to escape poverty.

The combination of family and neighborhood poverty has been especially devastating for black families. Although income and education gaps have significantly narrowed, according to a recent National Urban League report,[5] black families' tenuous holds on prosperity—steady progress and devastating setbacks—continue to burden family life. Historically barred from buying homes in certain neighborhoods, black families and their children are 20 times as likely as white children to live in severely distressed neighborhoods. Additionally, Hispanic children are about 10 times as likely as white children to live in a severely distressed neighborhood. Like many contemporary ills, the loss of the community hit the poorest hardest.

Capturing the many ways in which these neighborhood and community conditions exact a toll on children's development, studies[6] report

- Social disorganization: the level of chaos, crime, and sense of danger that permeates the neighborhood
- Stress: the damaging developmental consequence of exposure to violence and to physiological hazards, such as elevated lead levels and asthma-inducing air pollutants
- Limited institutional resources for children's development, such as playgrounds, child care, health care facilities, parks, and after-school programs
- Isolation, the consequence of extreme protectionism and insulation: strategies that parents use to keep children away from the negative influences of peers who may spread problem behaviors

Children turn early in life to the "streets"—away from the mainstream. These threatening environments are characterized, according to sociologist Robin Jarrett, by their individualistic, competitive, predatory ethos. "Hustling" becomes a valid way of securing scarce resources, and "getting over" is seen as a strategy that works.

Children learn to survive in a world where violence is common. To read just a week's worth of police calls in North Philadelphia is to read of rapes, robberies, drive-by shootings, knifings, gang frays, drug deals, vandalism, and prostitution. One study[7] reports that 1 in 10 American children witness a violent event prior to age six, and another estimates that about 1 in 4 urban youths have seen someone murdered during childhood. Walking to school for young children is like navigating a minefield, pushing past drug dealers catering to their daily customers. By day, you'll hear playgrounds ring with language and shouts of children at play. By night, you'll hear gunplay.

Children come under the influence of these predators while seeking a sense of identity. Ghetto street culture, according to one ethnographer,[8] can be glamorous and seductive to youngsters, promising its followers the chance of being "hip" and popular with certain "cool" peers who hang out on the streets or near the neighborhood school. Feeling that the mainstream culture and its institutions are unreceptive and unyielding to their interests, they look for credibility and influence in other ways.

Efforts to counter these trends have grown significantly over the past decade. Targeted at specific threats to our society, the federal government has put substantial funding into preventing such problems as teen smoking, sexually transmitted diseases, unintended pregnancy, and alcohol and drug abuse, albeit with modest effects. Further targeted programs by cities include outlawing outdoor pay phones believed to be used in crime; boarding up property if landlords fail to evict tenants engaged in drug crimes, prostitution and outdoor gambling; and creating a housing code to address vacant and blighted housing.

The mistake that we make about these neighborhoods of severe distress, however, is to stereotype them as unrelieved stretches of hopelessness. The reality has more dimensions. Residents in these neighborhoods will often give a more sanguine view of their neighborhood, like Mary Green in North Philadelphia who tells me, "I don't like it at all, with all the drugs and crime going on. But people have to live where they can afford to live." When she looks at her neighborhood, she sees not only crime and gangs but the sidewalks where she and her friends used to straddle bikes, the churches where they were baptized, and the homes where she and her siblings, aunts, uncles, and cousins used to spend Christmas. Many of her friends have found a way out—often by moving far away. But not Mary: "I'll be here 'til I die."

These neighborhoods, with the help of community partners and institutional supports, may build on their once-proud histories to create opportunities for promoting children's development. Many of these cities have vital assets and strengths, including libraries, museums, and national parks that can connect young children with a broader vision of positive outcomes. Programs in this chapter are finding ways to bring these assets back to the local neighborhoods, reaffirming a sense of community and helping children move into more healthy and productive futures.

Changing the Geography of Opportunity

Why is it critical to build on community assets? Instead, why not just uproot these neighborhoods? For years, academic and poverty researchers have debated whether it might be more productive to simply relocate families from neighborhoods of concentrated poverty to more middle-class neighborhoods. In the past, these discussions were largely theoretical, because such extensive resettling of the poor would have been political suicide, as well as impossible to pull off.

Yet two relocation experiments, occurring at different times, under different circumstances, offer some revealing insights on the influences of neighborhoods, as well as on some of the downsides to mobility.

The first experiment, known as Gautreaux, occurred as part of a court-ordered settlement of a racial discrimination lawsuit against the Chicago Housing Authority. From 1976 to 1998, the housing authority moved nearly 25,000 poor African Americans from crumbling public housing to subsidized housing in suburbs where no more than 30% of the population was African American.

Studies led by James Rosenbaum,[9] sociology professor at Northwestern, showed that heads of households were more likely to be employed than their inner-city counterparts, although they still earned poverty-level wages. But their children did even better. They were much more likely than their inner-city colleagues to be successful on educational measures, to graduate from high school, and to get good jobs. These new suburbanites were much more likely to interact with both whites and blacks. As one student reported to the researchers, "We went into a new school and had the opportunity to be with white people, Indian people, just a mix of races and actually get to know people and have people get to know you."

In the 1990s, the federal Department of Housing and Urban Development tried another program called Moving to Opportunity,[10] which gave vouchers to thousands of residents in five poor city neighborhoods—Baltimore, Boston, Chicago, Los Angeles, and New York. The participants were required to move to neighborhoods with lower poverty levels. Two-and-a-half years into the program, the results looked somewhat positive. But by the seven-year mark after leaving their old neighborhoods, the study found that children who took part in the program were doing no better in school than their peers who stayed behind in public housing projects.

Study authors suggest that the differences in findings relate to specific migration patterns. In the Gautreaux experiment, according to Rosenbaum, the families scattered to different census tracts; in the voucher program, families moved in groups to neighborhoods with less poverty. Jeanne Brooks-Gunn, a coresearcher on the project, noted that the hoped-for learning gains of the voucher program may have failed to materialize because the affected children did not end up in schools that were markedly better than the schools they left behind.

Some others might argue that such a diaspora of the poor only poses new challenges, such as community and political disempowerment. Disappearing from public view, poverty might be swept underground, hiding but not solving the problems. It may add to the turbulence of family mobility, detrimentally affecting children's achievement. Without the friends and neighbors so vital in the poorest neighborhoods, this migration may only deepen a cycle of dependence. At its best, it may create a survival strategy targeted to isolated individuals rather than a plan that can evoke the energies of an entire community.

Social fragmentation and indifference to one another can lead to rising crime, failing kids, and polarized politics. It can also pose health threats—a daunting array of risks beyond the reach of individual control or understanding. Without a sense of community, people can lose the conviction that they can improve the quality of their lives through their own efforts.

The alternative path—one that creates a new "geography of opportunity"—builds on the capacities, skills, and assets of the families in these highly distressed neighborhoods. Even in the poorest neighborhoods, there are individuals, organizations, and resources that can help connect families, multiply their power and effectiveness, and begin to harness their energies for regenerating community. These families can learn to count on their neighbors, rebuild local relationships, and get out and engage in a place rich with social life and commerce, taking charge of their lives and their community's future.

The regenerating community assembles its strengths, organizations, and residents to work with those on the outside to build a wide array of opportunities to promote positive outcomes for young children. These programs range from those intended to build parenting skills to arts and recreation activities, and they also give us a large research base from which to study the features of programs that make a tremendous positive difference in children's lives.

Features of High-Quality Community-Based Programs

Picture a group of young families somewhat warily entering the doors of a community-based program. What kind of welcome might make them want to return for another day? What features might maximize their development? What programs might promote positive behaviors rather than merely preventing problems from happening?

This was a question put to a group of experts from the National Academy of Sciences[11] on promoting youth and community development. Synthesizing the limited empirical research, the review highlighted a number of key features of programs that maximized children's development. Children crave havens where they can feel welcomed and appreciated for who they are. They need safe and healthy facilities and a place to belong. They need clear, consistent rules and expectations. And, most centrally, they need supportive, caring, and responsive staff members who help them build skills, giving them a sense of pride and ownership in learning.

Reviewing the evidence of prevention and promotion programs, and empirical research in the fields of psychology, anthropology, sociology (among others), the Committee found that these key features in community programs make a tremendous difference in children's lives. The type of program is actually less important than the kinds of interaction it supports. Programs with these features expand children's opportunities to acquire personal and social characteristics and to experience positive developmental outcomes. Jacquelynne Eccles, chair of the committee, reports, "We found strong evidence to conclude that these programs reduce risk, and show evidence of higher rates of positive outcomes."

Striking in this list is its focus on creating connectedness, building social networks, norms, and developing social trust. Social scientists such as Bob Putnam[12] argue that it rests on the concept of social capital and the features of social organizations that facilitate coordination and cooperation. Participation in sports clubs, religious organizations, special interest groups, and civic programs— places where children can see and get to know each other, where adults work together and share the pleasures and responsibilities of the place where they work, build social capital. They facilitate civic engagement and create solidarity among people. They help to broaden the individual sense of self, turning "me" into "we."

There are many wonderful examples of community-based programs operating in this country that promote children's well-being. Boys' and girls' clubs, faith-based organizations, community clubs, and special interest groups are only part of the wide landscape of community-based programs that are revitalizing neighborhoods and supporting youth development. Yet a surprising few of these programs have been evaluated for child outcomes. Struggling to fund services, they often focus on serving and supporting programs rather than on research and evidence.

Without research, however, we have no evidence—and without evidence, it's difficult to claim victory. A number of community-based programs are taking this to heart, recognizing the critical role of evaluation in determining what works, and why—actually defining the attributes of effectiveness. Using an outcomes orientation, these efforts are providing compelling evidence that community-based programs can have a powerful effect on children's lives. Further, by carefully documenting the effects of these programs, they demonstrate how to develop sustainable, replicable, and affordable models for changing the odds.

Carnegie's Dream Comes Alive

If you visit the Cecil B. Moore branch of the Free Library of Philadelphia in the heart of North Philadelphia after school lets out, "you might have to wait your turn," says the security guard responsible for crowd control. Spilling over with the pent-up energy of kids on any given weekday afternoon, you'll find anywhere from 30 to 80 children at this bright, attractive library. Many will stay until their parents pick them up after work, using the computers to play games, do homework, and write school papers. They sit around the tables, read, and talk about books. They play chess, hold tournaments, watch movies, and have discussions groups. Sometimes the noise level will be anything but library-like, overwhelming all but the most tolerant or hearing-impaired senior citizens.

This is the state where Andrew Carnegie founded the public library. His dream was to create spaces where children and their families could have free access to books and information. But Carnegie's vision and his beautifully constructed buildings were in such sorry shape by the 1980s that city officials seriously considered scaling down operations and closing branches, especially in the poorest, most depressing neighborhoods in Philadelphia. Even worse, a report[13] indicated that 4 out of every 10 fourth-graders in the area couldn't read even the most basic materials, 30 points below the national average.

Recognizing the critical if little-understood role that libraries may play in hard-pressed communities, Philadelphia's William Penn Foundation, along with the leadership of the Free Library's president, Elliot Shelkrot, set about a five-year comprehensive community-based initiative. They reasoned that innovating libraries that added technological and physical improvements and what they described as a "wow" factor might help bring families and children out in the community. This, in turn, would help children and families in the community overcome isolation, supporting neighborhood activity and employment and creating learning opportunities for children, youth, and adults.

"We decided that we could really make a difference in the lives of everyday people if we could renovate the library branches," says Elliot Shelkot, "the small—sometimes store-front—neighborhood libraries that attract six times as many visitors as the Central library."

After five years of demanding effort, their hard work paid off. Documenting the renovations over six years, my colleagues and I, evaluating their efforts,[14] found that more people were using libraries, more kids were coming in for summer programs, and more kids were part of the after-school community. Acting as havens in blighted neighborhoods, these libraries became community gathering places and resources for information and social interaction. In some places, librarians added rugs, couches, and coffee machines to welcome any and all patrons.

"The people in this neighborhood, even with all their problems, have a real strong sense of community and look at this library as a place to get together and hold meetings," Audrey Rowl says. "And I'll try anything to get them to come. We may even open up a thrift shop." Audrey adds, "Because while for decades it might have been about books, now it's about community if we're going to survive."

With circulation figures up and increasing numbers of people from all economic and social walks of life now in standing room only at some libraries, city leaders and library administrators began to see the transformative power of libraries on urban communities. But, to their credit, Shelkrot and his team began to look at some troubling numbers reported in our ongoing evaluations.

Despite the good news of increased circulation, the not-so-good news was that the *quality* of reading activities in the library for children in poor communities was not equal to those of their middle-income counterparts. Differences started early on, with young children—even three or four years old—in poor neighborhoods. They often came to the library and were unaccompanied for long periods of time, engaged in little purposeful activity, spending lots of time just hanging around. Similarly, the older children from these neighborhoods often read low-level books and spent most of their time playing computer games with little educational value. For example, we found a 50% gap in the overall quality of books read between middle- and lower-income children.

Perhaps even more troubling, computers seemed to actually exacerbate the learning gap, with middle-class children reading far more text at more sophisticated levels than poor children, who spent much of their time playing games on computers. For example, 93% of the materials read by children in the middle-income communities were approximately on grade level, compared to 58% for children in the low-income communities. This means that a striking 42% of the materials read by poor children was *below* reading level.

Yet a number of the 52 libraries—particularly in deeply poor, troubled neighborhoods—broke out of these patterns. These libraries were more than safe havens for needy children. They had especially talented librarians who developed a steady following of children and seemed to make a difference despite overwhelming odds. Librarians like Audrey, a middle-aged African American, would greet children by name, take time to joke with them about the latest hairstyles, and get them involved in writing clubs. She even ran a program on Civil War militia three days a week. Patty, a Caucasian in a mostly Hispanic neighborhood library, crammed in 35 preschool visits a month to local child care centers because she recognized that it was the best way to create a library–reading connection. Whether through chess clubs, reading groups, field trips, or yard sales, these librarians created circles of "human connectivity," as Bob Putnam would put it, building relationships and tacit understandings and sharing the intimacy that develops through close communication.

It was the bonds of friendship, of longing for attachment, that ended children's sense of isolation. Collaboratively, librarian administrators, foundation officers, and even city officials recognized that neighborhood libraries had yet another responsibility in revitalizing poor communities. They needed to reach out more directly to these neighborhoods. As Hedra Packman, chief children's librarian for the city, said, "We can't sit and wait for people to come to us. We have to go out to them."

What emerged from these insights about a successful—but still fragile—victory in high-risk neighborhoods was an outreach plan that has stood the test of time, affecting the literacy lives of thousands of young children and their caregivers. Now over a decade old, a campaign designed to "put books in children's hands" by reaching children "where they are" has transformed the language and literacy opportunities for children and their families in this proud City of Brotherly Love.

Books Aloud: A Campaign to "Put Books in Children's Hands"

You won't find much to read on the street in South Philadelphia where three-year-old Deon travels every day to his child care center. In the windows of row houses, "For Sale" signs have long since given way to plywood. Illegible signs and graffiti tags mark much of the former candy-making factory and warehouse. A rusting teacher's desk, barely visible through a blown-out window is the only vestige of what was once a neighborhood school.

But inside this decrepit building with uneven walkways and stairs, we watch as Deon looks at his favorite book, *Where the Wild Things Are*, along with a gaggle of similarly aged children who implore him to read it again. He flips the pages, jabbing his little finger hard at Sendak's witty monsters and carrying out a running commentary with his friends on the actions of the wild things "dancin' in the trees," and the sea monster "breathin' fire."

It looks so simple and natural. And yet there is nothing simple about what Deon is doing—or where he is doing it, or when. On this bleak street, at this struggling child care center, at this age, it seems nearly a miracle that Deon has a book in his hands and is able to choose from so many. That Deon is able to enjoy the power and pleasures of reading is the result of Books Aloud, the library's outreach campaign to "put books in children's hands."

Recognizing that literacy habits and literacy learning begin early, Books Aloud was designed to get poor children mentored in reading as early as possible. But its target focus was perhaps its most innovative feature: supporting child care centers in the poorest areas of the city, as well as the child care providers who shepherd those toddlers and preschoolers through long days that stretch from before dawn to past suppertime. "We knew that these children often spend more waking hours at child care centers than they do at home," reported Dick Cox, now-retired vice president of the William Penn Foundation, which helped conceive the program. "And we hoped that if we could get teachers motivated to use printed material, then perhaps children would get excited about books and would take them home to parents."

The effort to put books in children's hands resulted in a dazzling display of ways in which the local library branches support children's literacy. With $2 million from the foundation and special library discounts of 40%, the project provided more than 89,000 brand-new storybooks to 17,675 toddlers and preschoolers in child care centers and home-based child care. The program also provided bookcases and storage and display racks to create library corners in classrooms. In a single month, 325 child care centers and 250 family child care homes, in the most high-risk neighborhoods across the city—at a ratio of five books per child—were flooded with sturdy board books, beautiful picture books, and books that rhymed and counted and told wonderful stories. "It felt like Christmas morning," remembers Ann Boyle, the director of Deon's facility. "We had tried to buy books a few at a time, and even then, it would kill the budget just for glue and scissors and construction paper. Now we got boxes and boxes of them, so many that we were able to have multiple libraries for children to use in one classroom."

But Hedra Packman, one of the conceptualizers of the outreach plan, balked at the idea of a mere "book flood." "I've worked in these communities long enough to know that it's just not enough to have books for kids. You must also immerse the adults. The adults must be comfortable with reading if you want children to learn."

Hedra's vision clashed with other library officials. But her take on Books Aloud could be turned into a larger vision of how libraries should operate. "I had this vision that libraries could be a real force in a child's life. Books can be a part of a child's life, as much a part of their life as a favorite toy."

With its focus on child care providers, Books Aloud required teacher training. The purpose of the training program was to emphasize the importance of the early years in establishing a foundation for literacy, to create environments that engage children in print activities, to foster effective read-aloud techniques, and to make books and story reading a constant presence in their everyday activities, not just a "fill-in activity wedged between arts and crafts and nap time."

They set up their Books Aloud training program at local library branches. Week-by-week, as the evaluators of the project, we watched as attendance at these trainings dropped markedly; by the third week, the numbers were abysmal. Reporting back to the Books Aloud team, a data-driven decision was made: no longer would the program expect people to come to them. Rather, they would go out to the people.

However, the outreach program would not be run in one-shot workshops, where caregivers would have to trek at night in these tough neighborhoods. Reaching out to them, Books Aloud dispatched a small army of 22 "preschool specialists"—goodwill ambassadors, many of them retired teachers—to help child providers set up library corners and display the new books in ways that would entice children to use them, play with them, and read them. Freda, a naturally gifted pre-K specialist, found that doing her workshops in child care centers rather than at the local libraries helped her better connect with teachers. The intimacy of the center made teachers more comfortable, willing to ask questions and try things out. Her workshops became wildly popular, attracting parents and other locals wanting to learn more about Books Aloud.

In weekly visits to the centers, trainers such as Jean Byrne encountered child care providers who, in the beginning, would hustle the new books out of children's reach in the belief that they were too precious to let children play with. Some caregivers simply did not see the point of exposing babies to books when they obviously could not read. Trainers heard some providers protest that they didn't read well aloud—a face-saving device, followed by a later admission that the caregivers couldn't really read well themselves. They found that some providers were so focused on teaching preschoolers the alphabet that they had no time and no patience for indulgences such as books.

These preschool specialists realized that although they lacked formal training, child care providers were hardly empty vessels waiting to be filled by expert knowledge from outside resource specialists. What they were teaching was based on their instincts, values, beliefs, and sense of what was right for young children. Trainers had to respect those values, trying not to change but to stretch their beliefs, selling what information they know about early literacy practices as something teachers might find of value and then encouraging them to 'take it out for a trial spin.'

And sell they did. In visits to child care centers, preschool specialists kept the message focused: "Put books in children's hands, whether it is potty time, free play time, or nap time. Read them stories and let them play with and touch the books and see the pictures and print. The children will learn that words tell stories. They will begin to recognize letters and sounds, and without seeming to try, they will build a foundation for literacy."

Throughout our evaluation of the impact of Books Aloud, my colleagues and I began to notice not-so-subtle changes in these child care centers. One day, for example, we entered a freezing classroom in a basement of a church. Children were sitting in this dark, windowless room, wrapped in sweaters and coats, the single fixture high up in the 14-foot ceiling adding little light to the room. Despite these discomforts, eight young children sat happily on the floor surrounding their caregiver Ms. Helen, who was quietly reading *Letters from Felix*. The children listened intently. "Can you smell the cookies being baked?" Ms. Helen asked as she sniffed the air. The children followed her lead. "Let's smell them together," she said, and each child touched the page with the cookies. After reading, Ms. Helen told the children to get a book from the nearby open-faced bookcase, which now had about 20 high-quality hardcover children's books. They gathered around the bookcase, asking questions and telling their own stories to go along with the words.

By the end of the year, there were significant changes.[15] Among the more than 18,000 young children affected by the program, we found striking differences in early achievement scores for children from Books Aloud centers compared to others not involved in the project. Before the project, we found that just 20% of the classrooms had some kind of book nook, although 30% had TVs. By the end, virtually all centers had a special book corner with child-size display bookcases.

Exposed to more storybooks, children were better able to tell and recount stories, recognize letters, understand the conventions of print, and grasp early writing skills. What was particularly interesting is that toddlers benefited just as much as preschool children. Evaluating the progress of 600 preschoolers, our data showed statistically significant gains in receptive language, phonological awareness, and concepts of print, approaching a six-month gain in skills compared to controls. The Books Aloud children arrived in school ready to learn.

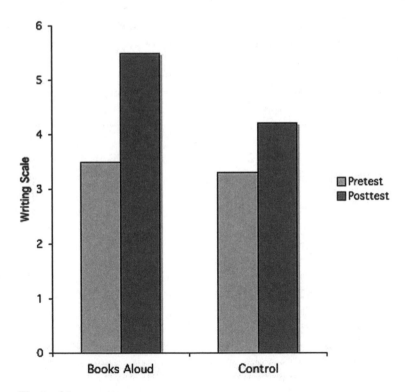

Figure 6.1.
The Effects of Books Aloud (Developmental Writing).

Watching children hold brand-new books, not recycled or donated, made all the difference in the world. Originally, there was some skepticism: some didn't believe in giving new books to children because they would be destroyed. Some centers didn't want teacher training. But, as Hedra found, "We were the library, we had credibility. We were not the government. We were not some agency downtown. We were the local library, located right in their neighborhood."

And as you watch highly active children like Deon in the act of turning pages gently and slowing down to gaze at pictures, you'll see, literally, what it feels like to learn. His teacher reports "You really can't teach a child to have enthusiasm or motivation, but if I can give them a love of reading, their natural desire to keep at it will take them far   farther than anything else I can do for them. It gives them a fighting chance."

Seeing its transformative effects, the City of Philadelphia now calls the program its "first line offensive in early literacy." Becoming more and more ambitious, Books Aloud has progressed to training about early learning standards, getting large numbers of parents to attend their workshops in addition to caregivers. Working alongside parents and teachers to benefit children, the program has become a brand name for good quality and outreach, with its modest costs (approximately $60 per child) now duplicated as an outstanding model to reach families "where they are" throughout the country.

As Packman wisely recognized, libraries today have a new mission. "Reaching out to families and children has changed neighborhoods but it has also changed libraries—forever."

The Doctor Is In

Knowledge dissemination is critical for revitalizing communities. Information on services on health needs to affordable, high-quality child care is often hard to find. In fact, trying to find health services in the heart of Ypsilanti's poorest neighborhood was a number of years ago harder than finding an endangered species. But no longer. Part of a small but growing trend in urban areas across the nation, the neighborhood clinic is becoming part of the landscape in revitalizing neighborhoods, offering health care, social support, and much, much more.

Despite the overwhelming numbers of obstetricians, pediatricians, and family/general practitioners in this country, many children and pregnant women face severe shortages of providers in the poor or rural areas where they live. Typically, most physicians concentrate in metropolitan areas, in private practices, and in higher-income neighborhoods, imposing a tremendous travel burden on substantial populations of families. Far too often, poor residents are forced to turn to hospital emergency rooms for treatments for things from ailments as minor as poison ivy to more life-threatening problems, such as cardiac arrest. In some of these inner-city neighborhoods, according to one estimate, there is only one primary care physician for every 32,000 people.[16] That's a ratio one might expect in Afghanistan.

But increasingly there are groups of health care professionals who have made it their business to work with children whose parents have low-paying jobs—and, in many cases, no health insurance. Working to prevent health problems for low-income and uninsured children in communities, these neighborhood clinics are providing much-needed therapeutic, nutritional, and quality care to children who often fall through the cracks.

In the heart of downtown Ypsilanti, Michigan, once a booming little auto town, now a beleaguered city with a median household income of $28,000—31% below the national average—stands a little clinic on the corner. Bordered by strip joints and bars along a set of semi-abandoned streets, even with its bright orange trim and bold cheery lettering, it's hardly noticeable to outsiders.

Insiders—those who live in the neighborhood, however, know it well. Its small size belies its huge influence in this community. As an adolescent clinic care service started by Joan Chesler, executive director, and David Share, medical director, some 25 years ago, health and social service professionals deal with problems not often seen in a typical pediatrician's practice, and they do it for more than 3,200 youngsters.

They deal with a higher-than-normal rate of lead poisoning in children, probably the result of lead-based paints still prevalent in older-than-average housing. They also deal with high rates of hypertension, adolescent obesity, and poor dental hygiene, and the problems that go with them. They counsel children who suffer from depression. An estimated 5% to 15% of the children who come to the clinic have attention deficit disorder. Others are aggressive and defiant, have sleep disorders, or suffer from other conduct disorders, such as temper tantrums. Many are plagued with acute asthma, and some have witnessed the horrors of domestic violence. The clinic deals with the high incidence of low-birth-weight and premature babies who are the results of smoking, drugs, stress, and poor nutrition.

With a multidisciplinary treatment team that includes doctors, social workers, nutritionists, health educators, and nurses, the clinic offers food and even toys and household essentials such as car seats, diapers, and cribs. It's all about preventing problems for children from birth through age 18, instead of managing crises once health problems have gotten out of hand.

To get families in the door, the Corner Clinic looks about as nonthreatening as a local storefront. Physicians and health care professionals have established a homey, community-like atmosphere where mothers stop in for short-term care, WIC services, and a little corner store. On a given day, they'll see clients every 15 minutes, with about 30% no-shows and 10% walk-ins. Most visits are scheduled from day to day.

The waiting room, though small, is beautifully designed with red brick and muted colors, making it extremely cheery. There are toys for the children, soft mats, activity books, storybooks, and magazines. Personally welcoming their patients at the door, the young doctors avoid wearing off-putting lab coats, preferring to dress casually in slacks and shirts.

It's the multidisciplinary focus that attracts doctors such as Pam Davis to the Corner Clinic. "Many of the kids we're seeing here have tremendous needs,"

Davis said. "You can't just give the child a pill. There are too many problems for anyone alone to make a difference. But with a multidisciplinary team at least you have a prayer."

Serving as an anchor for child and adolescent health care in the city, the Corner Clinic is helping reclaim the downtown. There are community outreach workers who get to know each family and expectant mother, who meticulously follow up when appointments are missed. The staff helps adolescents surmount the numerous logistical and administrative obstacles necessary to access a wide variety of social services, including WIC nutrition benefits and medicine for their babies. The clinic also supplies social workers who visit Head Starts, schools, and churches, establishing a full support network for their clients. Obstetrical nurses and other staff are also available to provide support—not only during crises, but also to help answer the myriad of questions the adolescent mothers may have.

It's the personal touches that seem to make a difference. Helping to support good health habits, adolescent mothers are awarded points for making scheduled appointments, which can be used to "purchase" necessities such as cribs, mattresses, diapers, as well as movie passes and restaurant coupons. Baby formula and food are always free from the "pantry." The little store is located in the basement, like a bodega; it is very neat and lovingly organized. Using points reminiscent of S&H green stamps, mothers buy brand-new items that have been donated by the local service organizations and church groups in the neighborhood to the clinic. But the truth is, even if these young parents don't have points, the staff gives away diapers, formula, or food without asking any questions.

By word of mouth, the good work of the clinic is spreading in a neighborhood that Davis and others are trying to reclaim one building at a time. Increasingly concerned over the pervasive health disparities, especially among minorities and the working poor, these health professionals are not waiting for the government to fix the nation's health care system. They're doing it now, undaunted by the depressing stretch of empty lots, boarded-up storefronts, and dilapidated houses that surround them. They go to great lengths to promote good health education, working toward a model of care far different from the world they learned about in medical school.

They recognize that health care today is more than just mumps and measles. It's about helping children thrive emotionally, socially, and cognitively, encouraging parents to take seriously the importance of stimulating brain development early on. And the prescription they use throughout their well-baby visits is to Reach Out and Read.

The Check-up That Comes with a Story

For small children, the doctor's office can be a pretty scary place. There's the anxiety of being in a strange environment, having to sit and wait for the pediatrician, fearing possibly getting a shot. But the scene in the waiting room at the Corner Clinic is hardly that. Converging around an open-faced bookshelf with

brand-new books, ranging from little cardboard books for little hands to colorful trade books, a small crowd of kids are reading about trucks as a volunteer
points to the pictures and asks children lots of questions. Far from being afraid
of the doctor's office, they all seem like they're having a great time.

Among its other programs, the Corner Clinic is part of the nationwide Reach
out and Read program.[17] The idea is to make better use of the time kids and their
parents spend waiting for care by encouraging children to read and urging parents to read to them. Children are given age-appropriate books to take home
when they go to the doctor—and are hopefully inspired to read them with their
parents. The point is to get children turned on to reading early, between the ages
of six months and five years, getting them excited about holding books in their
hands.

Like many simple ideas, it's deceptively powerful. Started in 1989 by Dr. Barry
Zuckerman, chief of pediatrics at Boston Medical Center, and by Dr. Robert
Needlman, now in Cleveland, the program has gone from a small project in one
waiting room at a single clinic to over 3,000 doctor's offices in all U.S. states and
territories.

The program was inspired when Needlman looked at his waiting room at a
medical center in a poor neighborhood in inner-city Boston and noticed that
something was missing: books. He called around, wrote letters to publishers, and
begged local donors, and before long, Boston's historic Old South Church came
through with $6,000, enough money to buy a fresh new supply of books.

He gave them away—one book to every child who came in for a well-baby
visit. At the same time, he rounded up volunteers to read to the children in the
waiting room, so parents could see how it was done. And during the well-baby
check, he talked to each child's parent, telling them how important it was for
children to grow up loving books, explaining that part of a healthy childhood
was getting them started listening to books early on.

Targeted at children who live in poor neighborhoods such as Ypsilanti without access to books, the program features three key elements: volunteers read
with children in pediatric clinic waiting areas, pediatricians educate parents
about the importance of reading with their children every day, and children
receive a new book to take home and keep every time they come in for a well-
child check-up. "Giving a book to a young child, along with age-appropriate
advice about sharing books for the parents, may be a powerful thing that pediatricians can routinely do to promote children development," write Needlman
and his colleagues.

According to these physicians, the rationale for making literacy a target of
pediatric intervention came about for several reasons. First, the medical community was becoming increasingly aware that illiteracy constituted a health risk.
Medical risks associated with low literacy have been extensively documented in
adult populations, and to a lesser degree in children. With limited literacy, adults
face increased risk of illness and hospitalization, as well as higher health care
costs. These medical risks extend from difficulties reading prescription labels and

poison warnings to inability to read and comprehend complex directions of particular medicines. Second, understanding that genetic predispositions and the quality of the environment are inextricably related, pediatricians had a biological rationale for efforts to enhance early learning. Third, the pediatric health check-up seemed like a natural context in which to promote reading aloud and other parenting practices that support literacy development.

Medical research supports Zuckerman's claim, showing that literacy promoting interventions by pediatricians have significant effects on parental behaviors, beliefs, and attitudes toward reading aloud. For more than a decade, they've developed a corpus of studies indicating that parents who get books and literacy counseling from their doctors and nurses are more likely to read to their young children, read to them more often, and provide more books in the home. In a 2005 study of a national sample of over 1,600 parents of children aged 6–72 months, implementation of the program was associated with more than simply increased parent support for reading aloud.[18] Regular bedtime reading increased to more than three times a week. What's more, a study by Mendelsohn in New York City[19] found that scores on standardized vocabulary tests were significantly higher in the Reach Out and Read clinics—8.6 points higher for receptive language (understanding words) and 4.3 points higher for expressive language (picture naming), both large, meaningful effects. Supported by these data, the program recently received funding from the U.S. Department of Education, providing 50% of start-up funds to doctors' offices for the first year and 25% for the second. Next year, the Reach Out and Read program will pass out 4.6 million books to 2.8 million children at 3,200 physician offices, hospitals, clinics, and health centers in the United States, Puerto Rico, Guam, and the U.S. Virgin Islands.

In my visits to the Corner Clinic, it's clear that the power of the intervention lies in its repeated message: read to your child. Inside the pedestrian's room, parents are given brief how-tos on reading and what they can expect, depending on their children's ages. It sounds relatively easy. But parents who aren't used to reading to their children—often because they do little reading on their own—pose a tremendous challenge. "Teaching them how a child will respond to a book isn't easy, but it's crucial,' Davis said.

Visiting eighteen-month Emanuel and his mother, Dr. Pam Davis gently begins with a series of probes or "trigger questions": "How's he doing?" "Is he saying any words?"

The young teenage mother answers somewhat hesitantly: "Uh, uh, no."

"Is he babbling and pointing to things?"

"No," says the mother."

Handing the book to her, Davis begins to talk about the advantages of reading. "Books are really good things for helping children learn new words. He'll point to things, and he should begin to tell you what they are. Sometimes he'll pretend to know what they are. He'll act like he knows a lot about things. You can have a conversation."

Dr. Davis then demonstrates and models how to read a book to Emanuel, who is acting very fussy after having his blood pressure taken. Pointing to the picture, she asks, "What's that? It's a snake, a snake." Instantly, Emanuel becomes engaged and stops whimpering. Pam gives it to the mom, who tries to follow her lead.

Tentatively, she asks, "What's that? It's a sheep."

As the mother continues, Pam tries to give her some benchmarks to consider, "He should know about 10 words by now and understand them. Next time, I'll expect him to know a few more words." She writes a prescription, adding, more directly, "You should read to him every day." She then hands the book and the prescription to Emmanuel's mother and tells her, "You're doing a great job."

For other mothers, it's like preaching to the choir. Baby Tyler's mother, also a teenager, is reading to her young one when Pam enters the room. Asking her the same trigger questions, this parent gives detailed answers, saying, "He likes to turn the book backwards, and he keeps turning it around. He has a few favorites—like books about trucks." Following up, Davis talks about the fact that children who look at books and have parents who read to them generally do better in school. But Tyler's too busy to listen as he continues to point to the pictures and ask his mother to read, hardly realizing that the doctor is in the room.

"One reason I like the program a lot is that if a baby like Tyler says, 'Mommy, Mommy, look at the truck!' you don't need to ask whether he can put two words together to form sentences. You can see it. You can see if the child is securely attached to the mother, what words he's using, whether he's pointing and getting new vocabulary words. It's kind of a natural for a well-baby visit." Davis knows the program has had an effect when she brings a new book to another teenage parent and her child, who says, "This is the same one you gave us last time. We've read this book a lot." Bringing another new book, this one a board book, she tells Alicia, the mother, "this book has hard paper—a six-month-old is going to put a book in her mouth." Alicia says, "I try to read to him, but he just eats it," to which Davis replies, "That's why they make cardboard books! You can do lots with it. It's great for the bedtime routine, great to use in winding down the day, and a great way to spend time together."

The program's aim is to help families create a home library for their child with as many as 12 new books. After going through the program, the parents of these children are expected to have learned new skills through which they can actively encourage their children to dive into books.

But the doctors admit there's a clever subterfuge in the program. Books hopefully entice parents to bring children in for their regular check-ups. Along with the repeated messages to read, regular health supervision and ongoing care can help not only by improving children's health, but by identifying and responding to problems that may not exclusively biological. Alert health professions can spot subtle problems in children's behavior that, if ignored, can become compounded later on, only further contributing to a downward negative spiral.

Adopting a wider lens than the norm, these physicians and health professionals recognize that children's physical, cognitive, social and emotional development are intimately related, especially in the early years. Therefore, despite the pressures of time, these physicians place a high priority on well-baby visits and promoting reading, emphasizing the importance of physical closeness and language interaction.

In these Reach Out and Read programs, these dedicated health professionals have taken on leadership responsibilities to bridge this program with other collaborating service organizations. Though they are very busy, they have committed themselves to ongoing training, creating connections with local libraries as well as regional and state coalitions. Providing technical support and quality control, the Reach Out and Read National Center includes a curriculum for reader training, as well as instructions and guidelines for other aspects of program implementation, headed by its passionate spokesperson, Dr. Perri Klass, who coordinates advocacy efforts at the national level.

This year, doctors and nurses in similar clinics throughout the country will distribute 4.6 million books to 2.8 million U.S. infants, toddlers, and preschoolers, with special emphasis on children such as Emanuel and Tyler, who are growing up in poverty. The total cost of the program per clinic is likely to come to about $1,705 if each clinic is giving away 620 books per year, at $2.75 per book. Each of the children who participate in the program will start kindergarten with a home library of up to 12 books. They will also have the benefit of a parent who has heard at every health supervision visit about the importance of books, reading, and good conversation with their children. Doling out books with shots and prescriptions, doctors at over 32,000 sites are helping children show up to school ready to learn and ready to read.

An Unlikely Ally

With their deep roots in a community, institutions such as libraries, clinics, and museums make for natural allies in helping to rebuild neighborhoods. But every so often, it takes an outsider with a different approach and a different way of thinking to make substantial changes in the learning of those living in the confines of concentrated poverty. The unlikely ally in this case is television and local public broadcasting stations who help build a learning-rich environment for children who live in circumstances of unrelenting poverty and despair.

Television—the much-maligned black box—might hardly seem the ideal partner for helping to boost children's achievement and parent's involvement. The truth is quite the contrary. Television has been considered the source of many of society's ills, from encouraging obesity and violence to low reading achievement.[20] Recently, the American Academy of Pediatrics warned families that television or any screen time at all—including television, video games, and computers—could be harmful for children younger than two years old.

But for preschoolers, this may not be the case. In a remarkable breakthrough in television programming, starting during Lyndon B. Johnson's War on Poverty, *Sesame Street*—still going strong after some 35 years—proved convincingly through two longitudinal studies[21] by Samuel Ball and Gerry Bogatz at the renowned Educational Testing Service that television could not only entertain but teach. Disadvantaged children could learn their letters, numbers, and other readiness skills through the medium—so well, in fact, that kindergarten teachers were left scrambling to up the ante in their kindergarten curriculum.

Brilliantly conceived by Joan Ganz Cooney and supported by Lloyd Morrisett at Carnegie Foundation, *Sesame Street* showed that children's love of slapstick humor, music, and formats such as cartoons, game shows, situation comedies, and fast-paced commercials needn't always be a bad thing. It could be used to children's advantage, helping them learn. Gathering together a talented group of scholars and out-of-the-box thinkers, including educational psychologist and Harvard professor Gerry Lesser as chairman of the board of advisors and Ed Palmer as director of research, they carefully examined how a program might be configured to support nontraditional young learners. It needed to appeal to children's interests, making them laugh, holding their attention, and at the same time entertaining parents well enough to tempt them to watch along with their children. Out of these discussions emerged a storyline centered in a neighborhood populated by beloved Muppets and characters who sang of the joys of learning, along with their tag-lines of "brought to you by the letters N and P, and the number 2."

But the Sesame team not only put together a classic children's program, they revolutionized educational programming. From the beginning, they insisted that the show be designed as an experimental research project that would bring together educational advisors, researchers, and television producers as equal partners. To an unprecedented degree, the creative, educational, and research components were to function as inseparable parts of a whole to ensure that every segment of the show that would be aired was "research-based." Developing the fine art of formative research,[22] each segment was assessed for its appeal, interest, and comprehensibility for two-and-a-half- to four-year-old children.

Children's Television Workshop, now known as Sesame Workshop, has gone on to create many wonderful programs for children, among them The Electric Company, 3-2-1 Contact, and Ghostwriter. Its model of using research to tap television's potential for learning has since spawned other companies to create programs for different ages and interests, including science, math, and writing.

To Chris Cerf and Norm Stiles, veterans of the creative team for *Sesame Street* and The Electric Company, it seemed only natural to take the Sesame concept a step further, to try to teach concepts of reading that are often difficult for teachers, parents, and others to explain. "We wanted to see how TV could help—what TV could do that no other medium could do," reports Cerf.

He tells the story of Dr. Seuss, visiting his office years ago, to talk to him about a problem he was having in writing a new book. "He wanted to create an alphabet book that used verbs instead of nouns. The problem, however, was that it's hard to illustrate verbs in a book—if you show a horse running to illustrate "r," the child might look at the horse, and not the action of running," he explained. "Television's power is that it can illustrate verbs and other concepts that print or individuals can't."

It can also illustrate *how* to teach. Television can show teachers and parents how to read a book to children—how to say words slowly so that the children can hear their distinct sounds. Television can also teach how to introduce word families that can give children the insight and confidence to tackle multisyllabic words. It can use its ability to zoom to focus on good models of teaching, mobilizing teachers and parents to help children learn how to read.

With a production team at WGBH in Boston, Cerf and his Sirius Thinking Corporation generated the idea of a magical neighborhood public library as a home base equivalent to the street on *Sesame Street*. A family of lion puppets would serve as the librarians, connecting viewers to the world of books. Using a magazine-like format, it would teach precise, systematic skills to children ages four through seven, simultaneously dramatizing the meaning and purposes of reading and writing.

They developed a "whole–part–whole" concept for teaching skills and concepts in reading. Just like a good teacher, the program would start with a story. They would then go on to teach a phonics or skill lesson, finally returning to the story to demonstrate how these new skills might work in reading. With recommendations from a panel of experts, they concentrated on vowel sounds, knowing that mastering these tricky sounds might "sink or swim" the emergent reader, according to advisor Bob Slavin.

But this was no boring drill and practice. The creative team came up with hilarious bits to help children learn. They used a Monty Pythonesque segment in which two knights crashed into at each other saying different sounds in order to teach verbal blending. Vowel sounds were sung by none other than Martha and the Vowelles, a Motown-style singing group (brought to the White House to delight Laura Bush), and phonics were presented by a strange, white-haired Fred Newman, who made every sound known to man, blending and playing with sounds.

Between the Lions, a delightful mix of skills and fantasy, debuted on public broadcasting stations across the country in 2000 to wide acclaim and numerous awards and Emmys. Using the research model that won *Sesame Street* its loyal following, its cast of characters and skill segments were appealing, interesting, and targeted to Sesame graduates who were now ready to learn the building blocks of reading achievement.

But unlike its predecessor, it didn't catch on. Despite all the evidence from formative studies, the show suffered abysmal ratings, hardly registering significant ratings in any market. The reason for the show's low ratings seems clear. Program developers had hoped the program would air at 7:00 a.m. or 7:00 p.m., when families were home and could watch with their children. As Linda Rath, curriculum consultant found, "That didn't happen. Local networks placed it on their schedules during off-peak times—hours that pre-K and kindergarten children are usually at school."

Rather than wait for an audience to eventually catch on, the *Between the Lions* team set out to build one. They brought *Between the Lions* to two of the hardest-hit communities in the Mississippi Delta: the Indianola region and Choctaw Pearl River Indian Reservation.

A bleak mountain of federal research suggests the extraordinary risks and hardships of children growing up in these settings. Native American youth commit suicide at twice the rate of other young people, according to the U.S. Commission on Civil Rights. Native Americans of all ages are 670% more likely to die from alcoholism, 650% more likely to die from tuberculosis, 318% more likely to die from diabetes, and 204% more likely to suffer accidental death. Despite considerable financial gains in the past 15 years, some of it the result of gambling operations, Native Americans remain the poorest single ethnic group in the country.[23]

Both the Choctaw Indian Reservation and the town of Indianola in the Mississippi Delta mirror these statistics, struggling with isolation and poverty, with children rarely getting beyond eighth grade, too early to be recorded as high-school dropouts. Leading the nation in childhood poverty, according to KIDS COUNT,[24] only 18% of their fourth-grade children read proficiently, one of the lowest rates in the nation. With language skills lower than any other urban or rural group in the United States, most of their children are in the highest-risk group for reading failure by the time they begin school.

Although reluctant to let outsiders in, the communities knew full well the likely trajectory for their children. They hoped to use the *Between the Lions* program to model good early literacy teaching early on. Bundling their Title I funds, in partnership with Mississippi ETV and the local public television station, they brought 50 preschool, kindergarten, and first grade teachers and nearly 1,000 children a year's worth of programs, along with teachers' guides, handbooks, posters, books, and information for parents. Teachers received ongoing training throughout the year on how to use the program in their classroom.

Children were encouraged to regularly watch half-hour episodes of the program in child care or grade school, followed by teacher-related activities. But the study designers were not prepared for the severity of the problem. As Dr. Cathy Grace, Coordinator of the Early Childhood Institute at Mississippi State University, and Director of the study reported, the language delay for many of the children was far more significant than anticipated. In addition, Grace found that some of the teachers were needy themselves, making it difficult to encourage consistent use of the program in centers. "When they saw the first episode of *Between the Lions*, you could see by their faces—they were learning too."

Although end-of-the-year assessments found improvements, results were not overly impressive. Children's language scores remained low, and their readiness skills were still far below benchmark expectations for their age levels. Examining these findings in preparation for another study, Deb Linebarger,[25] a professor at the University of Pennsylvania, commented that, "[g]iven their very low initial scores on most literacy tasks, these children clearly needed a more intensive reading intervention." Following up in the Mississippi region, Cathy Grace acknowledged, "We need to be more deliberate in how it is used, more focused."

According to Grace, in these extremely poor Head Start child care centers, the program had rolled out like so many interventions that have shown to be weak or ineffective. Teachers were trained, given materials, and asked to use these materials two or three times a week. They did not have to show the program at a specified time each day, or in a particular sequence. Without strong direction, some teachers just stopped viewing, despite their delight in receiving the materials.

These experiences yielded some important changes in the next trial of *Between the Lions* in New Mexico, initiated by Judy Stoia and Beth Kirsch of WBGH, working closely with KNME, the PBS affiliate. Teachers were given complete curriculum guides, spelling out how to use the program in the classroom. They were also given more training sessions and more coaching in the classroom. In addition, the team worked diligently to make sure the curriculum guides offered suggestions on how to "springboard" the program segments into activities that were more culturally relevant to children of different backgrounds. All this effort was made to finally tap the power of television to easily reach an audience of at-risk children at little cost.

The Laguna Pueblo Head Start Center is located on the Laguna Pueblo Indian Reservation about 50 miles west of Albuquerque. Approaching the site, the landscape turns from the lush green of the city to the deserted dust of the mesas. Surrounding the Laguna Pueblo Family Center are small, ramshackle cabins, cobbled together with adobe, aluminum siding, and tin, their front yards littered with broken-down pickup trucks, bikes, a few children's toys, and curiously enough, the occasional satellite dish. The land is hard-packed dirt with no trees or grass—just endless sun and dust.

The Family Services Center springs up among the houses, a series of well-kept trailers, flanked by a playground, a parking lot, and two kivas, the Pueblos' traditional adobe ovens for baking bread. Outside the Head Start trailers, a few lizards run among some new corn plants.

All of the children at the Laguna Head Start are children of the Laguna Pueblo tribe. Although the tribe is concerned about children's education and well-being, the children are extremely needy. Most parents are young—teens and early 20s—and work sporadically in local casinos. Most of the grandparents are retired, are also very young, and are very involved in caring for the children.

Like other Indian tribes, the Pueblos in this region struggle to maintain their culture and help their children become educated about the mainstream world outside the reservation. But the isolation is extreme. Teen pregnancy is common. There are few jobs outside of the local casinos. There is no running water or electricity in many places, few paved roads, no programs, and most importantly, no hope. The people often maintain a wary, supercilious attitude toward the federal government, which they see as an oppressor and destroyer of their culture, a view that isn't totally unreasonable, given that the Bureau of Indian Affairs used to yank reservation children from their homes and place them in boarding schools where they were forbidden to speak their native language.

As a result, most Pueblo are not fluent in their native language. However, they perceptively view that reconnecting with their native language and cultural traditions may be a key to their survival and to changing the sharp trajectory of decline that so many children experience here.

Working alongside the public broadcasting production company in Mississippi, the *Between the Lions* group sought to help, creating new segments to help the show coincide with the Native American children's experiences. "We used kids and scenes from the area. We had to get over our cultural references. We realized that what we know as a house in the Northeast is not the same as a house in New Mexico." "Our goal was to help create a 360 surround for children." Conceivably, if children could watch the program at home and in the classroom, coviewing with their parents and teachers, they might have more opportunity to learn the key building blocks of reading instruction.

"Pushing the envelope to help the neediest children," Chris Cerf felt that television segments might be especially helpful. Knowing that video could model skills or content for children, giving them clear demonstrations of proficient performance, they could use segments that encouraged children to sound out words and think out loud. They could also model for teachers, providing "just-in-time" professional development. For example, showing children working in cooperative groups could provide teachers with a clear idea of what cooperative learning should look like.

Furthermore, with the language differences of the children, the complementary nature of words and moving pictures has been shown to greatly increase children's initial learning of concepts, helping in both retention and transfer as long as the picture and text or narration are closely aligned with each other. Cerf's group took these research findings seriously, developing special segments to create the explicit connections between words and pictures.

A visitor to the four-year-old class at Laguna Head Start is greeted by the sounds and sights of beautiful Pueblo children busily engaged in activity. Although the outside may be arid, brown, and dry, a step inside the class reveals a different world: clean, colorful, and vibrant. On this particular day, the class is preparing to watch a segment that revolves around the book *Abiyoyo*. The teacher, Carol, has gathered the children around her and has told the class that they are about to watch a TV show about a boy and his dad who help save the village from a monster. The dad is a magician and the boy plays the ukulele. "What do magicians do?" She asks. "Have you ever seen anyone play a guitar?"

As the show starts, the children rise up and sing and dance along to the theme song with the song from *Abiyoyo*. When Abiyoyo's shadow first appears, Carol pauses the television and asks, "What do you think was making the great big shadow and the group shake?" "A monster!" the children cry.

As the story progresses, there is a near-constant stream of words superimposed on the TV screen that gives the kids reading practice without them knowing it. The new episode focuses on the vowel sound in words such as coat, boat, and goat.

In a highly engaging way, those three words appear in a *Cliff Hanger* book about a silly goat in a coat on a boat. Other words, which appear at appropriate moments in the various skills, include toad and croak, boat and okay, soak and soap. Each time, the word with "oa" highlighted is overlaid on the screen. After half an hour, it's an easy bet that most of the kids catch on to the "oa" pattern. "Can we watch it again?" they cry when the show ends.

Afterward, Carol seizes opportunities to use the curriculum to teach the Laguna Pueblo culture, as well as to explore facets of American life that these children have no experience with. She talks about traditional instruments, such as drums and rain sticks. She exposes children to a violin and other instruments for them to explore. *Abiyoyo* also deals with magic. The children make their own magic wands, which are now displayed in the classroom. Carol, unsure that the children knew what a magician was, spent time exploring this concept with them.

Shana Hyer, the educational coordinator at the Head Start, was initially skeptical about bringing any kind of television into the center. "I did *not* want our children watching TV!" Through training, she worked with teachers to make the children's viewing an active experience. "When I go in the class, the children are singing and clapping along with their favorite songs. The teachers will stop the program at an important part to reinforce concepts."

Chock full of rhythm and rhyme, and designed to trigger phonological awareness and new vocabulary to foster and build background knowledge, the program has helped teachers learn on the job. Most have little formal education. Because of their efforts, skills have improved over the past two years not only for the children, but for the teachers as well. Says Carol, "Most of my staff has never had a job outside the reservation. They've never had to interact in the outside world. This is a whole new world to them."

So far, the percentage of children considered at risk in these communities has decreased from 39% to 12%. The proportion of children performing at "above average" increased from 23% to 64% by the project's end.[26] In addition to creating measurable changes from the beginning of the project to the end, there is also provocative evidence showing that children are accelerating in skill development. Using a highly predictive measure for examining children's phonemic awareness skills, a method often used to determine whether a child is at risk for reading failure, 100% of the Choctaw and 74% of the Indianola children have reached benchmark level or better. Children's language scores continue to rise as the teachers work with parents to intensify the instruction even further.

For families in these isolated reservation lands, considered the "worst poverty pockets" in the country, the playful characters of *Between the Lions* are giving them a new language—a language connected with the skills children need in order to be successful in reading. Families are learning that children need to identify the initial sounds of words, that 37 vowel combinations can help their children unlock nearly

500 primary grade words. If they watch at home along with their children, they can reinforce these skills and better prepare children to be successful in school. But the show is no bitter pill to swallow in the name of education. Although the program's theme is literacy and skills, the episodes are put together in such a way that books and reading are shown as a fun and engaging way to spend time. "Teachers looked forward to coming to work every day because the program is just as exciting for the teachers as it is for the children. They learn because they're having fun."

Using the power of television and its enormous reach, these communities are helping to build a common language for learning about literacy for the most at-risk children at very little cost. Weaving together culture and curriculum, they are beginning to reap the fruits of their labors, celebrating their children's developing early literacy skills.

Community Programs that Work

Low-income and neighborhood poverty together pose near-lethal risks for children and their families. When economic conditions bode ill, unemployment rises, the real value of the minimum wage declines, and—as most of society's ills—it hits the poorest hardest. Our nation has seen an alarming growth in the ratio of poor families living in concentrated poverty, increases that have been even more dramatic for black and Hispanic children.

In the past, our public investments for children who face such risks have focused on problems: violence, alcohol, substance abuse, teen pregnancy, obesity. Billions of federal dollars have been spent on creating "safe and drug-free communities," despite the evidence from three national evaluations[27] that these programs have made communities neither safer nor more drug-free. Counseling methods that encourage children to "just say no" have wasted billions of dollars, proving to be totally ineffective in changing behavior.

These programs have ignored the root of the problem—the limited choices for children and their families in these neighborhoods and the often daunting array of risks that confront them. In Kensington, Maria Rodriquez, 34, is a divorced mother who is rearing six kids, aged 2 months to 10 years, in a crowded apartment. She lives within sight of the more gentrified Fishtown, and she tells me, "No one imagines what it's like for the children. But in this bad neighborhood here, the children just sit for hours on end with nothing to do."

Programs in libraries, health clinics, and public broadcasting stations provide alternatives to problems. They offer solutions. Taking on the important role of information disseminators in their neighborhoods, they become fulcrums of activity on issues related to health, education, and early childhood. By gaining people's trust in their own capacity to improve their lives, these programs are serving as important touchpoints in their community, helping restore a sense of dignity, pride, and ownership among diverse residents.

Although a plethora of well-meaning organizations exist in urban America, what makes these programs stand out is not only their vigilance for quality but their determination to get results. Take, for example, the Book Aloud program:

studies show that children come to kindergarten with greater knowledge of letters, sounds, and words, fulfilling their teachers' expectations for school readiness skills. Families in Reach Out and Read double the rate of frequent book sharing with children, increasing children's receptive language by almost a standard deviation. *Between the Lions* demonstrates how televised models of good phonics instruction can improve children's phonological development, a key predictor of reading success. These interventions focus on outcomes, knowing that specific problems and threats to children's health and education, especially in the early years, can severely compromise their well-being in the long run.

In fact, each project tells a somewhat similar story. Beginning with a sound foundation of research, each program started with great aspirations. But each found bumps along the road to implementation. In the case of Books Aloud and Reach Out and Read, for example, program developers underestimated the sea change that would be necessary to help caregivers and parents read to their children regularly. Programs certainly needed books, but the participants also needed strategies to read books, especially when their own reading skills might be underdeveloped. Similarly, teachers using *Between the Lions* needed more explicit instruction on how to use it effectively to impart literacy skills. Whether in waiting rooms and child care centers or on television, participants needed to see good models of practice. They needed to look at it, reflect on it, and practice its strategies to make it their own.

Instead of waiting for negligible outcomes, each project carefully monitored its progress. Each used data to develop mid-course corrections. Books Aloud and Reach Out and Read, for example, grappled with questions of practical importance, such as "How do we intensify the experience? What training do people need in order to better implement the program? What methods of reading aloud are most effective?" Despite teachers' many years of experience, the *Between the Lions* team found that these teachers needed additional training and specialized knowledge to help develop children's skills. The teachers needed to enhance their existing skills' repertoire—it had to be modeled frequently through coaching and mentoring by project leaders. Each program made data-driven decisions to intensify the intervention, all in greater efforts to improve child outcomes.

In each case, programs returned to the seven essentials. They recognized that to be successful they had to begin early and target their efforts to children who needed help the most. They needed to reach families "where they are" by connecting them to comprehensive services that acknowledged the integral nature of health, educational, and social–emotional development. They learned—sometimes through trial and error—to intensify their treatment and to provide the kind of coaching and support that was needed to improve outcomes. They relied on highly trained staff with deep roots in the community and an even deeper commitment to their people. During each intervention they held them themselves accountable, with the ambitious goals to improve children's outcomes and achieve powerful results.

The linchpin of success lies in accountability, the focus on results. But none of these programs would have succeeded nearly as effectively, if they hadn't been monitored for progress along the way. If the staff of these programs had simply waited until the end of the year to measure whether or not they had achieved their intended purpose, they all would have missed the mark. Community programs needed retooling once in the field to adapt to the needs of the community. In each case, programmers learned that no intervention is ever able to be scaled up without being embraced and linked to the culture of the community.

In doing so, they not only benefited the individual children and families in these communities, they set in motion the belief that neighborhoods, even those that have been devastated by unemployment and poverty, can once again be revitalized, building a sense of community where children and adults can play and work and join in the pleasures and responsibilities of the places where they live.

CHAPTER 7

CHANGING THE ODDS THROUGH AFTER-SCHOOL PROGRAMS

When it comes to explaining the roots of inequality and why poor children do worse academically than their middle-class counterparts, analysts typically focus on the differences in the quality in schooling. There is a widespread perception that poor children are routinely short-changed by their schools. This is how the No Child Left Behind Act of 2001 is understood—as being mainly about failing schools—and this understanding has been used as a rationale for the greatest federal encroachment on local school governance in the history of the United States.

But what if the supposed failure of schools to close the achievement gap is altogether misleading? Children spend only 20% of their waking hours in school, leaving many hours free each day, including 185 fully free days. What if the large proportion of out-of-school time accounts for the gap in achievement? This is the great insight exploited by Doris Entwisle and Karl Alexander in their 1997 book *Children, Schools and Equality*.[1] Back-mapping high school achievement scores for over 900 Baltimore students into their developmental precursors at the time of school entry, they found to their astonishment that poor and middle-income children make comparable achievement gains during the school year. It was the out-of-school time that made a difference. Although the middle-class children continued to make gains during after-school hours and in the summer, poor or disadvantaged children lost ground academically.

Entwisle and Alexander liken this unsettling discovery to the metaphor of a faucet. When school is in session, the resource faucet is turned on and all children gain pretty much equally. When it is not, the resource faucet goes off—at least for a majority of poor children. During out-of-school time, better-off children engage in extracurricular activities that help them move substantially up the ladder of achievement. But in neighborhoods that have been depleted of resources and opportunities for learning, poor children languish and fall precipitously behind.

Documented first by Barbara Heyns in the 1970s in her landmark study of summer learning for children in Atlanta, Georgia,[2] the seasonality of learning has shown remarkable generality across other localities and nationally in the Early Childhood Longitudinal Study. Findings from this literature support an unequivocal conclusion:[3] the source of learning gains and loses occur when children are *out* of school, not *in* it. Family resources, both financial and psychological, do not strongly predict how much children learn when school is open. They only predict children's gains when school is closed.

This may explain not only why poor children start school behind, but why they continue to lag behind later on. It is the continuing press of environment. Poor children depend on schooling to increase achievement; without it, their rate of growth is slowed or even reversed. This is precisely why early intervention, such as preschool and high-quality child care, has such a powerful impact. It attenuates the influence of socioeconomic status, reducing the direct dependence of outcomes on family and neighborhood resources.

But this also highlights a key element for changing the odds: if we are to improve achievement for disadvantaged children, we must keep the faucet flowing—both in and out of school. Today, more than 78% of mothers of school-age children are in the work force, with as many as 10 million children between the ages of six and nine left in "self care."[4] Children become increasingly vulnerable to the consequences of high-risk behaviors related to sexual promiscuity, drugs, and violence. No wonder the increasing sense of urgency to turn the equation of downtime into productive time for children who are likely to spend about 80% of their waking hours outside of school. As writer Jonathan Alter of *Newsweek* comments, "[T]he most dangerous time of the day for children isn't late at night. It's from 2:00 p.m. to 8:00 p.m., when children are out of school and their parents are still working."[5]

That is also the prime time to provide opportunities for nurturing healthy social relationships in alternative, cognitively stimulating environments in which children can learn about themselves and their worlds. Across the country, there is a growing recognition that after-school programs can provide opportunities for positive development, putting in place the kinds of safety nets that are needed to support a healthy and positive passage through the rough waters of early and middle adolescence. With supportive efforts at the federal, state, and local levels, schools are partnering with community agencies to open their doors earlier and keeping them open later in the evenings for after-school and summer programs.

What had once been a modest effort in education at the margins of social awareness has now become known as a "distinctive child development institution of learning."[6] This chapter examines this fragile and unique institution—one that bridges the traditional boundaries of formal and informal learning. It highlights community-based organizational efforts that offer zones of safety and comfort for children to master new skills from adults who are available to catch them if they go astray.

It also recognizes that the years from six through adolescence are times of great developmental change when children will either begin to feel competent and productive or inferior and insecure. Helping those that have felt the brunt of failure and despair will be a formidable, though not impossible, task. Even though we must recognize that early intervention would have been better, there is no excuse for neglecting these youngsters. Nevertheless, the more long-standing the neglect, deprivation, and failure, the more difficult and costly will be the remedies.

The great promise that these programs hold is that they offer a form of learning laced with experiential activities *different* from what happens during the school day. In some cases, the very success of these programs hinges on their nonschool flavor, their ability to create an alternative learning environment from school. In other cases, they offer personal learning spaces for children to develop skills without emphasizing differences in abilities or grade-level distinctions. Having greater autonomy than schools, these after-school programs allow children to safely explore their independence and new peer relationships, providing opportunities to form positive and long-lasting relationships with adults outside their families.

Evidence for the benefits of after-school programs, an emerging institution, is still in its formative phases. To date, there are no randomized controlled trials, nor are there highly detailed cost–benefit analyses. Although some pioneering efforts integrating best practices are in their initial phases, rigorous research evidence is currently lacking. Nevertheless, to dismiss after-school programs because of their "freshman status" would be to ignore a quiet revolution—a revolution that begins when school is out at 3:00 p.m., with community groups all across America keeping the faucet flowing for thousands of children long after the sun has faded.

What Is After-School Education?

After-school programs are held in schools, churches, and community associations where children aged six through the young teens explore expressive arts, sports, and other developmentally enriching activities. Most offer a mixture of extracurricular activities, including homework help, athletics, computer clubs, and other activities tied to an academic program.

Although they have been operating for many years in some communities, after-school programs and the national awakening to their potential for learning is still just a few years old. Known by many different names, such as supplementary learning, complementary learning, or out-of-school learning, after-school programs represent the collaboration among public and nonprofit agencies and businesses to create supervised environments for young children and youth during nonschool hours.

The original impetus for after-school programs was keeping children safe and away from the neighborhood violence that frightens many young children and attracts older children to its risks. Initial studies[7] indicated that being engaged in extracurricular activities was associated with lower rates of involvement with such risky behaviors. A national survey of tenth-graders, for example, compared students who spent one to four hours weekly in school-sponsored activities with those who spent no time in such activities: nonparticipants were 57% more likely to drop out, 49% more likely to use drugs, 37% more likely to smoke, and 27% more likely to be arrested.[8] Organizations such as Save the Children and America's Promise, an umbrella group for hundreds of nonprofits and corporations, recognized the potential of after-school programs to promote positive youth development, an alternative to gang membership and unproductive time. Working with foundations such as Charles Stewart Mott and George Soros to secure millions of dollars, practitioners and scholars from many disciplines pushed up the demand for high-quality programs that provided safe places for children to spend time when school was not in session.

Initial studies,[9] however, cast new light on the prevalence and character of after-school activities. These studies indicated that the availability of programs not only kept children safe but seemed to change their lives. Growing up in neighborhoods filled with crime and drug use, children could escape into a different world—even for just a few hours each afternoon. Results from L.A.'s Best,[10] an after-school enrichment program in 24 Los Angeles elementary schools, showed that 75% of the children liked school more after participating in the program; their parents reported less tension at home; teachers reported improved behavior; student grades improved; and school-based crime dipped by a striking 40–60%.

Today, nearly 7 million of the nation's children are in after-school programs, with nearly an additional million under the auspices of the federal 21st Century Community Learning Center program. Still, as many as 5 million low-income children between ages 6 and 12, from working poor families, do not have access to after-school programs. Not surprisingly perhaps, findings from Public Agenda,[11] a nonpartisan New York City–based research group reports stark inequities in the availability of programs, with more than two-thirds of low-income parents facing significant obstacles in finding high-quality, affordable after-school programs.

Too many children must fend for themselves in libraries, malls, subway stations, and neighborhood stores, or behind locked doors in housing developments. We need to break this grim cycle by making out-of-school time productive for children. By helping children explore new skill areas, discover talents within themselves, and experience the thrill of doing something just because they love doing it, successful after-school programs across the country are building a new three R's in children's lives— resiliency, resourcefulness, and responsibility.

Entry into Middle Childhood

Children's remarkable growth in the early years is now well established. During these early years, they transition from helplessness to growing independence— from thinking primarily about themselves and their inner drives to more external demands. The energy and capacity of children to learn about their universe and the people in it flourish during these years, transforming newborns into five-year-olds who are usually well prepared to embark in school.

Although these early years are marked by striking changes, the developmental and social changes that occur between ages 6 and 14 are dramatic as well. These are the years when children move from home into wider social arenas that strongly influence their development. According to developmentalist Erik Erikson,[12] during these years children develop a sense of industry, a feeling of competence and productivity. It is in middle childhood that children learn to cooperate, seeing themselves as part of a larger enterprise both embracing their energies and broadening their experiences. With successful experiences in different situations, children develop a healthy sense of competence in academic, social, and other domains; they develop confidence that they can master and control their worlds.

There is also a broad consensus that children develop key intellectual and conceptual skills during these middle-school years. According to psychologist Jacquelynne Eccles,[13] middle childhood is marked by several critical advances in learning and understanding. Children develop metacognitive skills, or techniques that help them develop a notion of how to go about learning new ideas. They discover that strategies such as studying and practicing can improve learning and performance. They begin to consciously coordinate their learning progress and modify their plans based on reflection and evaluation. Alongside these metacognitive strategies, they develop an ability to take on different perspectives, perceiving events and states as others see them and developing empathy and understanding for other people's viewpoints.

Nevertheless, these years are fragile ones. According to a study conducted by Deborah Stipek,[14] when children were asked how good they were in reading, most kindergarteners ranked themselves near the top of the class—but there was essentially no relation between their own ability ratings and actual performance levels. By age 10, however, children were typically far less optimistic, and there was a greater relation between self-ratings and performance. Some say this decline occurs as a result of growing self-consciousness. Social slights can make children more pessimistic about their abilities, shying away from activities where their performance is questionable. Others describe it as the "calm" before the adolescent storm. Nonetheless, problems with anxiety, low self-esteem, and withdrawal in the face of challenges begin to emerge during these crucial middle years. Outside the safe confines of family, parents feel increasingly helpless in directly intervening in their children's lives.

Researchers have since corroborated Erik Erickson's stages of development, the understanding that feelings of competence and personal esteem dominate children's sense of well-being. Children who do not feel competent in these middle-childhood years, whether in academic, social, or physical activities, seem more depressed and socially isolated than their peers. They feel anger and aggression. These frequent feelings of frustration and incompetence coalesce early on into a negative pattern toward school and other activities.

Their problems can become our problems. Early adolescence—the years from 9 to 14—often marks the beginnings of a downward spiral, leading to academic failure and school drop-out. These children see their school grades decline precipitously when they enter middle school, along with their interest, motivation, and confidence in their intellectual abilities. Negative responses to school increase as students become more prone to learned helplessness and growing self-consciousness. Rates of truancy, drug dependency, and juvenile crime rise dramatically as a result.

Some suggest that all this occurs as a result of the psychological upheaval and biological changes associated with development. Many argue, however, that the antecedents of adolescent school failure and crime lie in our failure to provide environments that respond to children's emerging desire to be competent and productive, to seek companionship and independence. There is now ample evidence that without intervention, gradual declines in various indicators of academic motivation, positive behaviors, and self-perceptions are sufficient enough to raise alarm.

A Distinctively Different Child Development Institution

After-school programs can play a vital role in buffering children against some of these problems. They come at an important time. Some have argued that the structural features of schools in the middle-childhood years may not be responsive to children's needs and developing capacities. Fragmentation and isolation may reduce opportunities for close interactions between teachers and students, precisely at a point when students need support from nonfamilial relationships. It is in these years that educational environments become more judgmental: grading and tracking practices can serve to undermine students' motivation and confidence. Competition for achievement and the inevitable social comparisons that accompany these higher stakes may heighten students' self-consciousness and further erode their self-esteem.

Especially in disadvantaged communities, school's penchant for discipline and teacher control and its limited opportunities for student decision-making come at a developmental stage when young adolescents need to build on their knowledge base and stretch their reasoning capacities. Consequently, the ill fit between the middle-childhood years and the school environment increases the risk of disengagement and disappointment, especially for those who were experiencing difficulties academically and socially even before this key transitional period.

After-school programs use a model different from that of school-based learning. Programs are based on "learning by doing," in settings with nonfamilial adults where students are encouraged to express their individuality and their ability to reason and solve problems. These programs highlight effort over competition, reasoning over rules. Such programs provide students psychological spaces to experiment with ideas, with adults who characteristically sponsor their talents and individual efforts. They combine security and comfort with expanding leadership opportunities that recognize and respect students' need to take control of their environment.

Lucy Friedman, founder and president of the After-School Corporation in New York City, and Jane Quinn use the term *stealth learning* or *learning on the sly* to describe many of the experiences that help students engage in the community and discover phenomena in their real world that they might otherwise not notice.

There is actually a large empirically based scientific literature that underlies Friedman's notion of stealth learning. Influenced by John Dewey's pedagogical theory of activity,[15] this learning model is based on the premise that children acquire knowledge, language, and social understandings through useful activity inherent in solving real problems or social challenges. Opportunities to engage in community service, for example, help young people understand how they can affect their immediate environment, providing new avenues for responsibility while helping them feel like valued members of their community.

Cultural theorists such as Jean Lave and Etienne Wenger[16] distinguish this type of learning from didactic instruction. Here in real-world settings, learning takes place in what they describe as "a community of practice." Communities of practice develop around things that matter to people, around some particular area of knowledge and activity that gives members a sense of joint enterprise and identity. For a community of practice to function, it needs to generate and appropriate a shared repertoire of ideas, commitments, and memories. It also needs to develop various resources such as tools, documents, routines, vocabulary, and symbols that in some way carry the accumulated knowledge of the community. In other words, it involves practices, or ways of doing and approaching things that are shared to some significant extent among members.

The interactions involved, and the ability to undertake larger or more complex activities and projects though cooperation, bind people together and help facilitate relationship and trust. Communities of practice, therefore, can be seen as self-organizing systems and have many of the benefits and characteristics of social networking, or what Bob Putnam and others have discussed as social capital.

Although informal learning and its traditions have been with us for many years, the ways in which Lave and Wenger have developed an understanding of the nature of learning within communities of practice, and how knowledge is generated allows us to think a little differently about the groups, networks, and associations with which children are involved. It is a form of learning that is based on a dynamic apprenticeship model as a central concept. Adults lend support and structure tasks sufficiently that the student can begin to take over responsibility for learning.

In the landscape of after-school programs, it is the practice-based approach to learning that provides its unique structure. Adults consider the complexity of learning activities and design strategies that encourage children to participate. Tasks are geared to activities that relate to students' lives, as well as to challenging new opportunities for growth. Adults "lead from behind" to support students' actions and involvement so they can successfully accomplish their goals.

Unlike school, in after-school programs, it is skilled performance that matters, not standardized test scores. Whether it is sports, creative arts, or an urban ecology project, programs focus on mastering the knowledge and skills necessary to carry out tasks. They may focus on purposefulness, high demand for immediate performance, and the instantaneous feedback that makes this type of learning especially well suited to children who in other circumstances have felt defeated, marginalized, and often invisible in schools.

A consensus is now emerging on the features of activity-based learning in after-school programs.[17]

- *There is an intimate connection between knowledge and activity.* Problem-solving and learning occurs through authentic experiences. Perhaps one of the most understudied areas in learning is the extent to which education involves informed and committed action. Some programs, for example, include advocacy efforts, volunteerism at Food Banks, and other community efforts. Such activities give voice to students' needs to become engaged in productive and meaningful work.

- *Mentors encourage students to become part of a community of practice.* Learning activities are planned by students as well as adults; mentors not only foster students' actions and activities but also learn from their own involvement with students. Communities of practice support teamwork and joint action, helping students to begin to think of "we" instead of simply "me."

- *Learning requires social interaction.* Activities support intentional relationship-building through cooperative learning and joint activity. Students work together on exhibitions, performances, and organized sports, all designed to recognize a variety of talents and to help them build capacities to work with well with others.

- *Students need a broad array of choices.* Interest drives engagement. Programs need to offer students choices and opportunities to consciously plan, coordinate, and evaluate their goals, contributing to their own learning. After-school programs give many students their first exposure to new learning opportunities in areas as various as dance, music, art, and organized sports. Providing many choices helps students expand their goals for their own schooling, careers, and avocations.

Such programs build on communities of practice that are strongly connected to real-world learning. Tied to authentic activity, they support problem-solving, collaboration, and opportunities to learn for students without the burdens or continual reminders of status differences or the norms of academic achievement. In many respects, they use immersion as their model of learning as students apprentice with more experienced mentors in fields as varied as sports, arts, and performance.

These programs allow students to safely explore their independence, developing strong, respectful relationships with adults outside of their families. But after-school programs may not only support healthy, positive development during middle childhood, they may also put in place a critical safety net for children who are juggling a volatile mix of family, school, and social pressures in harsh, disadvantaged communities.

Learning beyond the Bell

As dance music thumps from the blaring tape nearby, I watch as Lilliona's feet seem to hopscotch around the gym floor in a dazzling performance before a group of students watching from the sidelines with admiration. Getting ready for an upcoming parent event, Lilliona and her group have been working steadily on dance routines for several weeks. After several practices, they take a rest and then quickly run off to another room for a light dinner before boarding the bus for home about 6:00 p.m. When I ask Lilliona why she attends the after-school program, she says, "I don't want to go home after school. It's boring at home."

Lilliona's life here is hardly boring. After 1:50 p.m., when school lets out in San Francisco, the after-school program begins at McKinley School. Run by the After-School Enrichment program, a nonprofit community-based agency licensed throughout California, there will be about 120–125 kids on an average day in the program involved in a schedule that ranges from community service to Chinese art. On the day of my visit, rain has spoiled their plans for a field trip to the Farmer's Market, but the students and teachers seem highly engaged in their dance routines, playing games and relaxing with some structured activities in between.

Mateo, the director and teacher of the program, is a striking figure in his mid-thirties, a mixed-race Latino with stark, black tattoos that look scary to the uninitiated. Taking a circuitous route to education, he first worked in the juvenile justice system, then as an aide in school programs, including special education. Frustrated with school bureaucracy, he turned to after-school education, convinced that the mentorship role might better suit his talents and sensibilities. Now into his sixth year, Mateo, a renaissance man, has shaped the program into an environment that is both safe and intellectually challenging. Students engage in poetry as well as sports, fine arts, and advocacy workshops. The program provides "zones of comfort" as well as challenging new opportunities for growth with well-defined rules, responsibilities, and expectations.

The second-grade students today are learning to take care of a teacher's treasured Gila monster over the one-week spring holiday. They gather round the cage, watching, as the teacher feeds the animal with live food. Mateo barks instructions. "You've got to make sure that there's water in the cage—who's going to be in charge?" he asks. As they go about their chores of cleaning and feeding, you hear words such as, "Hey dude, I'm getting some books on how to take care of him . . . . Sorry, you can't pet him, dude," in casual and relaxed conversations.

Mateo is joined by some other renaissance men in the program as well. Nick, a late-twentyish, handsome, pony-tailed man has been with the program for about a year, and Ryan, just a bit older, has been around for more than six. A true fashion plate, he wears a brown baseball cap sideways with a brown jacket, earrings, untied shoes, and the tiny glasses currently in fashion. He is a local rap star who spends his days in the after-school program and his nights with his band.

Staff are very young—early 20s and 30s, about 50% male, clearly reflecting the demographic characteristics of the students they serve: largely Hispanic, Asian, and mixed-race families. Low wages—about $10 per hour, a problem that has plagued after-school programs—seem not to have deterred them; staff turnover is low. Responding to why they stay on, these mentors say that they play a crucial role at a critical time in students' development. In fact, "I love working with them" becomes a common refrain throughout my visits to programs.

In this and other programs, the qualifications for teachers are different than for those in school learning: real-life skills. None of these staff has formal teaching training credentials; some do not have a bachelor's degree. Carrie, for example, a widely respected after-school teacher, works as an aide during the school day and hopes to get her associate's degree a year from now.

Each staff member, however, brings a distinctive expertise to the program. One is a poet and another a professional musician. Each has specialized knowledge in art, photography, or music. Working their way up through perseverance, skill, and determination, they wish to give back to the community, drawn to the institution of after-school programs for its unique character in shaping students' development during the transitional and often turbulent years of middle childhood. They seem to enjoy their roles as coaches, mentors, teachers, and friends to these students, who are coping with the trials of pubescent change, school transitions, and the other stressors of life.

It would be wrong to assume that teachers get only on-the-job training, however. There is a strong training component in this program. Each teacher is required to spend a considerable number of hours in training workshops. Collaborating with community agencies and scheduling activity blocks that engage over 125 students a day involves a heavy dose of administrative time and attention. Carefully crafted student choices of activities that range from science, foreign language, literature, drama, sports, jazz, and hip-hop have to be meticulously organized to provide for engagement, social-skill development, and other achievable outcomes.

The unique features that characterize an after-school program from more formal educational environments become all that more evident when one observes a structured lesson for students who have been struggling with academic challenges. Mateo, a poetry buff, is engaging students in the writing process, using a program known as Kidzlit that is targeted at children with academic challenges and reading difficulties.

This is no phonics lesson or serious drill or practice. Rather, Mateo starts the lesson holding a giant stuffed goose to the delight of all the children. Apparently, the goose is a signal for students to listen attentively. "What does this mean?" he asks? Sasha responds, "We must show mutual respect and pay attention when others are talking."

Lilliona adds, "Don't tell nobody that he's stupid."

"Very good, thank you," Mateo adds.

Today, these 20 children will work with their mentor to create a community poem, one dedicated to their beloved city. Throughout the room, Mateo has placed charts with sentences and beginning phrases and words, such as "In my city, I hear . . . see . . . smell . . . touch . . . say," reflecting each of the five senses. Soon all the children are dispatched to different areas to fill in personal words and adjectives for different senses, before coming together as a group some 20 minutes later. Encouraged by his colleagues, Marcello chooses to read his group's poem aloud:

> In my city, I smell . . .
> In my city, I smell burritos, plants, transmission smoke, chicken, Chinese food . . .
> In my city I smell flowers, daffodils, pansies . . .
> In my city, I smell hard work, oil, garbage . . .
> In my city, I smell . . ."

The children clap after each poem is read and make a joint decision to create a class book, an ode to the city they love. Nick, the rap star, now takes over and reads them a story about a child in a Third-World country. The children remain transfixed, even clapping after he finishes the book. He grabs for the big stuffed goose and tosses it to a child, saying, "Ask a question."

They start a wonderful conversation. Maesmo asks how the artist blended the colors to make watercolors. He pitches the goose to Cairo, who asks whether the story is real or not. She pitches the goose to another student who says, "What country is he from?" Nick then pushes it up a notch. "Let's think about the differences in this country and the other country. Can you guys go to work in this country?"

"No," they answer.

"That's right. The child labor law protects you from having to work. But in some countries, they make you work for 14 hours at a time," he explains. He then asks the students to get in small groups to explore what community actions they might take as a result of the story. After interesting discussions, a group leader reflects the consensus: "Since the governor gives us the money for our after-school program, we should only buy things that say 'made in America.'"

Nasha's mom comes to get her. Still in the thick of a conversation with Nick, she asks if her mother can wait outside until they're finished. Sensing that the hour is getting late, Mateo, once again, pulls out the goose and says, "You have 30 seconds to say an appreciation. If you don't come up with something, you'll have to pass."

The remaining children begin:

> I appreciate everyone here.
> I appreciate Davon because he helped me.
> I appreciate my mom.
> I appreciate Nick's beautiful reading of the story.
> I appreciate my teachers helping me learn.
> I appreciate my caregiver, who taught me German.
> I appreciate everyone.

Without labeling or defining, restricting or demanding, children engaged in a wonderful array of conversations. They had opportunities for problem-solving, decision-making, and working collaboratively as a community of practice. Far from the highly regimented school day, these learning activities allowed children to explore ideas, feeling, and identities, giving them avenues for self-expression, exposure to their own heritage as well as that of the larger culture, and time for unstructured play and simple fun.

What was perhaps most striking, however, was the relationship between teachers and children. One might think of these adults as camp counselors, big brothers, or coaches—authority figures who use their character, charisma, and expertise to win students' confidence and respect. These adults seemed to have an empathetic understanding of students' character and an insight into the various paths of their development. They also regularly demonstrated a genuine regard for the students, building on the strengths that—according to Nick—"ninety-nine out of a hundred naturally have."

Interestingly, throughout my visits to programs, none of the disciplinary problems that have traditionally plagued inner city schools were evident in these after-school programs. Even in the case of highly troubled students, Mateo responds, "We try to work with families. We don't turn anyone away. In some cases, where the children are very needy of help, we'll have someone who shadows them, and we may need an extra adult, but we'll work with any and all kids. That's our job."

People who think and talk about inequality often ask why it is perpetuated. Yet we must remember that life is very different for a family in which a single parent works at two minimum-wage jobs to make ends meet, and a family with one highly paid wage earner, with a spouse or partner at home caring for a child. The children of many poor families will be left on their own in unsafe neighborhoods crisscrossed by traffic, plagued by street violence, and peopled by strangers. The disintegration of community buffers has led directly to a decline in positive youth outcomes. Surrounded by a pervasive sense of hopelessness, children's lives become self-fulfilling prophecies of limited expectations and rewards.

Eight-year-old Derek, who lives with his mother and two younger siblings in a small apartment on a family income well below the threshold of poverty, is one such child. His mother works nights as a waitress, leaving him and his sisters to fend for themselves after school and at night. Like so many other children who are challenged by stressful situations such as poverty, divorce, illness, and other catastrophes, Derek's teachers report that he has behavioral problems and is likely to be held back in school.

It used to be a forgone conclusion that Derek, starting along this negative trajectory, would eventually fail in school. But recently, studies[18] charting the lives of families such as Derek's are identifying protective factors that highlight children's remarkable "recovery" and adaptability. When children are able to draw strength or support from someone outside the family, they are able to compensate for a variety of constitutional and environmental misfortunes. In fact, these researchers found that early biological problems actually disappeared in children who were able to grow up in a stable and supportive environment by the time they were in middle childhood.

Among the external protective factors identified by these researchers is a positive and safe learning environment, accompanied by high, yet achievable, expectations. Feeling safe—not just physically but also psychologically—is essential for students to take risks associated with new activities and learning. Nonetheless, the key protective factor that seems to build children's resilience is their ability to become attached emotionally to another adult, an individual who gives the child a sense of belonging and purpose, values his or her abilities, and promotes opportunities for success.

In Derek's case, that adult is Lincoln Chavez, a local musician and a teacher in Derek's after-school program. Although a wide array of services and activities are available through the program at P.S. 163, that's not what keeps Derek coming every day to the after-school program. It is getting to hang out with Lincoln.

In his late-twenties, with long dreadlocks and black uniform T-shirt, Lincoln cuts quite a figure as an after-school leader. He never expected to be an educator. After graduating college, where he was involved in the campus radio station, he went into the automobile business and ended up as a coowner. "But I always wanted to work with kids," Lincoln said. "I wanted to be a role model for kids— black, white, Hispanic, whatever—to show how important education is. I see too many kids who think they can become sports stars or music stars without getting an education. I think education is the key to opening doors, and that doors will open for them if they have the qualifications."

Lincoln is hardly your typical educator, however. Like Mateo, he is a tough and demanding taskmaster. Getting ready for a dance performance, the students are practicing their moves. "OK, Santiago," he instructs, "let your hand go in a motion that looks like you're hugging yourself. Let's take it from the top . . . five, six, seven, eight."

The moves are incredibly complicated, yet none of the children seems to give up, even after the tenth go-around. Like an effective coach, Lincoln teaches by modeling. "Watch, this is what it's supposed to look like." "Try it with me." "Yeah, Derek, you got it!" he says with tremendous excitement. With his back to the students, he demonstrates the moves, turns around quickly to assess the students' progress, and gives specific feedback without mincing words in a rhythmic pattern: *here's how to do it, here's how you did it, here's how to do it now.* Sometimes he even scolds students: "How many times have I told you to follow through on that move?" At various stages of the dance, he will yell "Freeze!" and point out what they are doing wrong, showing them how to do it the correct way.

All through these moves, Lincoln praises, provides encouragement, smiles, and builds on the children's momentum, always finding tiny bits of activity to reinforce. At the same time, he places responsibility for learning on the learners and fosters each child's skills through vigorous teaching, practice, and repetition. He works on teamwork—unity, team spirit, and cooperation—reminding children that there are only a few days before their community performance.

The phrase *role model* crops up everywhere—in the media, in sports, and in community programs. Lincoln, as his words and actions illustrate, is clearly one for students such as Derek. But it is not only his striking appearance and his energy toward his work that capture attention. It is who he is and what he does—his interpersonal interactions, character, and professional demeanor leave a strong impression. Later on, I learn that he is pursuing his master's degree in music, but it is his personality that has a more lasting effect than all his professional accomplishments. As a coach, he nourishes, prods, and teaches children such as Derek to believe and to achieve, giving them a sense of belonging and purpose within their community of practice.

School after 3:00?

Especially for low-income children, the widening achievement gap has brought on simultaneous efforts to use out-of-school time to improve and complement students' academic achievements. These efforts reflect the growing recognition that extra time spent in learning may be essential for poor children to progress effectively.

Setting out to provide reliable data on what America's parents and young people want for kids during after-school hours, for example, a study commissioned by the Wallace Foundation and Public Agenda[19] recently surveyed over 1,000 parents of school-aged children. Providing a wealth of information, it described the very real challenges faced by all families, especially poor families, when it comes to finding productive things for their children to do when they aren't in school. Findings revealed an all-too-typical picture of haves and have-nots. Too many families feel that their children are not getting the kinds of after-school opportunities that could genuinely help them thrive. Over 46% of low-income parents, for example, said they worry that their children "hanging out with the wrong crowd" might lead them astray.

This survey also uncovered an important finding—often missed in the debate over the content of after-school programming. By extremely wide margins, parents at or near the poverty line, given a choice, prefer after-school programs that emphasize academic learning to improve achievement and sharpen their children's competitive edge. They look to after-school programs to be not just havens but extensions of school offering their children more education. Recognizing the enormous gap in school achievement, parents worry about their children falling behind (60%) and not getting the help they need (67%); they also worry about their children needing a better match that would focus on "providing extra academic preparation and skills" rather than sports or the arts (56%).

These statistics lead to an important proposition: no one size fits all. The burgeoning field of after-school programs reflects a diversity of programs, sensitive to the fact that different children and their families want different things. Yet for children who attend highly dysfunctional schools—schools in such disarray that districts are subject to state takeover—such extra efforts to boost children's achievement in after-school programs may be the last stop before giving up.

A visit to Adventure Island—an after-school program developed by Robert Slavin and Nancy Madden, professors at Johns Hopkins University and creators of Success for All, a comprehensive school reform program practiced in hundreds of schools across the country—could be the poster-child for what some might call the academic approach. Targeted to especially needy kids with reading problems, it is a highly teacher-directed program, now implemented in about 100 places across the country. It may not be to everyone's liking in the after-school community who prefer its nonacademic flavor; nonetheless, the program and approach are beginning to show some stunning effects.

Whitehall Elementary and Norristown High are located on a winding road outside the borough of Norristown, Pennsylvania. Across the street from these institutions is vast farmland, which belongs to Norristown State Hospital; it is a massive sprawl of creepy gothic-style buildings housing severely mentally ill patients. The schools, even though modern and comfortable, are part of a troubled school system for a changing population of immigrant and lower-income families. Although the schools sit on a fairly deserted road outside of town, nearly all the students are bussed from the center of the borough, a crime-riddled area of shabby row houses.

Children are streaming from the building when we arrive at 3:30 p.m., while another mass is streaming into the auditorium, readying up for the after-school program. Unlike the other programs I've seen, the after-school routine is planned to the minute, following a precise order each afternoon: 3:30, snack; 3:40, lesson begins; 4:25, lesson ends; second round for some who stay; 4:30, teachers plan or meet with reading coach until 6:00.

Adventure Land—the name, at least—is a bit of a misnomer. The adventure in this case is related to improving reading achievement. Alfie's Lagoon, Captain's Cove, Discovery Bay, and Treasure Harbor stand for groups with different reading abilities, starting with beginners and moving up to those who can read more independently. The program is staffed by master teachers, each with about 10 years of experience.

As we enter Miss Sherri's class, two groups are together, preparing boxes of trinkets. These trinkets serve as prizes for attendance, cooperating with teachers, good behavior, and reaching goals. When children finish all their work, they get prizes from the cart, which, from all indications, keeps the regular attendance up around the 80–90% level.

After the prize-picking, the other class leaves, and the next group of seven children settle around a table with Sherri. All of the children are in second grade and reading significantly below grade level. The children are working in a workbook as Sherri sits at the head of the table with the teacher's book in front of her.

Sherri: Look at the word. What word is that? Let's sound it out.
Jose: aw-aw-f-f-f—awful?
Sheri: Yes, awful, What does that mean?
Jose: Not so good—right?

Sherri then picks up a stack of cards. They review the "ur," "oy," "ai," and "ea" sounds, adding today the "ow" sound. Throughout the presentation, Sherri moves quite rapidly. The children are quiet and attentive, with the exception of Jose, who tends to squirm a bit without being disruptive. When his attention starts to drift, Sherri quickly reminds him to look at his book. She also awards the other three for their good behavior. "Celine, give your team a point," she'll say as Celine sits quietly. By the end of the session, Celine, Taylor, and Shane rack up a bunch of points, while Jose has accumulated little but reprimands.

Like its elder, Success for All, Adventure Island is a tightly woven, fast-paced, program that suggests there is not a moment to lose. Children spend 45 minutes each afternoon reading in small groups; they often read aloud in unison to reinforce the sounds of words, with teachers following a highly detailed script that tells them what to say and when. Whenever they hear their teacher give the signal that says "Point, ready, read!" the children chant phrases from their storybooks in response. They read silently. They read aloud. They pair up to critique each other's reading, with an emphasis on phonics and cooperative learning. And the teachers, sometimes with kitchen timers in hand, remind students that there is still more to do.

We walk around to "Discovery Bay" and find a group of 11 children reading *The Zack Files*. Carolyn, one of the teachers, says, "OK, make sure to ask your partner some Q&A questions."

At one table, Zoe is sitting with Manuel. "What did the kids in the book say?" Zoe asks.

Mumbling to himself as he reads, Manuel tries to find the answer. "Um . . . oh!" He said, "I'm so sorry."

"Now it's your turn [to ask a question]," says Zoe. Manuel hesitates a little and then asks, "What color is the charm?"

Zoe, obviously irritated, answers, "Hey, that's not a thinking question! It's gotta be something like 'How did you know' something . . ." Before Manuel can come up with a question, Carolyn ends the session as Zoe protests, "Oh, come on! It was just getting good!"

Cooperative learning, by actively engaging children in problem-solving tasks, plays a major role in the program that is based on Slavin's extensive research.[20] Children work on "think, pair, share" activities, all within a consistent framework that emphasizes reading, retelling, along with frequent testing. Teachers monitor the students closely, and work with small groups. Samantha, a third grader, says, "You have teachers here who help you with your work. And they make it fun and exciting—we're not sitting around bored."

For students needing a bit more help, developers have created additional materials in the form of a computer-assisted program that gets children to apply their newfound reading strategies. We watch children react to Alfie, who, like a beginning reader, pops on the screen to offer some reading pointers. At one point, he says, "We need more cl-cl-cl. . . . Oh, I don't know what that word says. This is tough—I need a strategy to figure it out." Jose, getting into the game and playing along, yells out, "Alfie, how about read and think?" His friend Sherri looks on. "OK, Alfie, sound it out!"

And yet, despite Adventure Land's success in helping very needy children learn to read, it is embroiled in controversy, much like Slavin's other program, Success for All. Some veteran educators bristle with anger over the "academic focus," claiming that the scripted lessons, emphasis on phonics, and testing seem in conflict with the vision and the mission of after-school programs. Nevertheless, for children who have significant reading problems, as Jose has, Slavin and his colleagues have shown that intervention efforts can scale up and remain true to the integrity and quality of the program. Students in this school from the first to the fourth quarter have gained, on average, over 10% more than the district as a whole on their benchmark assessment, which is correlated with their state assessment.[21] Over 51 separate studies[22] tell the story, painting a solid portrait of the program's achievement.

Children in early elementary school are painfully aware that learning to read, spell, write, and do arithmetic is their number-one mission. Failure to do these things well places them on a precipice of low achievement, eroding whatever self-confidence they may have started with in school. Poor readers may stop even trying to learn the things that are valued in school, turning into a downward spiral known as the Matthew Effect. In the absence of rigorous intervention, hostility, truancy, and misbehavior are likely to become chronic and serious as children conclude that the future holds so little promise that it is simply not worth their effort.

Programs such as Adventure Land provide an important choice for children who need additional support for acquiring basic literacy skills. Seriously behind in their reading, children receive intensive support from highly trained teachers, and, from all indications—especially considering they had already spent six hours in school—all were engaged, attentive, and learning the skills needed to be successful in reading.

We saw no evidence of "drill, skill, and kill" activities in our visits to Adventure Island. Although mirroring "school" activities more than other programs, it reminded us of a learning camp, with children casually interacting with adults, using first names and snacking along while engaged in their activities.

Kelley Harmer, the director of the after-school programs, points to significant academic strides as the best evidence for continuing the program: "80% of our students who came in with 'unsatisfactory' and attended 30 days or more are doing better on their report cards." Partly he attributes these differences to changes in better attitudes toward school. "The students develop a relationship with teachers as real people as they work with them in smaller groups. And the teachers get to see students in a different light," he says. Jose, a second grader, probably says it best, "They help me to read the books; they make me proud."

As a robust, distinctively different institution, effective after-school programs support not just one but many models to meet student needs. Although most young children, according to Public Agenda's report, do not want additional academic work after school, there are a surprisingly large number of students who do. Programs such as Adventure Land meet this need, recognizing that closing the achievement gap has to be a joint responsibility. As Kelley Harmer noted, "I don't think that anybody can do it alone."

The Impact of After-School Programs

When the public-elected officials and child advocates focus on the risks and opportunities inherent in after-school hours, discussions invariably focus on the potential benefits they might offer. Are such expenditures a wise investment? What do they achieve? Do they expand academic enrichment opportunities? As the concept of after-school programs continue to evolve, much of the knowledge base and empirical foundations of the field is based on professional experience. Central to this perspective is the firm belief that after-school programs are clearly beneficial for many children, especially in contrast to the risks associated with self care. In this context, a broad patchwork of out-of-school programs with a wide variety of service providers have proliferated; they are guided by a clear conviction that their efforts benefit student development.

The evaluation of these after-school programs on students' developmental outcomes, however, has proven to be a complex task. The growing diversity of programs and the heterogeneity of purposes and goals intensify this complexity. For more than a decade, researchers and service providers have struggled with both the identification of significant and appropriate outcomes and their valid and reliable measurement. Superimposed on this formidable challenge, the high-stakes assessment of competence in children who are adapting to a wide variety of biological vulnerabilities and environmental challenges remains one of the more complex issues facing the after-school education field.

The evaluation literature, which has increased considerably over the last 10 years, as a result, has been vast and diverse in focus, highly variable in its methodological rigor, and often inconsistent in the particular outcomes it examines. Debate has been lively in both the academic and policy circles about the way to measure the effects on the elusive constructs of social and emotional behaviors and middle-childhood development. The debate centers on the general challenges inherent in developmental assessment in these middle-school years, and on what may constitute the most appropriate targeted outcomes—such as grades, dropouts, and emotional adjustment.

Nevertheless, a convergence of research on the impact of programs on students' social and emotional adjustment,[23] although varied in the different outcomes measured, is remarkably robust. There is a clear pattern in the effects of after-school programs on children's adjustment, both short-term and over time.[24]

The Ecological Study of After-School Care,[25] for example, showed that third graders who spent more time than their peers in enrichment activities were better behaved in school and had better relationships with their peers; they were also better adjusted emotionally. Following students from third through fifth grades, researchers found longitudinal benefits: children who spent more time in enrichment activities showed better emotional adjustment in fifth grade. The most striking impact, however, was on poor children and those with biological vulnerabilities: evidence for the beneficial effects of after-school programs was strongest for children in urban, high-crime neighborhoods.

Similarly, studies[26] on social and emotional development demonstrate that programs

- Help children develop social skills by providing opportunities to interact with more diverse groups.
- Show positive effects on students' level of effort, increased sense of belonging in school.
- Demonstrate striking decreases in deviant behavior such as gang-related activity, alcohol, and substance abuse.

On the other hand, evidence for the benefits of after-school programs on academic achievement has been far less definitive and far more contentious. There is some evidence to suggest that low-income children may be making targeted gains. For example, a meta-analysis by Mid-Continent Research for Education and Learning (McREL) of 56 out-of-school-time program studies[27] (i.e., after-school, weekend, and summer programs) revealed small positive effects on student achievement in both reading and math. Similarly, a study by the University of California at Irvine and Research Report Services found that students in the YS-Care program[28] (aimed specially at children from families on welfare in Los Angeles) had higher reading and math gains on the Stanford-9 test than did children who were not participating in the program. In addition, the second year of an evaluation of the TASC program[29] found small but significant differences among participants and nonparticipants in the lowest math-proficiency level.

Conversely, other large-scale program evaluations, such as the 21st study by Mathematica Policy Research, Inc.,[30] have not demonstrated any statistically significant impacts on test scores. Some suggest that the study was seriously flawed. In fact, Mathematica acknowledged in its report that 3 out of 10 programs were not designed to measure achievement. Others suggest that the outcome measures may be among the least of its problems.

In fact, evaluation theorists might say that these designers, as well as some others in the field, have often ignored the logic and complexities of after-school programs as a unique and distinctive learning institution. Evaluation planners have often lacked a conceptualization of how their activities and efforts are expected to connect to outcomes for program participants and the communities in which the programs are implemented. Some evaluators have closely modeled their designs on laboratory social science research rather than facing the difficulties inherent to community settings, not understanding how a program's effectiveness may depend on community participation. Furthermore, some evaluators have appeared to take on the role of adversaries of the program, requiring nothing less than absolute assurance of statistical improvements in student achievement.

All of this debate suggests there is a pressing need to construct evaluation designs aimed at better understanding the effects of intervention and its abilities to influence developmental outcomes. At present, evidence is, at best, haphazardly translated into design and evaluation of initiatives. In addition, those who study interventions lack systematic opportunities to feed their insights and questions back into improvements for program designs.

There are some pioneers whose experiences can pave the way for greater efforts in the future. Psychologist and after-school specialist Deborah Vandell and her research team,[31] for example, are systematically gathering information on program features that appear to enhance students' academic, social, and emotional development, and testing the hypothesis that disadvantaged youth between the ages of 8 and 14 who participate in these after-school programs will achieve great development and learning gains over a two-year period. In essence, the approach attempts to focus on promising after-school programs rather than on a random or representative sample in order to assess the potential for programs to exert positive effects on youth development. Similarly, the After-School Corporation[32] has examined shared features of high-performing after-school programs that may help to further enhance quality through extensive training and technical assistance.

Evaluations that build on promising practices may be especially useful for an emerging learning institution, such as the after-school programs, for several reasons. Taking into account program diversity, evaluations provide a basic framework for examining program quality. They build on examples of programs where kids are safe, engaged, and attending consistently. They use multiple forms of evidence to determine the nature and magnitude of expected effects. And finally, they recognize that any evaluation of after-school programs must be based on the entire range of potential benefits to children—their social, emotional, and cognitive growth—as well as to their families and their communities.

The Promise of After-School Programs

For many children, the years between 6 and 14 are exciting times of positive group development; for some, however, they are a time of frustration, alienation, declining motivation, and decreasing involvement with schools. After-school programs may serve a valuable role in buffering children against some of these harsh realities. Offering a rich array of activity with highly qualified staff, they support a different type of learning, one based in practical activity involving young people in opportunities to interact with mixed age groups of children and to feel like valued members of their community.

As an emerging institution of learning, after-school programs are continuing to evolve; their future vitality will be served by a creative blend of critical self-evaluation and openness to fresh thinking from evidence of best practices. The developing nature and imprecise measurement of outcomes in these programs, however, have underscored the critical need for more descriptive, exploratory, and formative investigations that measure not only outcomes but conditions—to understand their effects. In this respect, subjecting programs to randomized controlled trials, the gold standard of research methodology at this stage of its development, might bring more harm than good.

Despite the methodological challenges of the existing scientific base and the marked diversity of disciplinary perspectives and program models that are represented in the research literature, the seven essential features clearly emerge across a broad spectrum of after-school programs. These are represented in both well documented empirical findings and state-of-the art guidelines based on professional consensus.

Again, they target children who need help the most. Quality after-school programs are especially powerful for children from low-income families in high-crime neighborhoods. In fact, Deborah Vandell, in a synthesis of studies,[33] found that targeted programs provided greater gains for children in low-income families than for children in suburban neighborhoods and middle-class families. Low-income children who attended programs had fewer behavioral problems and higher social competence. She attributes these finding to the problem of self-care for children in poor and dangerous surroundings.

A variety of small-scale studies point to the second essential element: the importance of beginning early. Enrolling children in the early years, particularly through grade 3, boosts attendance and reduces behavioral problems during the school day; it also improves academic performance in class and on standardized tests. Surveys conducted for the After-School Corporation, for example, found that younger children in the programs were more likely to finish homework, read, use computers, and feel comfortable solving math problems, and their parents report being able to work full-time while also developing closer relationships with their children's schools. Similarly, Vandell found that beginning early in children's schooling helps create a pattern of attendance that is reinforced through developing friendships with fellow students and connections with staff. Enrollment in after-school programs in her studies has been at its highest in the kindergarten years, suggesting that the needs of parents are especially acute in the early years.

Promising programs tend to attract and retain children's participation by offering a comprehensive array of activities, the third essential factor. Such programs keep children busy with experiential learning, athletics, arts, and academic support, all of which help to enhance, not replicate, the school day. The activities run the gamut, from playing games such as Double Dutch to homework help to "grossology," kitchen chemistry programs that explore topics of insects and endangered animals. For students whose development may be compromised by unsupportive environments, programs that are tailored to their needs have been shown to be most effective in producing desired outcomes. Witness Chicago after-school programs, where youngsters with low test scores—about 237,000 of them—have seen their test scores rise considerably. Similarly, in an after-school program in the Cabrini Green housing project, the portion of students who met national average scores jumped to 21% from 14% in reading, and to 29% from 15% in math.

Programs that support a more intensive approach, the fourth essential feature, are more effective. Intensity involves a greater "dosage" of treatment. Supporting a more intensive model, advocacy groups have recommended a student–staff ratio of 10 to 1. When a smaller children-per-adult ratio exists, evaluations indicate that children receive more individual attention and establish closer relationships with peers and other staff members, who are sensitive to their needs. Children spend less time waiting and more time doing. At P.S. 163, where children cook sophisticated meals or stage mock trials after apprenticeships with volunteer chefs and lawyers, the small groups seemed to boost involvement. Says Kim Baranowski, the director of the program, "The students develop a relationship with teachers who get to work with them in smaller groups. And these teachers get to see students who sometimes have pretty bad behavior problems in school in a totally different light."

Intensity is also reflected in more regular attendance in programs. Students who attend once or twice a week are likely to be less invested than those who attend regularly. In most Mathematica evaluations, programs with poor attendance had little effect.

The nature of performance-based activity is itself intensive. Instruction is embedded in action, with instant feedback, correctives, and information. Watching children get ready for a dance performance was a study of intensity. Lincoln, with his coach-like actions, drills, and practices, urged children to increase their accuracy of movement, wanting things to become automatic through repetition. Practices were nonstop, electric, supercharged, and demanding, requiring children to think and act. Although varying dramatically in its focus, Adventure Land, with its call-and-instant-response strategies and small groups, also provided an intensity of instruction that children rarely experience in school learning.

A substantial body of research[34] clearly links staff qualifications, the fifth essential element, to better after-school attendance and outcomes, particularly for low-income children who are at risk for later educational underachievement. Effective teachers in after-school programs often lack formal educational credentials; nevertheless, they have something more important: credibility in the community. These teachers create supportive, challenging learning environments and help push children to achieve beyond their expectations, encouraging them to persevere and praising their accomplishments. They often act like a hard-nosed coach—demanding, tough, and influential in students' lives.

Programs that compensate for limitations in family resources or opportunities are more successful than others. These programs combine security and comfort with expanding leadership opportunities, recognizing students' needs to be competent and independent. For instance, jazz sessions and rap groups give children and early adolescents a chance to discuss issues that concern them while allowing significant adults into their lives. These programs are about building social capital that celebrates children's cultures, respects their interests, validates their voices, and affirms work and cooperative teamwork, demonstrating the relevance of learning to the dynamics of everyday life.

But there is also scant evidence supporting a one-size-fits-all model of after-school programs. After-school programs that provide homework assistance to compensate for students' lack of reading and writing skills have an important place in the rich array of program offerings. LeAp, the after-school program at P.S. 163, for example, combines a wide variety of activities, along with tutoring programs for students at risk. These programs recognize that instruction targeted to students' skill needs is critically important for self-esteem and feelings of competence and connection.

Finally, promising programs employ a variety of accountability mechanisms, the seventh essential feature, to address a more focused set of questions. Some programs use progress-monitoring strategies to refine their program. For example, what can be learned about improving attendance and retention in programs? What can be learned about thresholds of program intensity that are necessary for measurable impact? What is required to sustain positive change, both in terms of processes that must be set in motion and ongoing services that must be continued? What are the major barriers and constraints that limit the possibilities for positive change? Other programs tie their work specifically to benchmarks and state standards, as in California. Still others, such as TASC, align their programs to outcomes on grade-level state assessments. Though varied in their mechanism, all successful programs are accountable for student achievement gains.

Future research will undoubtedly provide answers to these and other compelling questions. Recognizing that after-school programs are complicated efforts that require constant mid-course corrections, accountability mechanisms drawing on larger bodies of evidence and more comprehensive measures of outcomes will need to be developed. By doing so, we can combine what we know about the theory of learning, experiences, and previous research to identify not only what works, but why it works to improve children's development during these crucial middle-childhood years.

No longer on the periphery of educational reform, after-school programs have the potential to keep the faucet flowing during a pivotal period of development for thousands of children. Although policy makers have focused on the school as the critical arena for remedying inequity in achievement, after-school programs offer alternative educational environments in which children can learn about themselves and their worlds and can discover opportunities for carving their own versions of success. Recognition of the power to make a difference in the lives of students is particularly important for changing the odds at a time when feelings of competence and personal self-esteem are forming and achievement trajectories are being determined. The stake for children's futures could not be higher.

CHAPTER 8

THE PUBLIC WILL: WHAT IT WILL TAKE TO CHANGE THE ODDS

Americans care about their children. They place a high priority on education, and as a people, believe in equality of educational opportunity. Most agree that poor children should not have to suffer the consequences of their family's economic circumstances—that all children should be *entitled* to a high-quality education and what its opportunities afford. But Americans are seriously conflicted about how to achieve these goals. Traditionally, liberals have recommended bootstraps to help the disadvantaged by giving more of everything—more services, more funding, and more government. Conservatives on the other hand, have recommended less—less federal interference, less red tape, and less funding.

The truth is that neither of these strategies has worked to break the cycle of disadvantage for poor families and their children. Today the gap between rich and poor children's achievement remains as large as it was when we first began tracking children's progress in the early seventies. And this gap represents a formidable reminder that despite our many efforts, a fair and equitable education is still outside the reach of millions of vulnerable children.

The fact that we have not made much progress in thinking about how to address the needs of poor children, despite spending billions trying to figure out how to, should provide the impetus for change. Per-pupil spending has risen by 240% in the last three decades, after correcting for inflation, but achievement scores for students have remained virtually flat.

Adding to a sense of urgency is our progress in international comparisons of achievement. Once the world's leader in educational attainment, the United States today has the dubious honor of leading all developed world countries in the proportion of students who drop out of high school. In fact, the Programme for International Student Assessment (PISA) and the Progress in

International Reading Literacy Survey (PIRLS), the two most widely respected comparative measures of achievement, now place the United States in 2006 anywhere from the middle to the bottom of the international rankings.[1] Unless we can improve the educational prospects of our young, particularly those who are poor and in minority groups, our place in the global economy and the strength of a democracy based on informed, participating citizens will be seriously threatened.

We now have a sound evidentiary base in the sciences to halt this pattern and to reduce the tremendous disparities in children's achievement and life chances. There now exist interventions that can help repair early damage—whether caused by prenatal injuries, poor health, or poor environment. By capitalizing on the knowledge gained from nearly half a century of considerable public investment, we can improve children's outcomes and change the odds that they will live productive lives.

To do so will require a new way of doing business, however—one based on evidence of what works. Illustrated in previous chapters across the broad spectrum of interventions, there are seven essential principles at work. These principles highlight the critical importance of targeting, and of beginning early. They emphasize the importance of coordinating services, particularly for children from families who bear the burden of multiple risks. They focus on boosting children's outcomes through compensatory high-quality instruction delivered by trained professionals, not by aides or volunteers. They show that intensity matters, and that any dilution of program quality has been a waste of money, having a disastrous and demoralizing influence on the public. Their watchword is accountability—both to themselves, their programs, and the public.

As this orientation takes hold and becomes the norm, not the exception, we will demystify the funding of programs, encourage greater citizen monitoring of progress, and create greater demands for information about program effectiveness. But most important of all, by funding what works, we will win back the public's confidence in the belief that well-designed, well-implemented programs can powerfully affect the developmental trajectories of children whose life course has been threatened by economic disadvantage and family disruption.

From Principles to Action

We can no longer defend an indefensible system that robs children of real opportunities to learn. We need to move from principles to action. Minor tweaking of existing programs won't do it. Reorienting policy so that it is about today's goals rather than yesterday's paradigms will require no small amount of vigilance and determination.

But the good news is that the search for better solutions is gaining momentum. Cities and states with support from private foundations are taking unprecedented steps to strengthen services for disadvantaged children and their families. Coalitions for funding what works through best practices are working to change the way educational services are financed, organized, and delivered. Added federal funding streams for research specially targeted to interventions that work are providing new knowledge of what works. There is an extraordinary convergence of increased awareness that something must be done to reverse the growing polarization between the haves and the have-nots.

By mobilizing this tremendous surge of talent, energy, and supports, we can move from principles to actions. At the top of my list are six key priorities.

1. Let's Admit That Schools Can't Do It Alone

There's an old time-worn story called the "drunkard's paradox": in the wee hours of the morning, a very inebriated drunk is on his hands and knees looking for his keys under a lamp post. Confronted by an Irish cop who asks, "Hey, buddy, what are you doing crawling under the light-post?" the drunk quickly replies, "I lost my keys over there in the bushes." With a tone of disbelief, the cop asks, "Why the hell are you looking for them here under the light-post?" "That's where the light is," the drunk unhesitatingly replies.

As a nation, we've been looking under the lamp-post—school reform and No Child Left Behind—as the answer to closing the achievement gap. But the search for the "educational reform" is actually over in the bushes.

It's in the early years, *before* children ever begin their schooling. We know of the rapid progress that children make in language and cognition in the first five years of life. They learn to think for themselves, to reason, and to bond and interact with adults and other children. They learn to wonder, to question, and to imagine beyond the here-and-now. Subsequent learning will depend on these foundational capacities, which will become the building blocks for successful achievement in school.

Our many dedicated teachers can help disadvantaged children significantly. But they can't begin to unravel the complicated and profound problems that children trapped in poverty may bring to the schoolhouse doors. Historically, schools were designed to educate students already provided by their families with the essential building blocks of learning and of motivation to succeed in school. Contrary to what you might hear from the Bush administration, most teachers are highly capable of successfully educating these children. Today, however, schools are being asked to take on an added burden that is beyond any one institution: educating children whose families are in tremendous disarray, ill health, and turmoil.

Placing too many responsibilities, and making too many extraordinary demands on school as the sole institution of hope, only derails it from its mission of teaching. Rather, schools must be part of the solution—but not the only solution. Other institutions, integrally tied with strengthening early care and education, families, neighborhoods and communities, are important agents of change and must be a part of any equation for improving the lives of disadvantaged children.

2. Redress Our Current Inherently Flawed Federal Funding Strategies

If we are serious about changing the odds, we need to reconsider our current federal funding strategies for disadvantaged children. Title I of the Elementary and Secondary Act, the cornerstone of federal aid for disadvantaged children and our largest funded program, for example, is based on "leveling the playing field" by helping districts provide services for children, ages birth through grade 12, that might otherwise be unaffordable because of the low property tax base in poor areas. The complex funding mechanisms are based on a formula of comparability that attempts to equalize the amount of funding across services in programs so that all children have equal access to a quality education.

Over the years, policymakers have attempted to adjust the formula to ensure that school districts provide these services to poor children. But despite all these efforts, it turns out that the formula is not the central problem. It's the premise that underlies it. Leveling the playing field policies, as they are often described, do not close the achievement gap. In fact, policies that provide equal resources to all children are likely to increase, not decrease, the achievement gap.

Here's why. As we have noted, there are significant knowledge and skills disparities between children who come from enriching environments and those who do not. These differentials are serious and, unfortunately, do not easily close. Instead, they grow as a result of the differences in the amount, rate, and speed of gathering information. Children who come from knowledge-enriching home environments are better prepared to begin reading, acquire skills easier, read more, engage more in conversations, and better use information for fulfilling specific purposes and needs. Unfortunately, the opposite is also true. Children who lag in skills are likely to take longer to learn them in school and read and learn less; over time, the knowledge gap actually accelerates between the rich and poor.

The 1965 debut of *Sesame Street*, designed specifically to narrow knowledge disparities during the War on Poverty, provides an illustrative example.[2] The first- and second-year evaluations of the program showed evidence of actually increasing knowledge differences, helping those children who were somewhat prepared for formal reading instruction do better than ever before; those who were less ready benefited far less. As a result of the program, studies found larger gaps in skills by kindergarten for middle- and lower-income children than before.

Here's another example. In a flourish of great media attention, Nicholas Negroponte announced his initiative of "One Laptop Per Child." The mission is to provide a $100 computer to nearly two billion children in the developing world with little to no access to education. Just imagine, he writes, "the potential that could be unlocked by giving every child in the world the tools they need to learn, no matter who they are, nor matter where they live, no matter how little they may have." Although the potential is laudable, three-and-a-half-years later there is no evidence that knowledge differentials have changed whatsoever. Students with little knowledge use computers as playthings; students who can read, write, and problem-solve use them to gain greater knowledge.

Our six-year study of technology uses in neighborhood public libraries confirms this unfortunate thesis:[3] rather than closing the gap between low- and middle-income communities, technology actually exacerbates the gap. Poor children use computers to watch movies and cartoons, reading less and attending less; middle-income children read more, and more frequently. After more than $20 million was spent to equalize resources, middle-income children were reading approximately three times as much content as poor children. In fact, 58 studies since 1983 have demonstrated the flaws in policies attempting to "level the playing field" in areas ranging from health and education to welfare.[4]

Providing equal resources to unequal groups will never close the achievement gap. Instead, funding formulas must go beyond mere comparability to provide substantial funds in addition to leveling the playing field. As an emergency response system, Title I funds—at more than $13 billion dollars per year, the single largest federal educational support program—were intended for these purposes. Still, we find throughout the country that programs designed to supplement, not supplant, services to the most needy children have been needlessly diluted to many programs (90% of all schools currently receive funds). We need to redirect these funds to provide additional resources for the children for whom they were intended.

3. Monitor Programs Relentlessly

The time is long overdue for federal and state agencies to take bold actions to design and implement effective monitoring techniques to ensure high-quality programs for children. More than process measures, program indicators must focus on results—a set of indicators reflecting expected outcomes. On one hand, it will help program designers to establish clear, well-defined goals and to determine whether or not their intended outcomes are being met. On the other, it will help program monitors to document interventions and to put in place a full set of provisions that will help to improve programs.

For example, a common feature of federal funding to states and districts is a requirement that they use funds to *augment*, not replace, monies they would have used if federal funds were not available. This requirement, known as "supplement, not supplant," has always been part of the Elementary and Secondary Education Act, and it appears in No Child Left Behind over thirty different places. Fundamentally, what this means for intervention is that children should be provided "supplemental" instruction in addition what they would normally have.

But in a now-classic article, "If they don't read much, how they ever gonna get good?", Dick Allington, professor at the University of Tennessee, found that additional instruction for poor kids may be the exception, not the norm. Rather, his observations of 21 classrooms found that what they often got was instruction provided in hallways, unused bathrooms, and gymnasiums by untrained aides. They actually received less instruction, according to the amount of "time-on-task," than those better off.[5]

Better monitoring for outcomes is essential. Results-based accountability requires immediate feedback to programs, not feedback six months or a year later. If we are serious in our concern about the very real consequences for children who are in programs that are not meeting expectations, then we must able to make adjustments right away. If necessary, we also need to be prepared to shut programs down when they fail to produce solid results.

High-quality program monitoring is not a metaphor for paperwork, or tying up programs needlessly in procedures or red-tape. Good monitoring does not micromanage. Instead, it focuses on results and leaves the details of program implementation to the agency or district. In this respect, it adheres to the basic premise of local control, understanding that the local community has greater knowledge and a greater stake in seeking better outcomes.

Mediocre programs that promise little and deliver less have proliferated in social services and education. Unfortunately, they have perpetuated a view that children, not their circumstances, are the problem. Knowing that high-quality programs make a difference, we must advocate and monitor progress to make sure that our most disadvantaged children receive the very highest–quality services. In the long run, the returns will be greater for our citizenry at large.

4. Make Government Programs and Policies More Transparent

Even the most active advocates for poor children struggle with untangling the complex web of policy. Programs change regulations, guidance redirects funding to different constituencies, and, more often than not, the average citizen believes that policy is something conducted under a veil of secrecy that none but the most informed advocacy community and lobbying groups understand. This has led many good citizens to believe that policy is something imposed on them rather than something that they might contribute to and better understand.

If we are to change the odds, we need to make policies more transparent, and we need to evaluate their effectiveness. As I mentioned in Chapter 2, one innovative strategy recently taken on by the Office of Management and Budget is the Program Assessment Rating Tool (PART). Officials use the PART to assess whether a program is well designed, whether resources are sufficient and well-managed, and whether the results are reported timely and with great accuracy. This approach has the potential to hold every federal program to a high standard of effectiveness. Rather than brand loyalty, it begins to tie programs to tangible results and to effective outcomes for families and children.

Businesses and consortia in states are also moving toward more transparent practices. Community leaders in Los Angeles, for example, have developed a report card that assesses children's school readiness skills and identifies groups that are at greatest risk. The report provides a state-of-the-art assessment on the quality of children's literacy environment at home, such as the average exposure to books and the amount of time parents read to their children, among other critical factors. This approach holds everybody accountable—parents as well as community programs for children's successful entry into schools.

KIDS COUNT, a national and state-by-state database, tracks the status of child well-being throughout the United States and provides another critical service for benchmarking progress. Using 10 key indicators, it shows the percentage of children in high risk categories, providing evidence from a nonpartisan source on the educational, health, and economic conditions of children in each state and in the nation. Such transparency not only helps highlight our challenges but also demonstrates our real gains to a public that has often grown skeptical of governmental solutions. It also has the potential to galvanize the community in support of prevention and early intervention programs.

Consolidating much of this work, the Editorial Projects in Education Research Center has developed an innovative "Chance-for-Success" Index. The index combines information from 13 different indicators that span an individual's life from cradle to career. Several indicators capture family support, early child education, and adult educational attainment—critical components of the social and economic fabric of the nation and its states. States significantly outpacing the national average receive a point, with the results given state by state. So far, scores for Virginia are the highest in the nation, revealing that chances for a successful adulthood are heavily dependent on the educational environment in which a person lives.

5. Repair the Fractured Bureaucracy in Federally Funded Early Care and Education Programs

We need to consolidate and streamline policies and programs aimed at improving the life chances of young children in poverty. Today's efforts to address the needs of high poverty children have been thwarted by silos of governmental bureaucracy that waste precious resources and prevent responsive, integrative systems of health, education and social services from working jointly to benefit children. For example, current programs in early care and education cut across at least seven different major agencies, all with different regulations and requirements, to create an unwieldy bureaucracy that often hinders our capacity to work with multi-risk families.

Children whose future prospects are threatened by socioeconomic disadvantage, family disruption, and unsafe neighborhoods will need comprehensive services that break down these traditional categorical barriers of education, health, nutrition, family support programs. In 2002, a joint task force was created by then-Secretary Rod Paige, charged with reviewing the entire portfolio of funding streams in child care and early education. Small steps were taken to define the problem, to identify public investments in early childhood, and to establish a set of priorities that would lead to improved child outcomes. Efforts such as these need to be supported in subsequent administrations.

Subsequently known as "Good Start; Grow Smart," this initiative, although important, did not tackle the integrative nature of quality interventions and how to use funding streams to support them. Currently, agencies have to cobble together programs that seriously constrain program implementation.

The scientific knowledge base guiding early childhood programs and policies demands collaboration among mental health specialists, nutritionists, developmentalists, and educators. Block grants could help eliminate fragmentation and cumbersome bureaucracy. Unlike in small categorical grant programs, recipients of block grants (normally states) have substantial authority over the type of activities to support, with minimal federal administrative restrictions or intrusion. The basic premise is that states should be free to target resources and design administrative mechanisms to provide better services. Given that states have different resources in place, block grants would give them discretion to use the funds where they are needed the most—all to improve children's outcomes.

6. Revolutionize Our Evaluation Strategies to Better Match the Oft-Complex, Multi-Dimensional Nature of Early Intervention Programs and Community-Based Initiatives

If we are to fund what works, we need research and evaluation strategies that more effectively examine the multiple dimensions of interventions programs. Too often evaluation designs have short-changed programs, failing to measure some certain factors or potentially diminishing effects by using nonvalid measurement techniques. Many problems arise, but among the most important are (1) measuring effects before the program has gotten sufficiently underway, (2) poor fit between program objectives and strategies and the measures used to assess them, and (3) inconsistent levels of implementation—all of which may serve to undermine or undervalue highly effective program features.

Furthermore, the persistent use of IQ scores in the policy arena, when these types of measures have been shown to be highly insensitive to behaviorally meaningful impacts of programs, has been one of the contributing factors to the so-called "fade-out" phenomenon. IQ tests were never designed to measure achievement. In the absence of dedicated attention to evaluation measures and designs that offer a richer array of assessment options, multiple opportunities for detecting important and consequential intervention effects will continue to be missed.

There is an urgent need for the development of empirical, rigorous research designs that better capture multifaceted interventions. Several challenges are central to this work. First, we need to develop, adapt, and refine instruments with greater sensitivity to developmental changes in children's social, emotional, and cognitive growth. Second, we need to continue to examine differential

effects of key program features that can then be applied to other effective pro
grams. Third, evaluation designers must recognize that adaptations are often the
norm in field-based research. These adaptations can be examined and used to
better understand the conditions under which programs are successful. Fourth,
it is imperative that multiple methods be used to substantiate and describe how
programs might affect different families and constituencies. Finally, there is a
compelling need to use evaluation techniques to draw explicit linkages between
the theory of action guiding the program and the assessment of program effects
in order to understand the mechanisms involved in successful change efforts.

Accept No Excuses

Taking action inevitably comes down to financing. Traditionally, there are those
who question, "Can we afford to change the odds?", claiming that reform for our
most at-risk children is outside the reach of current funding—that it's far too
expensive and too politically untenable to undertake. But the truth is there really
are no excuses. Claims of limited funding ring hollow when we survey what is
possible with better implementation of policy. Rather, the real question should
be, "Can we afford not to change the odds?", knowing that the cost of low
achievement and the loss of income from lack of productivity take a tremendous
toll on our society.

Some people and programs have adopted a "no excuses" approach for improving low-income children's chances for better achievement and school success.
The visionary Governor Jim Hunt, for example, refused to take 'no' for an
answer when confronted with evidence of the extraordinary needs of families and
children in North Carolina. Recognizing that children's success in school
depended not only on funding but on community commitment, he gathered the
state's top corporations together to ask their support. Smart Start, a public–private
initiative to improve high-quality early care and education services for all children, from birth to age five, and their families, has become a national model for
ensuring that children under six are healthy and prepared for success when they
enter school. Today this public–private initiative has the support of 82 nonprofit
organizations in the state, coordinating health and family supports to address the
needs of each community's young children and their families.

Another example of "no excuses," First 5 LA, came about by recognizing that
an unprecedented number of children in Los Angeles continued not to thrive.
Through community meetings, public forums, residents set an agenda for
improving children's outcomes in five areas (First 5): good health, safety and survival, economic well-being, social and emotional development, and school readiness skills. They allocated their funding on the basis of need and at the same time
established a research partnership with the RAND Corporation to discover
whether their goals and strategies for improving children's early learning were
being met. Involving both private and public sectors, First 5 LA has successfully
begun an implementation strategy to target specific outcomes such as high

school graduation rates. With plans already in place for Next LA, the initiative is becoming a dynamic force for change in the entire Los Angeles county. "RAND's findings confirm that if we want to improve our children's success at school, we need to address the issue at both the community and family level," said Evelyn V. Martinez, executive director of First 5 LA, which funded the study.

These and other programs, such as the United Way's Success by Six, prove that a nation that prides itself on its generosity and entrepreneurial spirit can change the futures of disadvantaged children. We have the knowledge. We have the support of corporate giants, policy makers, administrators, and citizens throughout the country. What we now need is to capitalize on this historic opportunity to help reverse the fortunes of millions of children who, without intervention, will run the risk of growing up unskilled, uneducated, unemployed, and unable to make it in America. In light of this extraordinary convergence of increased awareness of the problem, knowledge of what works, and renewed commitment toward educating *every* child in America, the bleak cycle of poverty and disadvantage that has until now appeared so intractable can be broken forever.

WHERE TO GET EVIDENCE

Best Evidence Encyclopedia (www.bestevidence.org) provides evidence on promising practices and interventions. Produced by the federally funded Center for Data-Driven Reform in Education at Johns Hopkins University in Baltimore.

Child Trends: What Works (www.childtrends.org) summarizes research and promising practices for improving children's health, education, and welfare.

Poverty Action Lab (www.povertyactionlab.com), at MIT, scientifically evaluates anti-poverty programs in the U.S. and in developing countries.

Promising Practices Network (www.promisingpractices.net), operated by the RAND Corporation, highlights research-based programs shown to be effective at improving children's outcomes.

Social Programs that Work (www.evidencebasedprograms.org), produced by the Coalition for Evidence-based policy, lists interventions in education and social sciences that have been evaluated by randomized controlled trials.

What Works Clearinghouse (www.whatworks.ed.gov) contains research reviews and effectiveness ratings for educational programs and practices.

THE MAZE OF FEDERAL PROGRAMS THAT PROVIDE OR SUPPORT EDUCATION AND CARE FOR CHILDREN UNDER FIVE YEARS OLD

Department of Education

Alaska Native Home-based Education for Preschool Children
Bilingual Education—Comprehensive School Grants
Bilingual Education—Program Development and Implementation Grants
Bilingual Education—Program Enhancement Grants
Bilingual Education—Systemwide Improvement Grants
Charter Schools
Child Care Access Means Parents in School
Comprehensive School Reform Demonstration
Demonstration Grants for Indian Children
Education for Homeless Children and Youth
Even Start—Indian Tribes and Tribal Organizations
Even Start—Migrant Education
Even Start—State Educational Agencies
Goals 2000—Parental Assistance Program
Goals 2000—State and Local Education Systemic Improvement
Immigrant Education
Impact Aid
Indian Education—Grants to Local Education Agencies
Innovative Education Program Strategies
Migrant Education—Basic State Grant Program
Native Hawaiian Community-based Education Learning Centers
Native Hawaiian Family Based Education Centers
Reading Excellence
Ready to Learn Television

Safe and Drug-free Schools and Communities—State Grants
Special Education—Grants for Infants and Families with Disabilities
Special Education—Grants to States
Special Education—Preschool Grants (IDEA)
Special Education—State Program Improvement Grants for Children with
    Disabilities
Special Education—Technology and Media Services for Individuals with
    Disabilities
Technology Innovation Challenge Grants
Technology Literacy Challenge Fund Grants
Title I Grants to Local Educational Agencies (basic, concentration, and
    targeted grants)
21st Century Community Learning Centers

Department of Health and Human Services

Child Care Development Fund
Child Welfare Services—State Grants
Community Services Block Grant Discretionary Awards—Community Food
    and Nutrition
Demonstration Grants for Residential Treatment for Women and Their
    Children
Grants for Residential Treatment Programs for Pregnant and Postpartum
    Women
Head Start
Mental Health Planning and Demonstration Projects
Refugee and Entrant Assistance—Discretionary Grants
Refugee and Entrant Assistance—State-Administered Programs
Refugee and Entrant Assistance—Targeted Assistance
Refugee and Entrant Assistance—Wilson/Fish Programs
Social Service Block Grant
Temporary Assistance for Needy Families (TANF)

Source: GAO, "Early Education and Care" (April 2000).

PART Scores for Department of Education Programs

Not Performing

Ineffective (6):

Department of Education Even Start (http://www.whitehouse.gov/omb/expectmore/summary.10000186.2005.html)

Department of Education Federal Perkins Loans (http://www.whitehouse.gov/omb/expectmore/summary.10001034.2005.html)

Department of Education Federal Support for Gallaudet University (http://www.whitehouse.gov/omb/expectmore/summary.10003306.2005.html)

Department of Education Safe and Drug Free Schools State Grants (http://www.whitehouse.gov/omb/expectmore/summary.10000200.2005.html)

Department of Education TRIO Upward Bound (http://www.whitehouse.gov/omb/expectmore/summary.10000210.2005.html)

Department of Education Vocational Education State Grants (http://www.whitehouse.gov/omb/expectmore/summary.10000212.2005.html)

Results Not Demonstrated (41):

Department of Education Adult Education State Grants (http://www.whitehouse.gov/omb/expectmore/summary.10000180.2005.html)

Department of Education American Printing House for the Blind (http://www.whitehouse.gov/omb/expectmore/summary.10003301.2005.html)

Department of Education Assistive Technology Alternative Financing Program (http://www.whitehouse.gov/omb/expectmore/summary.10002074.2005.html)

Department of Education B.J. Stupak Olympic scholarships (http://www. whitehouse.gov/omb/expectmore/summary.10002078.2005.html)

Department of Education Byrd Honors Scholarships (http://www.whitehouse. gov/omb/expectmore/summary.10002080.2005.html)

Department of Education Child Care Access Means Parents in School (http://www.whitehouse.gov/omb/expectmore/summary.10002082.2005.html)

Department of Education College Assistance Migrant Program (http://www. whitehouse.gov/omb/expectmore/summary.10002084.2005.html)

Department of Education Comprehensive Regional Assistance Centers (http://www.whitehouse.gov/omb/expectmore/summary.10002086.2005.html)

Department of Education Developing Hispanic-Serving Institutions (http:// www.whitehouse.gov/omb/expectmore/summary.10003303.2005.html)

Department of Education Enhancing Education Through Technology (http://www.whitehouse.gov/omb/expectmore/summary.10003305.2005.html)

Department of Education Federal Work-Study (http://www.whitehouse.gov/ omb/expectmore/summary.10001031.2005.html)

Department of Education Graduate Assistance in Areas of National Need (http://www.whitehouse.gov/omb/expectmore/summary.10002092.2005.html)

Department of Education High School Equivalency Program (http://www. whitehouse.gov/omb/expectmore/summary.10002094.2005.html)

Department of Education IDEA Special Education—Parent Information Centers (http://www.whitehouse.gov/omb/expectmore/summary.10002098. 2005.html)

Department of Education IDEA Special Education—Research and Innovation (http://www.whitehouse.gov/omb/expectmore/summary.10001040.2005.html)

Department of Education IDEA Special Education—Technical Assistance and Dissemination (http://www.whitehouse.gov/omb/expectmore/summary. 10002100.2005.html)

Department of Education IDEA Special Education Grants for Infants and Families (http://www.whitehouse.gov/omb/expectmore/summary.10000190. 2005.html)

Department of Education IDEA Special Education Personnel Preparation Grants (http://www.whitehouse.gov/omb/expectmore/summary.10001039. 2005.html)

Department of Education IDEA Special Education Preschool Grants (http://www.whitehouse.gov/omb/expectmore/summary.10000198.2005.html)

Department of Education Impact Aid Basic Support Payments and Payments for Children with Disabilities (http://www.whitehouse.gov/omb/expectmore/ summary.10003308.2005.html)

Department of Education Impact Aid Payments for Federal Property (http://www.whitehouse.gov/omb/expectmore/summary.10002096.2005.html)

Department of Education Independent Living for People with Disabilities (http://www.whitehouse.gov/omb/expectmore/summary.10001042.2005. html)

Department of Education International Education Domestic Programs (http://www.whitehouse.gov/omb/expectmore/summary.10002102.2005.html)

Department of Education Leveraging Educational Assistance Partnership (http://www.whitehouse.gov/omb/expectmore/summary.10002106.2005.html)

Department of Education National Writing Project (http://www.whitehouse.gov/omb/expectmore/summary.10002110.2005.html)

Department of Education Neglected and Delinquent State Agency Program (http://www.whitehouse.gov/omb/expectmore/summary.10003312.2005.html)

Department of Education Parental Information and Resource Centers (http://www.whitehouse.gov/omb/expectmore/summary.10002112.2005.html)

Department of Education Physical Education Program (http://www.whitehouse.gov/omb/expectmore/summary.10003313.2005.html)

Department of Education Ready to Learn Television (http://www.whitehouse.gov/omb/expectmore/summary.10002116.2005.html)

Department of Education Smaller Learning Communities (http://www.whitehouse.gov/omb/expectmore/summary.10003314.2005.html)

Department of Education State Grants for Innovative Programs (http://www.whitehouse.gov/omb/expectmore/summary.10003315.2005.html)

Department of Education States Grants for Occupational and Employment Information (http://www.whitehouse.gov/omb/expectmore/summary.10000182.2005.html)

Department of Education Strengthening Historically Black Colleges and Universities (http://www.whitehouse.gov/omb/expectmore/summary.10003316.2005.html)

Department of Education Strengthening Historically Black Graduate Institutions (http://www.whitehouse.gov/omb/expectmore/summary.10003317.2005.html)

Department of Education Supplemental Educational Opportunity Grants (http://www.whitehouse.gov/omb/expectmore/summary.10001033.2005.html)

Department of Education Teacher Quality Enhancement (http://www.whitehouse.gov/omb/expectmore/summary.10001038.2005.html)

Department of Education Teaching American History (http://www.whitehouse.gov/omb/expectmore/summary.10002072.2005.html)

Department of Education Tech-Prep Education State Grants (http://www.whitehouse.gov/omb/expectmore/summary.10000204.2005.html)

Department of Education Training and Advisory Services (http://www.whitehouse.gov/omb/expectmore/summary.10002122.2005.html)

Department of Education Tribally Controlled Postsecondary Vocational and Technical Institutions (http://www.whitehouse.gov/omb/expectmore/summary.10000206.2005.html)

Department of Education Vocational Rehabilitation Demonstration and Training Programs (http://www.whitehouse.gov/omb/expectmore/summary.10003319.2005.html)

Performing (27)

Adequate (21):

Department of Education 21st Century Community Learning Centers (http://www.whitehouse.gov/omb/expectmore/summary.10001028.2005.html)

Department of Education American Indian Vocational Rehabilitation Services (http://www.whitehouse.gov/omb/expectmore/summary.10002124.2005.html)

Department of Education Charter Schools Grant (http://www.whitehouse. gov/omb/expectmore/summary.10003302.2005.html)

Department of Education Comprehensive School Reform (http://www. whitehouse.gov/omb/expectmore/summary.10000184.2005.html)

Department of Education Federal Family Education Loans (http://www.whitehouse.gov/omb/expectmore/summary.10001032.2005.html)

Department of Education Federal Pell Grants (http://www.whitehouse.gov/ omb/expectmore/summary.10000188.2005.html)

Department of Education Federal Support for Howard University (http://www.whitehouse.gov/omb/expectmore/summary.10003307.2005.html)

Department of Education Federal Support for the National Technical Institute for the Deaf (http://www.whitehouse.gov/omb/expectmore/summary.10003311. 2005.html)

Department of Education Gaining Early Awareness and Readiness for Undergraduate Programs (http://www.whitehouse.gov/omb/expectmore/summary. 10001037.2005.html)

Department of Education IDEA Special Education Grants to States (http://www.whitehouse.gov/omb/expectmore/summary.10000192.2005.html)

Department of Education Impact Aid Construction (http://www.whitehouse. gov/omb/expectmore/summary.10003309.2005.html)

Department of Education Javits Fellowships (http://www.whitehouse.gov/ omb/expectmore/summary.10002104.2005.html)

Department of Education Magnet Schools (http://www.whitehouse.gov/omb/ expectmore/summary.10002108.2005.html)

Department of Education National Institute on Disability and Rehabilitation Research (http://www.whitehouse.gov/omb/expectmore/summary.10001041. 2005.html)

Department of Education Projects with Industry for People with Disabilities (http://www.whitehouse.gov/omb/expectmore/summary.10002114.2005.html)

Department of Education State Assessment Grants (http://www.whitehouse. gov/omb/expectmore/summary.10002120.2005.html)

Department of Education Student Aid Administration (http://www.whitehouse. gov/omb/expectmore/summary.10000202.2005.html)

Department of Education Transition to Teaching (http://www.whitehouse. gov/omb/expectmore/summary.10003318.2005.html)

Department of Education Troops-to-Teachers (http://www.whitehouse.gov/ omb/expectmore/summary.10001030.2005.html)

Department of Education Vocational Rehabilitation State Grants (http://www.whitehouse.gov/omb/expectmore/summary.10000214.2005.html)

Department of Education William D. Ford Direct Student Loans (http://www.whitehouse.gov/omb/expectmore/summary.10001185.2005.html)

Moderately Effective (4):

Department of Education Advanced Placement (http://www.whitehouse.gov/omb/expectmore/summary.10003300.2005.html)

Department of Education Improving Teacher Quality State Grants (http://www.whitehouse.gov/omb/expectmore/summary.10001029.2005.html)

Department of Education TRIO Student Support Services (http://www.whitehouse.gov/omb/expectmore/summary.10000208.2005.html)

Department of Education TRIO Talent Search (http://www.whitehouse.gov/omb/expectmore/summary.10001036.2005.html)

Effective (2):

Department of Education National Assessment for Educational Progress (http://www.whitehouse.gov/omb/expectmore/summary.10000194.2005.html)

Department of Education National Center for Education Statistics (http://www.whitehouse.gov/omb/expectmore/summary.10000196.2005.html)

NOTES

Introduction: The Seven Essential Principles

1. E. D. Hirsch, *The Knowledge Deficit: Closing the Shocking Educational Gap* (Boston: Houghton-Mifflin, 2006).
2. D. Olds et al., "Effects of Nurse Home-Visiting on Maternal Life Course and Child Development: Age 6 Follow-up Results of a Randomized Trial," *Pediatrics* 114 (2004).
3. R. Needlman, P. Klass, and B. Zuckerman, "A Pediatric Approach to Early Literacy," in *Handbook of Early Literacy Research*, eds. D. Dickinson and S. B. Neuman (New York: Guilford Press, 2006).
4. R. Halpern, *Making Play Work* (New York: Teachers College Press, 2003).

Chapter 1: The Critical Early Years for Changing the Odds

1. G. Orfield, "Schools More Separate: Consequences of a Decade of Resegregation," in *The Civil Rights Project* (Cambridge, MA: Harvard University, 2001).
2. J. Heckman, A. Krueger, and B. Friedman, *Inequality in America: What Role for Human Capital Policies* (Cambridge, MA: M.I.T. Press, 2005).
3. C. Jencks, *Inequality* (Cambridge, MA: Harvard University Press, 1973).
4. L. Terman, ed., *Genetic Studies of Genius* (Stanford, CA: Stanford University Press, 1925).
5. M. Rutter and M. Rutter, *Developing Minds: Challenge and Continuity across the Life Span* (New York: Basic Books, 1993).
6. K. Pugh et al., "Neurobiological Investigations of Skilled and Impaired Reading," in *Handbook of Early Literacy Research*, eds. D. Dickinson and S. B. Neuman (New York: Guilford, 2006).
7. B. A. Shaywitz et al., "Development of Left Occipito-Temporal Systems for Skilled Reading Following a Phonologically-Based Intervention in Children," *Biological Psychiatry* 55 (2004).

8. R. Shore, *Rethinking the Brain: New Insights into Early Development* (New York: Families and Work Institute, 1997).

9. J. Shonkoff and D. Phillips, eds., *From Neurons to Neighborhoods* (Washington, D.C.: National Academy Press, 2000).

10. M. R. Gunnar, "Stress Physiology, Health and Behavioral Development," in *The Well Being of Children and Families: Research and Data Needs*, ed. A. Thornton (Ann Arbor, MI: Institute for Social Research, 1998).

11. W. T. Greenough, "Experience as a Component of Normal Development: Evolutionary Considerations," *Developmental Psychology* 27 (1991).

12. B. Perry and M. Szalavitz, *The Boy Who Was Raised as a Dog and Other Stories from a Child Psychiatrist's Notebook: What Traumatized Children Can Teach Us About Loss, Love, and Healing* (New York: Basic Books, 2006).

13. E. Turkheimer et al., "Socioeconomic Status Modifies Heritability of IQ in Young Children," *Psychological Science* 14, no. 6 (2003).

14. C. Capron and M. Duyme, "Assessment of Effects of Socioeconomic Status on IQ in a Full Cross-Fostering Study," *Nature* 340, no. 6234 (August 17, 1989).

15. J. Bruer, *The Myth of the First Three Years: A New Understanding of Early Brain Development and Life-Long Learning* (New York: Free Press, 1999).

16. Author, "The Santiago Declaration" (2007).

17. G. Dawson et al., "Preschool Outcomes of Children of Depressed Mothers: Role of Maternal Behavior, Contextual Risk, and Children's Brain Activity," *Child Development* 74, no. 4 (2003).

18. S. M. Grantham-McGregor et al., "Nutritional Supplementation, Psychosocial Stimulation, and Mental Development of Stunted Children: The Jamaican Study," *Lancet* 338 (1991).

19. R. Feurstein, *The Instrumental Enrichment* (Baltimore: University Park Press, 1980).

20. S. Shaywitz, "A Conversation with Sally Shaywitz, M.D." (San Mateo, CA: Schwablearning, 2003).

21. P. K. Kuhl, "Early Language Acquisition: Cracking the Speech Code," *Nature Reviews Neuroscience* 5 (2004).

22. Rutter and Rutter, *Developing Minds: Challenge and Continuity across the Life Span.*

23. U. Bronfenbrenner, *The Ecology of Human Development* (Cambridge, MA: Harvard University Press, 1979).

24. R. G. Barker, *Ecological Psychology: Concepts and Methods for Studying the Environment of Human Behavior* (Stanford, CA: Stanford University Press, 1968).

25. W. J. Wilson, *The Truly Disadvantaged* (Chicago: University of Chicago Press, 1987).

26. G. Duncan and J. Brooks-Gunn, eds., *Consequences of Growing Up Poor* (New York: Russell Sage Foundation, 1997).

27. E. Askari, "A 7-Month Free Press Investigation on Lead: 2.5 Million Lives Changed Forever," *Detroit Free Press*, September 15, 2003.

28. V. Lee and D. Burkam, *Inequality at the Starting Gate* (Washington, D.C.: Economic Policy Institute, 2002).

29. D. Helfand, "Nearly Half of Blacks, Latinos Drop Out, School Study Shows," *Los Angeles Times*, March 24, 2005.

30. S. Mayer, *What Money Can't Buy: Family Income and Children's Life Chances* (Cambridge, MA: Harvard University Press, 1998).

31. G. Farkas, *Human Capital or Cultural Capital?* (New York: Aldine De Gruyter, 1996).

32. J. Piaget, *The Language and Thought of the Child* (New York: Meridian, 1955).
33. L. S. Vygotsky, *Thought and Language* (Cambridge, MA: M.I.T. Press, 1962).
34. A. Lareau, *Unequal Childhoods* (Berkeley: University of California Press, 2003).
35. J. Bruner, "The Ontogenesis of Speech Acts," *Journal of Child Language* 3 (1975).
36. B. Hart and T. Risley, "The Early Catastrophe," *American Educator* 27 (2003).
37. K. Denton, J. West, and J. Walston, "Young Children's Achievement and Classroom Experiences: Special Analysis on the Condition of Education" (Washington, D.C.: National Center for Educational Statistics, 2003).
38. National Reading Panel Report, "Teaching Children to Read" (Washington, D.C.: National Institute of Child Health and Development, 2000).
39. N. Zill et al., "Head Start Performance Measures Center: Family and Child Experiences Survey" (Washington, D.C.: Office of Planning, Research, and Evaluation, Administration for Children and Families, U.S. Department of Health and Human Services, 2006).
40. K. E. Stanovich, "Matthew Effects in Reading: Some Consequences of Individual Differences in the Acquisition of Literacy," *Reading Research Quarterly* 21 (1986).
41. P. Bourdieu, "Cultural Reproduction and Social Reproduction," in *Power and Ideology in Education*, eds. J. Karabel and A. H. Halsey (New York: Oxford, 1977).
42. Kids Count Data Book, "Getting Ready" (Baltimore: Annie E. Casey Foundation, 2005).
43. M. McLaughlin, M. Irby, and J. Langman, *Urban Sanctuaries* (San Francisco: Jossey-Bass, 1994).
44. E. Hoff, "The Specificity of Environment Influence: Socioeconomic Status Affects Early Vocabulary Development Via Maternal Speech," *Child Development* 74 (2003).
45. S. B. Neuman and K. Roskos, "Access to Print for Children of Poverty: Differential Effects of Adult Mediation and Literacy-Enriched Play Settings on Environmental and Functional Print Tasks," *American Educational Research Journal* 30 (1993).
46. W. Labov, "The Logic of Non-Standard English," in *Language and Poverty: Some Perspectives on a Theme*, ed. F. Williams (Chicago: Markham, 1970).
47. Hart and Risley, "The Early Catastrophe."
48. Heckman, Krueger, and Friedman, *Inequality in America: What Role for Human Capital Policies*.
49. J. Coleman et al., *Equality of Educational Opportunity*, vols. 1–2 (Washington, D.C.: U.S. Department of Health, Education, and Welfare, Office of Education, 1966).
50. Lareau, *Unequal Childhoods*.
51. R. Putnam and L. Feldstein, *Better Together* (New York: Simon & Schuster, 2003).

Chapter 2: Changing the Odds by Funding What Works

1. M. Friedman, "A Guide to Developing and Using Performance Measures in Results-Based Budgeting" (Washington, D.C.: The Finance Institute, 1997).
2. E. A. Hanushek, "The Failure of Input-Based Schooling Policies," *Economic Journal* 113, no. 485 (2003): 64–98.
3. Friedman, "A Guide to Developing and Using Performance Measures."
4. S. Barr, "'Performance Reports' Faulted: GMU Researchers Find Agencies Lacking on Clarity, Access," *Washington Post*, October 17, 2000.

5. S. Raudenbush, "What Is Scientifically-Based Research?" (paper presented at the Symposium on Scientifically-based Research, U.S. Department of Education, 2002).

6. J. Currie, "Early Childhood Education Programs," *The Journal of Economic Perspectives* 15 (2001); J. Currie and T. Duncan, "Does Head Start Help Hispanic Children?" *Journal of Public Economics* 74, no. 2 (1999); J. Currie and T. Duncan, "Does Head Start Make a Difference?" *American Economic Review* 85, no. 5 (1995); V. Lee et al., "Are Head Start Effects Sustained? A Longitudinal Follow-up Comparison of Disadvantaged Children Attending Head Start, No Preschool, and Other Preschool Programs," *Child Development* 61 (1990); Administration for Children and Families, U.S. Department of Health and Human Services, "Head Start Impact Study: First Year Findings" (Washington, D.C.: 2005); N. Zill et al., "Head Start Performance Measures Center: Family and Child Experiences Survey" (Washington, D.C.: Office of Planning, Research, and Evaluation, Administration for Children and Families, U.S. Department of Health and Human Services, 2006).

7. B. Wasik, "Volunteer Tutoring Programs in Reading: A Review," *Reading Research Quarterly* 33 (1998).

8. S. Kellam and J. Anthony, "Targeting Early Antecedents to Prevent Tobacco Smoking: Findings from an Epidemiologically Based Randomized Field Trial," *American Journal of Public Health* 88, no. 10 (1998).

9. R. St. Pierre, J. Layzer, and H. Barnes, "Two-Generation Programs: Design, Cost, and Short-Term Effectiveness," *The Future of Children* 5 (1995); R. St. Pierre et al., "Third National Even Start Evaluation: Description of Projects and Participants" (Washington, D.C.: Planning and Evaluation Services, 2001).

10. S. B. Neuman, "Books Make a Difference: A Study of Access to Literacy," *Reading Research Quarterly* 34 (1999).

11. D. Reinking and J. Watkins, "A Formative Experiment Investigating the Use of Multimedia Book Reviews to Increase Elementary Students' Independent Reading," *Reading Research Quarterly* 35 (2000).

12. D. Gomby, P. Culross, and R. Behrman, "Home Visiting: Recent Program Evaluations—Analysis and Recommendations," *The Future of Children* 4, no. 26 (Spring/Summer).

13. Neuman, "Books Make a Difference."

14. B. Heyns, *Summer Learning and the Effects of Schooling* (New York: Academic Press, 1978).

15. C. Bruner et al., "Early Learning Left Out: An Examination of Public Investments in Education and Development by Child Age" (Washington, D.C.: Voices for America's Children, 2004).

16. St. Pierre, Layzer, and Barnes, "Two-Generation Programs."

17. J. Heckman, A. Krueger, and B. Friedman, *Inequality in America: What Role for Human Capital Policies* (Cambridge, MA: MIT Press, 2005).

18. Government Accountability Office (GAO), "Early Education and Care: Overlap Indicates Need to Assess Crosscutting Programs" (Washington, D.C.: Office of Management and Budget, 2000).

19. Heritage Foundation, "Education Notebook: New Year's Resolution for Congress: Rein in Runaway Education Spending" (Washington, D.C.: Heritage Foundation, 2005).

20. P. Barton, *Parsing the Achievement Gap* (Princeton, NJ: Educational Testing Services, 2003).
21. W. Galston, *National Public Radio Weekend Sunday* (1998).

Chapter 3: The Seven Essentials for Changing the Odds

1. J. Shonkoff and D. Phillips, "From Neurons to Neighborhoods" (Washington, D.C.: National Academy Press, 2000).
2. C. Bruner, "Many Happy Returns: Three Economic Models That Make the Case for School Readiness" (Washington, D.C.: State Early Childhood Policy Technical Assistance Network, 2004).
3. W. S. Barnett, K. Brown, and R. Shore, "The Universal Vs. Targeted Debate: Should the United States Have Preschool for All?" (New Brunswick, NJ: NIEER, 2004).
4. Bruner, "Many Happy Returns."
5. P. Wolf, "Sisyphean Tasks," *Education Next* 1 (2003).
6. R. St. Pierre, J. Layzer, and H. Barnes, "Two-Generation Programs: Design, Cost, and Short-Term Effectiveness," *The Future of Children* 5 (1995).
7. Ibid.
9. B. Bowman, S. Donovan, and M. S. Burns, "Eager to Learn: Educating Our Preschoolers" (Washington, D.C.: National Academy Press, 2000), eds. Shonkoff and Phillips, *From Neurons to Neighborhoods* (Washington, D.C.: National Academy Press, 2000).
9. D. Olds et al., "Prenatal and Infancy Home Visitation by Nurses: Recent Findings," *The Future of Children* 9 (1999).
10. D. Gomby, P. Culroos, and R. Behrman, "Home Visiting: Recent Program Evaluations—Analysis and Recommendations," *The Future of Children* Spring/Summer (1999).
11. L. Karoly, M. R. Kilburn, and J. Cannon, *Early Childhood Intervention* (Santa Monica, CA: RAND Corporation, 2005).
12. E. Hanushek and M. Raymond, "Does School Accountability Lead to Improved Student Performance?" *Journal of Policy Analysis and Management* 24 (2005).
13. Ibid.
14. D. Stone, *Policy Paradox and Political Reason* (New York: HarperCollins, 1988).

Chapter 4: Changing the Odds by Helping to Strengthen Families

1. "Sustaining Philadelphia," *Philadelphia Inquirer*, August 1, 2002.
2. U.S. Department of Health and Human Services, ed., *Summary Health Statistics for U.S. Children: National Health Interview Survey*, DHHS Publication No. (PhS) 2006-1555 ed., *Data from the National Health Interview Survey* (Hyattsville, MD: Centers for Disease Control and Prevention, 2004).
3. National Center for Health Statistics, "Health: United States, 2005 Chartbook," (Hyattsville, MD: Center for Disease Control and Prevention, 2005).
4. J. Roberts and M. Burchinal, "The Complex Interplay between Biology and Environment: Otitis Media and Mediating Effects on Early Literacy Development," in *Handbook of Early Literacy Research*, eds. S. B. Neuman and D. Dickinson (New York: Guilford, 2000).

5. J. Currie, "Health Disparities and Gaps in School Readiness," *The Future of Children* 15 (2005).

6. J. Shonkoff and D. Phillips, eds., *From Neurons to Neighborhoods* (Washington, D.C.: National Academy Press, 2000).

7. Currie, "Health Disparities."

8. J. Belsky, B. Spritz, and K. Crnic, "Infant Attachment Security and Affective-Cognitive Information Processing at Age 3," *Psychological Science* 7 (1996).

9. M. R. Gunnar, "Stress Physiology, Health and Behavioral Development," in *The Well Being of Children and Families: Research and Data Needs*, ed. A. Thornton (Ann Arbor, MI: Institute for Social Research, 1998).

10. J. West, K. Denton, and E. Germino-Hausken, "America's Kindergartners: Findings from the Early Childhood Longitudinal Study, Kindergarten Class of 1998–99, Fall 1998," (Washington, D.C.: National Center for Educational Statistics, 2000).

11. G. Farkas and K. Beron, "The Detailed Age Trajectory of Oral Vocabulary Knowledge: Differences by Class and Race," *Social Science Research* 33 (2004).

12. D. Olds et al., "Long-Term Effects of Home Visitation on Maternal Life Course and Child Abuse and Neglect: Fifteen-Year Follow-up of a Randomized Trial," *Journal of American Medical Association* 278, no. 8 (1997).

13. J. Love et al., "Making a Difference in the Lives of Infants and Toddlers and Their Families: The Impacts of Early Head Start: Executive Summary," (Washington, D.C.: Administration on Children, Youth, and Families, U.S. Department of Health and Human Services, 2002).

14. D. Olds et al., "Improving the Life-Course Development of Socially Disadvantaged Mothers: A Randomized Trial of Nurse Home Visitation," *American Journal of Public Health* 78 (1988).

15. D. Olds et al., "Long-Term Effects of Nurse Home Visitation on Children's Criminal and Antisocial Behavior: 15-Year Follow Up of a Randomized Trial," *Journal of American Medical Association* 280, no. 14 (1998).

16. M. Marcenko and M. Spence, "Home Visitation Services for At-Risk Pregnant and Postpartum Women: A Randomized Trail," *American Journal of Orthopsychiatry* 64, no. 3 (1994).

17. J. Love et al., "Making a Difference in the Lives of Infants and Toddlers."

18. J. Lombardi and M. Bogle, eds., *A Beacon of Hope* (Washington, D.C.: Zero to Three Press, 2005).

19. G. Will, "Sustaining Detroit," *Washington Post*, August 7, 2005.

20. "Detroit Becomes Nation's Most Impoverished Big City," *Detroit Free Press*, August 30, 2005.

21. Michelle Trudeau, "Program Matches Poor Mothers with Nurses," *NPR Morning Edition*, December 8, 2004, http://www.npr.org/templates/story/story.php?storyID=4208447.

22. This outcome reflects a reanalysis of data from the Elmira trial using an updated analytic method conducted in 2006. For more information, refer to the interview of Dr. Olds at http://www.nursefamilypartnership.org/resources/files/PDF/DavidOldsinterview1-24-06.pdf.

23. CBS News, in *Programs that Work*, August 16, 2001.

24. L. Karoly, M. R. Kilburn, and J. Cannon, *Early Childhood Intervention* (Santa Monica, CA: RAND Corporation, 2005).

25. S. Aos et al., "Benefits and Costs of Prevention and Early Intervention Programs for Youth" (Olympia: Washington State Institute for Public Policy, 2004).

26. D. Olds et al., "Effects of Home Visits by Paraprofessionals and by Nurses: Age 4 Follow-up Results of a Randomized Trial," *Pediatrics* 114 (2004).

27. P. Levenstein et al., "Long-Term Impact of a Verbal Interaction Program for At-Risk Toddlers: An Exploratory Study of High School Outcomes in a Replication of the Mother-Child Home Program," *Journal of Applied Developmental Psychology* 19 (1988).

28. Carnegie Corporation of New York, "Starting Points, Meeting the Needs of Our Youngest Children," (New York: Carnegie Corporation of New York, 1994).

29. Author, "2006 Report of Academic Outcomes for Children Graduates of the Avance Parent-Child Education Program 2004–2005" (Dallas: Dallas Unified School District, TX, 2006)

30. G. Rodriquez, *Raising Nuestros Ninos: Bringing up Latino Children in a Bicultural World* (New York: Simon & Schuster, 1999).

31. A. Schaller, L. Rocha, D. Barshinger, "Maternal Attitudes and Parent Education: How Immigrant Mothers Support Their Child's Education Despite Their Own Low Levels of Education," *Early Childhood Education Journal* 34 (April 2007).

Chapter 5: Changing the Odds through High-Quality Early Care and Education

1. J. Shonkoff and D. Phillips, eds., *From Neurons to Neighborhoods* (Washington, D.C.: National Academy Press, 2000).

2. V. Lee and D. Burkam, *Inequality at the Starting Gate* (Washington, D.C.: Economic Policy Institute, 2002).

3. M. Greenberg et al., "The 1996 Welfare Law: Key Elements and Reauthorization Issues Affecting Children," *The Future of Children* 12 (2002).

4. R. Wertheimer, "Poor Families in 2001: Parents Working Less and Children Continue to Lag Behind" (Washington, D.C.: Child Trends, 2003).

5. Detroit Free Press, February 21, 2006.

6. Fuller et al., "Welfare Reform and Child Care Options for Low-Income Families," *The Future of Children* 12, no 1. (Spring 2002): 97–119.

7. Ibid.

8. P. Morris et al., *How Welfare and Work Policies Affect Children: A Synthesis of Research* (New York: MDRC, 2001).

9. NICHD Early Child Care Research Network, "Early Child Care and Children's Development in the Primary Grades: Follow-up Results from the NICHD Study of Early Child Care," *American Educational Research Journal* 42 (2005).

10. NICHD Early Child Care Network, "Early Child Care and Children's Development in the Primary Grades: Follow-up Results from the NICHD Study of Early Child Care," *American Educational Research Journal* 42:537–570.

11. E. Peisner-Feinberg, M. Burchinal, R. Clifford, et al., *The Children of Cost, Quality, and Outcomes Study Goes to School: Executive Summary* (Chapel Hill: University of North Carolina, Frank Porter Graham Institute, 1999).

12. E. Smith, B. Pellin, and S. Agruso, *Bright Beginnings: An Effective Literacy Focused Prekindergarten Program for Educationally Disadvantaged Four-Year-Old Children* (Arlington, VA: Educational Research Service, 2003); Charlotte-Mecklenburg

Schools, "Bright Beginnings Program Cost-Benefit Analysis Project Report" (Charlotte-Mecklenburg, NC: Charlotte-Mecklenburg School District, 2004).

13. Charlotte-Mecklenburg Schools, "Cost-Benefit Analysis Project Report."

14. National Center for Rural Early Childhood Learning Initiatives, "Preliminary Rural Analysis of the Early Childhood Longitudinal Study—Kindergarten Cohort" (Oxford: Mississippi State University, 2005).

15. C. Grace, "Rural Disparities in Baseline Data of the Early Childhood Longitudinal Study: A Chartbook" (Oxford, MS: National Center for Rural Early Childhood Learning Initiatives and Child Trends, 2006).

16. Newark Star Ledger, "New Classrooms Are Nice. Textbooks, Too. But What About Parents? Chronicling a Quiet but Necessary Revolution in New Jersey's Schools," *Newark Star Ledger*, December 5, 2005.

17. C. Lamy et al., "Giant Steps for Our Littlest Children: Progress in the Sixth Year of the Abbott Preschool Program" (New Brunswick, NJ: NIEER, 2005).

18. G. Zellman and A. Johansen, *Examining the Implementation and Outcomes of the Military Child Care Act of 1989* (Santa Monica, CA: RAND, 1998).

19. G. Zellman and A. Johansen, *Examining the Implementation and Outcomes of the Military Child Care Act of 1989* (Santa Monica, CA: RAND Corporation, 1998).

20. N. D. Campbell et al., "Be All That We Can Be: Lessons from the Military for Improving Our Nation's Child Care System" (Washington, D.C.: National Women's Law Center, 2000).

21. Ibid.

Chapter 6: Changing the Odds through Community-Based Programs

1. L. Collins, "Professor Links Poverty to Host of Ills," *Deseret News* August 4, 1994.

2. R. Jerrett, "Successful Parenting in High-Risk Neighborhoods," *The Future of Children* 9 (1999); U. Torassa, "Researchers Question Theory of Innate Capacity to Succeed," *The Commercial Appeal*, September 2, 1999..

3. W. J. Wilson, *The Truly Disadvantaged* (Chicago: University of Chicago Press, 1987).

4. Ibid.

5. R. Jerrett, "Successful Parenting in High-Risk Neighborhoods."

6. M. Mather and K. Rivers, "The Concentration of Negative Outcomes in Low-Income Neighborhoods," (Baltimore: Annie E. Casey Foundation and Population Reference Bureau, 2006).

7. J. Osofsky, "The Impact of Violence on Children," *The Future of Children* 9 (1999).

8. J. MacLeod, *Ain't No Makin' It* (Boulder, CO: Westview Press, 1995).

9. J. Rosenbaum, "Changing the Geography of Opportunity by Expanding Residential Choice: Lessons from the Gautreaux Program," *Housing Policy Debate* 6, no. 1 (1995).

10. L. Sanbonmatsu et al., "Neighborhoods and Academic Achievement: Results from the Moving to Opportunity Experiment," *Journal of Human Resources* (forthcoming).

11. J. Eccles and J. Gootman, eds., *Community Programs to Promote Youth Development* (Washington, D.C.: National Academies Press, 2002).

12. R. Putnam and L. Feldstein, *Better Together* (New York: Simon & Schuster, 2003).

13. G. Gaul, "Libraries in Distress," *Philadelphia Inquirer*, June 1–4, 1997.

14. S. B. Neuman, "Getting Books in Children's Hands: Final Report to the William Penn Foundation" (Temple University, Philadelphia, PA, 1997).

15. S. B. Neuman, "Books Make a Difference: A Study of Access to Literacy," *Reading Research Quarterly* 34 (1999).

16. Ibid.

17. R. Needlman, P. Klass, and B. Zuckerman, "A Pediatric Approach to Early Literacy," in *Handbook of Early Literacy Research*, eds. D. Dickinson and S. B. Neuman (New York: Guilford Press, 2006).

18. R. Needlman, "Effectiveness of a Primary Care Intervention to Support Reading Aloud: A Multicenter Evaluation," *Ambulatory Pediatrics* 5 (2005).

19. A. Mendelsohn, "The Impact of a Clinic-Based Literacy Intervention on Language Development in Inner-City Preschool Children," *Pediatrics* 107 (2001).

20. S. B. Neuman, *Literacy in the Television Age* (Norwood, NJ: Ablex, 1991).

21. S. Ball and G. Bogatz, *The First Year of Sesame Street: An Evaluation* (Princeton, NJ: Educational Testing Service, 1970); G. A. Bogatz and S. Ball, "The Second Year of Sesame Street: A Continuing Evaluation" (Princeton, NJ: Educational Testing Service, 1971).

22. G. Lesser, "Learning, Teaching, and Television Production for Children: The Experience of Sesame Street," *Harvard Educational Review* 42 (1972).

23. D. Weyermann, "And Then There Were None," *Harper's Magazine*, April 1998.

24. KIDS COUNT Data Book, "Getting Ready" (Baltimore: Annie E. Casey Foundation, 2005).

25. D. Linebarger, "The Between the Lions American Indian Literacy Initiative: Research Component Report Prepared for the United States Department of Education" (Philadelphia: University of Pennsylvania, Annenberg School of Communication, 2003).

26. Ibid.

27. N. McCluskey, *Feds in the Classroom* (Lanham, MD: Rowman & Littlefield Publishers, Inc., 2007).

Chapter 7: Changing the Odds through After-School Programs

1. D. Entwisle, K. Alexander, and L. S. Olson, *Children, Schools, and Inequality* (Boulder: Westview, 1997).

2. B. Heyns, *Summer Learning and the Effects of Schooling* (New York: Academic Press, 1978).

3. K. Alexander, D. Entwisle, and L. Olson, "Lasting Consequences of the Summer Learning Gap," *American Sociological Review* 72 (2007): 167–180.

4. D. Vandell and L. Shumow, "After-School Child Care Programs," *Future of Children* 9 (1999).

5. J. Alter, "It's 4:00 P.M.: Do You Know Where Your Children Are?" *Newsweek* 101 (1998).

6. R. Halpern, *Making Play Work* (New York: Teachers College Press, 2003).

7. J. Dryfoos, "The Role of the School in Children's Out-of-School Time," *The Future of Children* 9 (1999).

8. N. Zill, C. Nord, and L. Loomis, "Adolescent Time Use, Risky Behavior, and Outcomes: An Analysis of National Data" (Rockville, MD: Westat, 1995).

9. P. Seppanen, D. deVries, and M. Seligson, "National Study of Before- and After-School Programs" (Washington, D.C.: Office of Policy and Planning, U.S. Department of Education, 1993).

10. Afterschool Alliance, "Formal Evaluations of the Academic Impact of Afterschool Programs" (Washington, D.C.: Afterschool Alliance, 2005).

11. Public Agenda, "Survey: Sports, Arts, Clubs, Volunteering—Out-of-School Programs Play Crucial Positive Role for Kids" (New York: Public Agenda, 2004).

12. E. Erickson, *Identity, Youth and Crisis* (New York: Norton, 1968).

13. J. Eccles, "The Development of Children Ages 6 to 14," *The Future of Children* 9 (1999).

14. D. Stipek, "Young Children's Performance Expectations: Logical Analysis or Wishful Thinking?" in *Advances in Achievement Motivation: The Development of Achievement Motivation*, ed. J. Nicholls (Greenwich, CT: JAI Press, 1984).

15. J. Dewey, *Democracy and Education: An Introduction to the Philosophy of Education* (New York: Macmillan, 1948).

16. J. Lave and E. Wenger, *Situated Learning* (New York: Cambridge University Press, 1991).

17. "Time for Achievement: Afterschool and out-of-School Time," *SEDL Letter* 18, no. 1 (2006).

18. C. Christle et al., "Promoting Resilience in Children: What Parents Can Do" (Washington, D.C.: American Institutes for Research: Center for Effective Collaboration and Practice, 2001).

19. Public Agenda, "Sports, Arts, Clubs, Volunteering."

20. G. Borman et al., "The National Randomized Field Trial of Success for All: Second-Year Outcomes," *American Educational Research Journal* 42 (2005).

21. Personal communication, Bette Chambers, Success For All Foundation, Baltimore, MA, February 14, 2007.

22. G. D. Borman, S. Stringfield, and R. Slavin, *Title I Compensatory Education at the Crossroads* (Mahwah, NJ: Erlbaum, 2001).

23. Vandell and Shumow, "After-School Child Care Programs."

24. Ibid.

25. D. Vandell and J. Ramanan, "Children of the National Longitudinal Survey of Youth: Choices in After-School Care and Child Development," *Developmental Psychology* 27 (1991).

26. Afterschool Alliance, "Academic Impact of Afterschool Programs."

27. "The Effectiveness of Out-of-School-Time Strategies in Assisting Low-Achieving Students in Reading and Mathematics: A Research Synthesis" (Denver: McREL, 2005).

28. "Evaluation of the YS-Care After School Program for California Work Opportunity and Responsibility to Kids (Calworks)" (Irvine, CA: Department of Education, University of California, Irvinie and Research Support Services, 2002).

29. J. Birmingham et al., "Shared Features of High-Performing After-School Programs: A Follow-up to the TASC Evaluation" (New York: TASC, 2005).

30. "When Schools Stay Open Late: The National Evaluation of the 21st Century Community Learning Centers Programs" (Washington, D.C.: Mathematica Policy Research, 2003).

31. D. Vandell et al., "The Study of Promising After-School Programs: Descriptive Report of the Promising Programs" (Madison: University of Wisconsin, 2004).

32. Birmingham et al., "Shared Features of High-Performing After-School Programs."

33. Vandell and Shumow, "After-School Child Care Programs."

34. Halpern, *Making Play Work*.

Chapter 8: The Public Will: What It Will Take to Change the Odds

1. M. Tucker, "Change the System, or Suffer the Consequences," *Education Week* 2007.

2. T. Cook et al., *"Sesame Street" Revisited* (New York: Russell Sage Foundation, 1975).

3. S. B. Neuman and D. Celano, "The Knowledge Gap: Implications of Leveling the Playing Field for Low Income and Middle Income Children," *Reading Research Quarterly* 41 (2006).

4. C. Gaziano, "Forecast 2000: Widening Knowledge Gaps," *Journalism and Mass Communications Quarterly* 74 (1997).

5. R. Allington, "If They Don't Read Much, How They Ever Gonna Get Good?" *Journal of Reading* 21 (1977).

BIBLIOGRAPHY

Adams, G., and M. Rohacek. "More than Work Support? Issues around Integrating Child Development Goals into the Child Care Subsidy System." *Early Childhood Research Quarterly* 17 (2002): 418–440.

Halpern, R. *Making Play Work*. New York: Teachers College Press, 2003.

Hirsch, E. D. *The Knowledge Deficit: Closing the Shocking Educational Gap*. Boston: Houghton-Mifflin, 2006.

Needlman, R., P. Klass, and B. Zuckerman. "A Pediatric Approach to Early Literacy." In *Handbook of Early Literacy Research*. Edited by D. Dickinson and S. B. Neuman. New York: Guilford Press, 2006, 333–346.

Neuman, S. B. "Examining the Impact of Model Urban Library Services for Children: A Final Report to the William Penn Foundation." Philadelphia: Temple University, 2001.

Olds, D., H. Kitzman, R. Cole, et al. "Effects of Nurse Home-Visiting on Maternal Life Course and Child Development: Age 6 Follow-up Results of a Randomized Trial." *Pediatrics* 114 (2004): 1550–1559.

Index

ABOUT THE AUTHOR

Susan B. Neuman is former U.S Assistant Secretary of Elementary and Secondary Education, 2001–2003, under President George W. Bush, and is now a Professor of Educational Studies, specializing in early literacy development, at the University of Michigan. In her role as Assistant Secretary, she established the Reading First program, the Early Reading First program, and was responsible for all activities in Title I of the Elementary and Secondary Act. She has directed the Center for the Improvement of Early Reading Achievement (CIERA). She is also a 2008 Leader for the American Library Association National Information Campaign on School Readiness. Neuman has authored more than 100 articles, and authored or edited 11 books, including *Educating the Other America* and *Multimedia and Literacy Development*.